Ōsugi Sakae
Anarchist in Taishō Japan

HARVARD EAST ASIAN MONOGRAPHS
102

Ōsugi Sakae, February 1922

Published with the permission of Nihon Kindai Bungakkan (Library of Modern Japanese Literature) Library Materials Section.

ŌSUGI SAKAE

ANARCHIST IN TAISHŌ JAPAN

The Creativity of the Ego

THOMAS A. STANLEY

Published by COUNCIL ON EAST ASIAN STUDIES, HARVARD UNIVERSITY, and distributed by HARVARD UNIVERSITY PRESS, Cambridge (Massachusetts) and London   1982

© *Copyright 1982 by the President and Fellows of Harvard College*

The Council on East Asian Studies at Harvard University publishes a mono-graph series and, through the Fairbank Center for East Asian Research and the Japan Institute, administers research projects designed to further scholarly understanding of China, Japan, Korea, Vietnam, Inner Asia, and adjacent areas.

Library of Congress Cataloging in Publication Data

Stanley, Thomas A., 1946-
   Ōsugi Sakae, anarchist in Taishō Japan.

   (Harvard East Asian monographs; 102)
   Bibliography: p.
   Includes index.
   1. Ōsugi, Sakae, 1885-1923. 2. Anarchism and anarchists—Japan—Biography. I. Title. II. Series.
HX947.O84S72   335'.83'0924 [B]   81-6916
ISBN 0-674-64493-X   AACR2

Contents

Contents

Acknowledgments

The author of a study like this is ultimately responsible for its gross mistakes. The contributions of others, however, are positive assets. I should like to admit debts to the following people for such contributions.

Gail Lee Bernstein provided delicate but decisive assistance at all stages. Even though she served as the chairperson of my dissertation committee, she remained willing to lend herself to my revisions. Her criticisms improved the manuscript, while her words of encouragement purged me of the uncomfortable feeling that I was the only one ever to face the problem of the moment.

Several other scholars have offered unselfish assistance. Charles H. Hedtke and Minoru Yanagihashi patiently edited several versions of the manuscript. I am pleased to acknowledge discussions with them which helped distill the major themes of Ōsugi's life. Albert M. Craig and Richard H. Mitchell offered valuable advice for the final revisions. Chitose Kitagawa and Don C. Bailey helped unravel linguistic knots, while Edward D. Putzar improved my translations immensely. Takeshi Ishida of the University of Tokyo provided much food for thought during the year he lectured at the University of Arizona as well as timely help when I was doing research in Japan. Ishikawa Tadao of Keiō University arranged my affiliation with that institution, where I was able to impose from time to time on the good will of Komatsu Ryūji. Kitanishi Makoto of Hiroshima University made it possible for me to begin research there. Frank Wong of Antioch College originally launched me into this general area of research and I have never regretted following his suggestion. Thanks are due, too, to W. Dean Kinzley for comments and discussions during the stage of final revision.

Several organizations provided financial support for various stages of research and writing. The Japanese Ministry of Education funded my field work for eighteen months in 1974–1976, and my first drafts were completed while employed thereafter by the Department of Oriental Studies, University of Arizona. Final revisions were undertaken in Tokyo in 1979–1980, thanks to postdoctoral fellowships from the Social Science Research Council and the National Endowment for the Humanities for a different project altogether.

Many friends in recent years kindly provided encouragement as well as necessary diversion, even while wondering if they would ever hear the end of anarchism. Especially helpful were David Andres, Barry Gartell and Ruth Gartell, Gilbert Facio and Joy Facio, William Kruse, Lee Learned and Jeannie Learned, Julia Phillips, and David Rees.

A special note of thanks must go to the Onos—Takeo, Toyoko, Atsuko, Setsuko, and Shinji—who provided gracious hospitality and assistance when I undertook language study and, later, research. The degree to which I remain mentally and physically healthy is attributable largely to them.

Yasue Aoki Kidd generously inscribed the characters for the bibliography and glossary in the manuscript.

Mary Boyd Stanley and Charles Johnson Stanley began and supported the process which led to this study: they sparked my interest in Japan rather than their own "homeland," China. It is to Mary and John, then, that I am most indebted.

Susan H. Kuyper typed some chapters, read others, and is still patient. She also put all minor and major revisions into the manuscript. Just when page proofs arrived, she delivered herself of our son, Johnson, but nearly died immediately thereafter. After five weeks in Tokyo hospitals and another two months of recovery, she is completely well, due to both the superlative medical care she received and the kindness and concern of so many friends. This book is dedicated to Susan.

Preface

Ōsugi Sakae (1885–1923) was the foremost Japanese anarchist of the Taishō period (1912–1926), even though his influence on his contemporaries was prematurely curtailed by his murder. Anarchist thought was the cutting edge of "progressive" thought in his day. Ōsugi's writings were solicited by liberals and radicals alike as respected additions to the debate on many of the most pressing current issues; often they were actually the starting point of discussion. Ōsugi's stature as a critic and a thinker guaranteed that reformers of every stripe would address topics first raised in one of Ōsugi's publications.

Ōsugi's ideas contain some of the roots of such dominant Japanese left-wing concerns as the united front, proletarian literature, centralism versus decentralism in the labor and political movements of the leftist camp, the role of socialist intellectuals with respect to the workers, the nature of post-revolutionary society, and the tactics to be employed by leftists of any persuasion. His influence was not limited to Japanese socialism and communism alone: he had great impact on a wider audience since reformist topics were easily transposed into those of interest to non-socialist intellectuals. Thus, topics such as the role of literature in society, the role of intellectuals themselves, the nature of the ideal society (and the negative corollary, the flaws of present society), as well as the long-lasting debate about love and marriage, were issues of interest to all intellectuals of Ōsugi's time. Whether his ideas were triggering a discussion or adding to it, they were always a force with which others had to reckon.

Ōsugi's influence stemmed from his articulation of the basic concerns of his generation. That generation confronted difficulties of a different order from those faced by the Meiji leadership. Looking back on the earlier Meiji period (1868–1912), one finds giants, heroes who accomplished astonishing tasks; they were nation-builders who transformed Japan in less than four decades from a collection of feudal domains into the major power in East Asia. During the Taishō period, however, Japanese society and the intellectual world faced the task of searching for solutions to a new set of problems. Whereas the Meiji leaders confronted the monumental question of how to modernize, Ōsugi's peers sought to cope with the effluent of modernization—pollution, labor discontent, increasing class inequities, and Japan's continuing economic instability.

Moreover, unlike the early Meiji generation, which found self-identity through service to the nation, many Taishō youths experienced the urgent need to define themselves as individuals in a society that still remained, despite rapid social change, dedicated to the virtues of self-fulfillment through submersion of the individual in the group. Self-identification became a severe problem in the Taishō period as constraints increased; the youth of Taishō found they could no longer hope to rise quickly to high positions as the Meiji leaders had done. The well-established political system of the twentieth century offered little opportunity, limited advancement, and no excitement. The individual was a minor cog in a mechanism that did not react to its smallest components.

Anarchism was one response, but an important one, to the problems of self-identity and modernization. Although it is now as misunderstood by contemporary Japanese as by Americans, anarchism was the leading radical socialist philosophy in the world before the success of the 1917 Russian Revolution replaced it with Marxism-Leninism. Before then, anarchism had been the main competitor with moderate social democracy for leadership of the socialist movement worldwide. In Japan, as elsewhere, Marxism-

Leninism and other forms of socialism ultimately became more important, but anarchism provided the start for the socialist debate early in this century.

Anarchism foresaw a new social and economic organization that would alleviate problems caused by modernization. Anarchist thought was a product of eighteenth-century liberal economic ideas carried to their logical extreme. It argued that people, given complete freedom from governmental restraint, would act in their own self-interest to solve their problems and, because human beings were by nature good, their actions would benefit both themselves and society. Moreover, in the absence of the artificial restrictions of government, human actions would be immediately and completely effective.

In Ōsugi's interpretation, anarchism provided a method for curing the social ills that plagued Japanese society. Further, it offered a method that gave the individual the responsibility and the ability to effect the cure. No longer would young Japanese need to feel excluded by a system in which opportunities were restricted; they could act with the knowledge that their efforts would not be in vain. Ōsugi's anarchism was not concerned exclusively with society and its organizational reform: it focused equally on the perfection of the individual by the individual's own action; by that means society too would be perfected. One is often left wondering whether he was not more interested in propagating individualism than anarchism. Anarchist theory, however, spans a wide spectrum of thought from individualism to collectivist syndicalism, and Ōsugi incorporated the seeming opposites, emphasizing them both.

Paradoxically, while Ōsugi's anarchism promised the elite youth of Taishō Japan self-identity and social significance on the one hand, it also accorded more importance and authority to the masses than ever before in Japanese history. In Meiji Japan, leaders had made decisions for the welfare of the nation on behalf of ordinary citizens. In the late Meiji and Taishō periods, some sectors of the elite attempted to tie the masses to the political system more securely in order to prevent their being captured by Western radical ideas, like anarchism, that would promote social disintegration.

Moral education courses, armed forces reserve organizations, and youth groups (*seinendan*) represented some of the methods they tried. Ōsugi too was attracted to the problem presented by the emerging masses; how could they be incorporated into society? However, whereas the elite strove to make the masses more docile, Ōsugi saw the masses as the source of ideas to which all elites should conform. He was unique in this respect both among establishment and radical thinkers, as he was unique in so many other ways.

Biographies of Japanese figures written in the English language have helped relieve much of the faceless anonymity of Japanese history. However, a vaguely disquieting feeling–that Japanese lack distinctive personalities–remains and is constantly reinforced by the omnipresent official portraits of imperial court figures and shoguns from ages past. The contemporary salary man of Tokyo–who seems to come equipped with a blue wool suit, a black umbrella, and a stereotypic personality–does nothing to dispel the image. A close encounter with Ōsugi, on the other hand, shatters such a notion forever, for he was eccentric enough to be considered exceptional anywhere in the world. Ōsugi was not a freak who appeared entirely by accident, however, but a man whose eccentricities are comprehensible against the background of his upbringing, his historical milieu, and the ideas that touched him. Each of these, the gist of this study, is in turn highlighted in him.

The reader should be warned that some chapters that follow are primarily biography while the rest are more resolutely intellectual history. The separation between the two types of approach may seem too sharp, but the chasm is imposed on the biographer by the available materials. Ōsugi's *Jijōden* (Autobiography) deals at length with his childhood and adolescence, but stops in 1906, at the point at which he enters irrevocably the socialist movement. Thereafter, autobiographical writings cover his months in prison from 1906 until 1910, his love affair in 1915–1916, and his trips to Shanghai in 1920 and to France in 1922–1923. None of these writings touches on Ōsugi's day-to-day life as a radical, his contacts with other radicals, workers, and ordinary people, or developments in the leftist movement, for the simple reason that Ōsugi did not want to reveal any important information to police authorities. Biographical information from Ōsugi's contemporaries is similarly very limited and mainly anecdotal. Thus, most of his life as a radical is obscure, and he must be dealt with in terms of his ideas for the most part. This unfortunately leaves the intellectual side of this study somewhat lifeless in places; but it is entirely unavoidable.

Chronology of Ōsugi Sakae's Life

1885	January 17	Ōsugi Sakae born.
1889	December	Father transferred from Tokyo to Sendai.
1891	April	Enters elementary school.
1894	July	Sino-Japanese War begins; father dispatched to war zone.
1895	April	Advances to higher elementary school.
1897	April	Enters Shibata Middle School.
1898	Summer	Travels to Tokyo, Nagoya, and Osaka to visit relatives.
1899	April	Enters Nagoya Kadet School.
1901	April	Receives 30-day disciplinary confinement to Kadet School, probably for homosexual activity.
	November	Stabbed during fight with another Kadet and expelled from Kadet School after returning to Shibata.
1902	January	Moves to Tokyo and enters Tokyo Academy.

1902   June   Mother dies.

       October   Enters fifth year of Junten Middle
                             School.

1903   September   Enters Tokyo Foreign Language School.
                             Experiments with Christianity.

       December   Begins to frequent the Heimin-sha.
       (approximately)

1904   February   Russo-Japanese War begins; father dis-
                             patched to war zone.

1905   July   Graduates from Foreign Language
                             School.

1906   March   Arrested in demonstration against in-
                             creasing the Tokyo trolley fare.

       June   Released on bail.

       September   Marries Hori Yasuko. Begins teach-
                             ing Esperanto.

       November   Begins editing *Katei zasshi*. Charges
                             filed against Ōsugi for writing "Shimpei
                             shokun ni atau."

1907   March   Charges filed against Ōsugi for writing
                             "Seinen ni uttau."

       May   Incarcerated in Sugamo Prison.

       November   Released from prison.

1908   January   Arrested for the Rooftop Incident. In-
                             carcerated in Sugamo Prison.

       March   Released from prison.

       June   Arrested for the Red Flag Incident.

       September   Incarcerated in Chiba Prison.

1909	November	Father dies.
1910	November	Released from prison.
1912	October	Begins publishing *Kindai shisō*.
1914	April	First meets Kamichika Ichiko.
	September	Stops publishing *Kindai shisō*. Introduced to Itō Noe.
	October	Begins publishing *Heimin shimbun*.
1915	March	Stops publishing *Heimin shimbun*.
	October	Begins publishing second *Kindai shisō*.
	December	Affair with Kamichika Ichiko has begun. Ōsugi removed from control of second *Kindai shisō*.
1916	January	Second *Kindai shisō* ceases publication.
	February	Affair with Itō Noe perhaps begins.
	May	Itō Noe leaves husband, Tsuji Jun, for Ōsugi.
	November	Stabbed by Kamichika Ichiko.
1917	January	Hori Yasuko renounces ties with Ōsugi.
	September	First daughter born.
1918	January	Begins publishing *Bummei hihyō*.
	April	Stops publishing *Bummei hihyō*. Begins publishing *Rōdō shimbun*.
	July	Stops publishing *Rōdō shimbun*.
1919	May	Strikes policeman Andō Kiyoshi.
	July	Charged for striking policeman.
	October	Begins publishing *Rōdō undō*.

1919 December   Incarcerated in Toyotama Prison. Second daughter born.

1920 March   Released from prison.

     June   Stops publishing *Rōdō undō*.

     October   Goes to Shanghai to attend Congress of Far Eastern Socialists.

     December   Taken into temporary custody at founding meeting of Nihon shakaishugi dōmei in Tokyo.

1921 January   Begins publishing second *Rōdō undō* in cooperation with bolshevik faction.

     March   Third daughter born.

     June   Stops publishing second *Rōdō undō*.

     December   Begins publishing third *Rōdō undō*.

1922 June   Fourth daughter born.

     September   Attends Osaka meeting to found national labor union—height of anarchist-bolshevik confrontation.

     November   Invited to attend the International Congress of Anarchists in Berlin in early 1923.

     December   Departs for Europe.

1923 February   Arrives in France.

     May   Arrested at May Day demonstration in St. Denis.

     June   Deported from France.

     July   Arrives in Japan. Last issue of third *Rōdō undō*.

     September   Murdered together with Itō Noe and a nephew in aftermath of the Great Kantō Earthquake.

ONE

Family, School, and Friends

The exact date of Ōsugi's birth, like the circumstances surrounding his death, is open to question. Although his autobiography (*Jijōden*) states that he was born in Marugame, Kagawa prefecture, on January 17, 1885,[1] the Ōsugi family registry and the official police record of his background and conduct[2] list the date of his birth as May 1. The discrepancy exists because his father, a young company-level army officer at the time, unwilling to post ¥300 in guarantee money required of junior officers when they married, did not register the marriage until the bride was visibly pregnant. The date of Ōsugi's birth was altered to maintain family respectability.

When Ōsugi was five months old, his family moved to Tokyo, where they lived in Kioi-chō, Kōjimachi (now in Chiyoda-ku), until moving to Shibata, in Niigata prefecture, northwest of Tokyo in December 1889. Although he never considered Shibata to be his home,[3] he resided there until entering Kadet School (*yōnen gakkō*) in 1898 and his family remained there until 1903.

Ōsugi was the eldest of nine children born to Ōsugi Azuma and his wife, Kusui Yutaka. Little is known of the other children: Ōsugi seldom mentions them in his autobiographical writings or letters, perhaps in an attempt to shield them from his own notoriety. Tragedy struck two of his sisters. The next to the youngest sister, Aki, committed suicide in 1916; no reason is offered by

any source.[4] The youngest, Ayame, married Tachibana Sōsaburō by whom she had a son, Munekazu, while living in Portland,
Oregon. Munekazu was killed together with his anarchist uncle in
1923.

Ōsugi's father was the third son of Ōsugi Kenkyūrō (or Kenshichirō—Ōsugi was not certain what the name was),[5] the village
headman (*shōya*) of Uji, located a short distance outside Nagoya.[6]
The village headship had been in the family for generations and was
inherited by Azuma's eldest brother, Inoko, when the father died
in 1894 or 1895.[7] Inoko held Azuma's share of the family property
but, to Azuma's dismay, managed to lose it all.[8] Thus, by the time
of Ōsugi's birth, the family's fortunes were so reduced that they
were forced to rely exclusively on Azuma's income, a circumstance
that encouraged Ōsugi to enter the army's Kadet School to take
advantage of reduced rates for officers' sons.

Despite the loss of his inheritance, Azuma became something of
a success. At first he left home to enter a Buddhist temple, but
abandoned the priestly life in the excitement of Saigo Takamori's
Seinan or Satsuma Rebellion of 1877 against the new Meiji Government. Azuma hurried to Tokyo and joined the army as a noncommissioned officer. After some study, he was able to enter
officers' school and afterward rose to captain before his death in
November 1909.[9]

Yet, despite his rise from the ranks, Azuma had an undistin-
guished record. Ōsugi reports a rumor that his father was transferred from the Tokyo Imperial Palace Guard division to Shibata
in disgrace; while on parade before the Emperor at the palace, the
story went, Azuma lost control of his horse and both rider and
mount reeled into the moat and were smeared with mud. The
Emperor is said to have laughed and said "Monkey, monkey."
Ōsugi questions the veracity of the story, noting unkindly that, in
any event, his father looked a good deal like a monkey.[10]

On the other hand, his father was a sufficiently adequate officer
at this time to come to the attention of his battalion commander,
Yamada Hōei, who thought enough of him to arrange for Azuma to
marry his young sister-in-law, Yutaka. Later, during the Sino-

Japanese War, Azuma saw action and was decorated with the Kinshi kunshō (Order of the Golden Kite).[11] Azuma was, however, known as a *seishin-ka,* or spiritualist, a term commonly applied to those of strong loyalist and patriotic sentiment in the army. The term implied praise, certainly, for loyalty and patriotism are desirable in any army, but it also hinted at inflexibility in military matters and thinking and weakness in military techniques. Azuma's reputation as a *seishin-ka* was strong enough that a guard at Chiba Prison, which Ōsugi entered after the Red Flag Incident (Akahata jiken) of 1908, recognized the name "Ōsugi Azuma" which was on Ōsugi's records as that of his former superior officer and remarked on his surprise at finding "that *seishin-ka*'s son" in prison.[12]

Ōsugi's father may have had an important though overall negative influence on his son. Ōsugi recalls that his father was unaffectionate and often absent from home. The Ōsugi children rarely saw him except at morning and evening meals. After dinner, Azuma would retire to his study to read or write. Although the nature of his father's studies is unclear, Ōsugi remembers seeing a Russian language book and a copy of the magazine published by the Kokuryūkai (Amur River Society or, improperly but commonly, the Black Dragon Society), a conservative organization dedicated to Japanese expansion in Manchuria. Later, Ōsugi also recalled being taught at Kadet School to focus his attention on the Liaotung Peninsula in southern Manchuria. After the Sino-Japanese War of 1894–1895, Russia, Germany, and France had joined in the Triple Intervention which forced Japan to return to China the Liaotung Peninsula, one of the spoils of war. In 1898, Russia secured from China a 25-year lease on the peninsula and built a major naval base at Port Arthur. Ōsugi recalled:

> Speaking of [a certain] instructor, I have one more memory of him. It concerns the interpretation of the word "retaliation" (*hōfuku*) in the Imperial Rescript on the restitution of the Liaotung Peninsula. I do not now remember any of the context surrounding that word. I imagine that it went something like "We shall endure hardship and privation and will devise our retaliation." This word "retaliation" had some formal meaning or other, but he told us that actually it meant revenge

(*fukushū*). I set so much value on this so-called real meaning that even now I cannot remember what the formal meaning was. . . .

After a meal [on the anniversary of the capture of Pyongyang], we all assembled in the lecture hall. There, right in front, hung a large map of Asia and on it China's Liaotung Peninsula was colored the same red color as Japan. All the school's officers and civilian employees were lined up to the left and right. This is where the instructor's talk on "retaliation" occurred.

When the instructor's lecture was finished, we were all taken to a military cemetery near a town to the east of Nagoya. Most of the school's officers . . . had comrades-in-arms buried there. One by one, they told us their memories of them.

"We must launch a war of retaliation without fail partly to comfort the spirits of these loyal and brave soldiers."

The conclusion of all the officers was a demand for this war of revenge against Russia, the ringleader of the Triple Intervention.[13]

If this story can be taken along with Azuma's reading material as evidence of the atmosphere in the army, we can assume that Azuma spent most of his free time planning and dreaming of exacting retribution from the Russians rather than attending to his children.

There seems to be little doubt that official policy-makers in the military and the government foresaw war with a European power, probably Russia, after the Sino-Japanese War. One writer concludes that the inner circles of the army were burning for revenge against the Triple Intervention powers, singling out Russia as the enemy, and states that the mood pervaded the military. Ōsugi saw a secret document to this effect on his father's desk and was overjoyed.[14] Much of the stimulus for a doubling of the number of army divisions from the Sino-Japanese War to the time of the Russo-Japanese War came from such assumptions.[15] Shumpei Okamoto notes that *gashin shōtan* (suffer privation for revenge) became the slogan of the day after 1895.[16] He adds that, even before a Russian naval base was established at Port Arthur on the Liaotung Peninsula, "clearly, the Triple Intervention made Russia, whom the Japanese public believed to have spearheaded the intervention, the enemy in the war of revenge that was, they thought, sure to come in the near future."[17]

There is little evidence, however, of widespread indoctrination within the army against Russia as a matter of official policy. Okamoto states that, because Russia was so slow in withdrawing from Manchuria after the Boxer Rebellion of 1900, Japanese generals "concluded, first, that war with Russia was inevitable; second, that the military situation vis-à-vis Russia would be favorable to Japan if war broke out soon; and, third, that the government should be urged to make the final decision immediately." Nevertheless, improvements in military preparedness did not begin until mid-1903. Further, the Kogetsukai—or Kogetsugumi —the first faction composed of second-echelon officers in favor of war with Russia, was only formed in May 1903.[18] None of this indicates a policy of planned and detailed indoctrination in preparation for war.

If Ōsugi's memory is correct, there was great excitement among junior officers like Azuma as individuals, not as official functionaries, in favor of a war with Russia even before the generals and government reached the same conclusion officially. If the Kadet School anecdote is correct, there were informal indoctrination sessions and a common assumption about war with Russia approximately one year before the same official conclusion.

Despite his own war fever, Azuma did not completely ignore Ōsugi. Shortly before he left to fight in the Sino-Japanese War, perhaps feeling a touch of mortality, he took his eldest son to the camp's rifle range every day and taught him how to shoot a pistol. He also gave his son rides on his horse. When he returned from the war, he tried to convey the experience of battle to his ten-year-old boy by placing him in a foxhole with live ammunition flying overhead and by giving him a few lessons in swordsmanship. Ōsugi had little other close contact with his father until he was accepted into Kadet School, when Azuma taught Ōsugi a little German in hopes of preparing him for language work at the school. He also took Ōsugi on a few one- or two-night trips during the boy's summer vacations, but was too busy for longer trips and offered his son little contact at home.[19]

Perhaps to compensate for lack of paternal affection, Ōsugi

came to seek attention from practically anyone who would give it. One form this took was a lifelong demand that he be a leader, preferably the sole leader, of any group with which he associated. Denied this opportunity, he would withdraw and have little or nothing to do with the group or individuals concerned. He constantly placed demands on others for their attention: he continually irritated his teachers by his unruly behavior, provoked his mother to beat him, and fought to obtain the regard and devotion of his friends. Little of this may have been calculated to gain his father's attention, which was in almost any case unavailable, but can perhaps be seen as displacement of his desire to do so.

Although Ōsugi had little contact with his paternal relatives, his mother's family exerted a great influence on him. To his maternal relatives he owed his early interest in a military career. The family's military background went back at least to his maternal grandfather, Kusui Rikimatsu, of Wakayama prefecture, of whom Ōsugi knew little except that he was a sake brewer, big and strong, given to practical jokes, and, though a merchant (*chōmin*) under the old feudal social system, much devoted to the martial arts—*kendō*, drilling with spears, and horse-riding. Family stories even said that he opened a school of martial arts which enrolled as many as six hundred students at one time. Ōsugi heard further from his younger maternal aunt that Rikimatsu lost the family's fortune by championing the interests of the *chōmin* against the samurai and died at the age of thirty-three.[20] Rikimatsu left no sons, but had three daughters, the youngest, Yutaka, becoming Ōsugi's mother.

Ōsugi's maternal connections came near to being famous. Yutaka's eldest sister married Yamada Hōei, who eventually became a lieutenant general. Their son, Ryōnosuke, also made a career in the army and was a lieutenant general in command of the Kyoto division at the time of Ōsugi's death in 1923.[21] Ryōnosuke's wife's eldest sister married Tanaka Kunishige, another army officer, who became a full general before his death and served as the army's representative to the Washington Conference. Although Ōsugi does not appear to have been well acquainted with Tanaka, the Yamada family considerably influenced him.

Ōsugi first met his aunt and her family in the summer of 1898 when he took a trip to Nagoya, Osaka, and Tokyo. His relatives introduced him to such Western luxuries as beef steak (which he cut too large to chew gracefully), a telephone, and a piano, as well as to such comforts of the rich as a separate house for Hōei's concubine. The Yamadas offered Ōsugi human warmth, acquaintance with luxury, and a model for success. That Yamada Hōei lavished affection on his nephew is evident from Ōsugi's autobiography, written twenty years later, where his father's lack of demonstrative love is contrasted with his uncle's loving affection. The month he spent with the Yamada family inspired him to study hard so that he could pass the entrance examinations to Kadet School and begin the climb to the lofty heights of success via a military career.[22]

Ōsugi's mother, Yutaka, seems to have played a more important role in Ōsugi's life than his father did. His relationship with her was a mixture of love and disappointment. Yutaka was a model for her son because her openness, tendency to speak her mind, and spontaneity were characteristics that later appeared in Ōsugi too. But she was also a foil; in addition to spoiling her first son, she responded unfailingly to his attention-claiming antics, thereby reinforcing his tendency to press himself on others by being unpleasant. In addition to the strikingly prominent eyes of her family, she passed on to him her strength of character: something of a tomboy before her marriage, she had the habit of riding brother-in-law Yamada Hōei's horse before he set off to work.[23]

Both mother and child were intransigent, and Ōsugi remembers, almost fondly one might say, that she had to punish him for one thing or another almost every day: he called it "one of mother's main daily chores." Sometimes she would order him to fetch a broom with which to be punished and, when he did, complain that he was a fool for bringing the instrument for a beating he could easily have escaped. Ōsugi, however, took pride in this ritual, reasoning that, since the broom did not hurt very much, there was no reason to flee.[24] Indeed, just as he later enjoyed testing himself against the police, he preferred the test of wills with his mother:

What were the rules for each side? How would each side enforce the rules? How could the rules be changed to his advantage? For example, when he was discovered playing with matches at the age of eight or nine, Yutaka scolded him. In response, he simply lit the *shōji* (sliding indoor paper partitions) and watched the maid help his mother extinguish the blaze. [25]

Only once does Ōsugi report that his mother actually hurt his feelings. He and a friend, Nishimura Torajirō, often played together. Nishimura was from a poor family and was, of dire necessity, very skilled at collecting foods like lily roots from the wild. Ōsugi would join in collecting, but then give his hoard to Nishimura thinking, "Since [his] house is poor. . . . " Once, when his mother was sick in bed and they had been collecting lily roots, Ōsugi remembered to select some lily flowers to take home to cheer her. She called him an idiot for bringing flowers when he could have fetched some good roots instead. "Had I only explained the reason, there is no doubt that she would have apologized for her exaggeration and praised me: this was the only vexatious memory of my mother, but a great one." [26]

Yutaka died in June 1902, half a year after Ōsugi was expelled from Kadet School and three months before he was admitted into middle school for the second time. After suffering a miscarriage, she had an operation in Niigata, but apparently expected to die: before leaving home she divided up her clothes into various piles, each labeled with a recipient's name. Ōsugi says she died of an ovarian abscess, although he adds that one of her friends told him that she was a victim of a surgeon's malpractice. The friend said that the doctor had operated again because of continuing pain and found an overlooked suture and massive infection. Azuma, though, refused to take any action in the matter: "What's done can't be undone." Though she was ill for some time, she refused to let any-one inform Ōsugi; yet, while she lay dying, she repeatedly asked if he had arrived. He was not in time to bid farewell. [27] By compari-son, there is only the barest mention of his father's death in Ōsugi's autobiographical writings.

Although Ōsugi inherited no heirlooms from his father, he did receive the most prominent possession of that side of the family, a stutter. Azuma had a stutter, though only a slight one, and his elder brothers as well as their great uncle all stuttered too.[28] Ōsugi's own stammer was fairly severe. He had the most trouble with syllables beginning with "k" or "g" and would go to some length to avoid these sounds whenever he wished to avoid stuttering. Once, he intended to ask Gotō Shimpei, then the Home Minister, for *gohyaku-en* (¥500) but ended up by asking for *sanbyaku-en* (¥300) instead, just to avoid the "go" sound.[29]

The stutter also made him very sensitive. Although he mentioned the fact explicitly only once, he indicated that he was very impatient with those who were unable to say exactly what they wanted to say, and that he was even more annoyed and distrustful of people laughing for reasons unknown to him, because he suspected they were laughing at him. His parents' reactions probably did not help him surmount his speech impediment. His mother thought that it was caused by a severe bout with bronchitis when young, while his father often put him on speech-correction programs, usually based on some book whose advertisement had caught his eye.[30] Since stuttering was a trait primarily associated with his father, we may speculate that Ōsugi let it become extreme as a means of bringing himself to Azuma's attention, particularly since his father never lost interest in correcting Ōsugi's impediment.

Oddly enough, Ōsugi's stammer disappeared under stress instead of becoming worse. Although Sakai Toshihiko praised Ōsugi's facility with foreign languages by joking that he stuttered fluently in five or six languages in the same way that Engels stuttered in twenty, his first wife, Hori Yasuko, maintained that he never stuttered in any foreign language.[31] She also related after his death that he was at times self-conscious in the extreme about his stammer: ". . . Every time he got out of prison he took care of nearly all his business for a month by [writing down everything he wished to say] (*hitsudan*) and therefore was occasionally mistaken for a newly arrived Chinese" but then she added that, "when he spoke in a foreign language, he never stammered at all."[32] Moreover, Ōsugi himself reported that, when he first began heckling

speakers in public meetings as a means of disrupting their pre-
established organization and order, he was uncertain whether he
would make a fool of himself by stuttering or not:

> However, as soon as I mounted the podium, I felt quite all right. I
> had made no preparations at all to speak. I thought I would try to dis-
> cuss with them the agenda of the meeting, which had become a prob-
> lem for all the people present. What I had thought to discuss with them,
> however, was already well understood by everybody. The meeting
> overflowed with feeling for the new agenda.
>
> I completely forgot my usual stammer and inexperienced timidity; I
> felt good, as if drunk; I talked to everyone in the audience. I debated
> with them. That was the first public lecture I had attended that left me
> with such a good feeling. [33]

While growing up, he took great pleasure in fighting. Sometimes
the fights were against one or more opponents, the number never
giving him pause, he professed. Just before leaving school in
Shibata one day, he had a premonition of danger, so he slipped a
long metal paperweight into a cloth bag. In a short while, the
"tough" kid from another class and six or seven of his friends
approached Ōsugi and threatened to beat him up. Ōsugi lost no
time in employing the paperweight to lay open the leader's head,
leaving a two- or three-inch scar. [34]

Ōsugi also had his own gang of followers whom he led in
numerous fights with other children. One series of fights in
particular reveals much about Ōsugi's competitive drive for
supremacy:

> On our side, there were about ten boys aged twelve and thirteen. I
> was the only officer's child; the rest were local residents [descendent
> from samurai]. At ten, I was the youngest. On the townie side, there
> were from twenty to thirty of them. In age, many were twelve or
> thirteen, but three or four fourteen- or fifteen-year-old boys were
> mixed in. . . .
>
> I gave everyone a suitable length of bamboo cut from the bamboo
> grove at home. In this way, the enemy, who came empty-handed, were
> completely beaten in the first battle.
>
> The next time, they too came with bamboo poles. Most had been
> used for a long time as clothes lines or had been plucked out of some

old fence. As soon as the hand-to-hand fighting began and we began to hit each other, their bamboo poles shattered.

Both times, I was at the very head [of our column] and, on the other side, the same fellow was at their head too. He was . . . the errand boy of a *tōfu* shop and had a big bald spot on his head that he concealed under a topknot. He was probably fifteen or sixteen and liked fights awfully; he was one who walked around buying into fights. In this instance too he had paid something to be included among our enemy. At the same time that I felt him to be weird, I found him odious and intolerable. I thought, somehow or other, I will make him cry for mercy.

The third time, it was a rock fight. Both sides had stuffed their pockets full of small stones and proceeded to heave them at each other from a distance. For some reason, our enemy's projectiles were used up first and they soon began to shrink back. I quickly closed in on them. The enemy were completely routed. However, Master Topknot was standing his ground alone without moving. Ultimately, everyone grabbed him, kicked and beat him mercilessly, then threw him in the nearby moat and retired singing a victory song. [35]

Only once did Ōsugi show any remorse when another child was hurt in these childhood pastimes. One day, a classmate was nearly killed by a needle or fishhook that lodged in the base of his neck in the course of a game. Ōsugi first disclaimed having done anything to him, then remembered an incident during a game of "king of the mountain" next to the barracks at the army encampment. Two groups or teams vied for control of a mound beside a building; one group held forth on the mound, while the other would send "heroes" to disrupt the kings by mounting the roof and jumping down into their midst. Ōsugi, of course, was the "hero" in this as in any other game. In this one, he remembered that he might have picked up a needle in his shoe while scurrying across the roof and then jabbed it into the other boy's neck when he jumped from the roof. In any case, Ōsugi, his mother, and his father all went to the boy's home and apologized. The other family declined to make an issue of the matter, saying that it was an accident and there was no knowing if Ōsugi had in fact done the damage. That was the end of the matter, except that Ōsugi reports that he was never again able to get along with the child. [36]

In addition to fighting, Ōsugi indulged himself in cruel rowdy-ism. He wrote that he often beat to death dogs and cats that he happened upon. Once though, after killing a cat, "I think because I used a particularly unfortunate killing method," he reacted to his own excess. He returned home for dinner but, feeling bad about the slaughter, he went to bed without eating much dinner. Worried, Yutaka checked and found he had a temperature. After he slept a little, he sat up in bed, made one hand into a cat's paw, and meowed. On seeing this, his mother knew exactly what was bothering him. Later, she often told Ōsugi and others:

> "I really felt nervous and everything; it was the first time ever that [I had seen anything] like it. But, thinking what a thing if I were defeated by a cat's spirit, I shouted 'Fool' at the same time that I slapped his cheek with all my strength. Even then, still making a cat's paw, his eyes grew round and bright. Unable to stand it, I shouted 'Fool! A hoodlum with no self-respect who kills cats and other weak things!' and really slapped his cheek again with all my strength. Then, he lay down and fell fast asleep. Really, I've never been so worried!" [37]

It was the last cat Ōsugi killed and the last parental exorcism.

It is difficult to determine exactly how well or poorly he did academically: he advanced normally from elementary school to higher elementary school to middle school and, on his second attempt, into the Kadet School. However, he reports that his grades declined in higher elementary school, when he dropped from third in his class in the first year to the "bottom" in the second year, and never again mentions receiving superior marks. Later, in middle school, he reports disliking a number of courses: painting, natural history, chemistry, and calligraphy he either found difficult or disliked. [38]

If he did not excel up until he entered Kadet School, neither did he do too poorly. He had no trouble advancing from class to class until he was briefly rebuffed attempting to enter middle school. At this point, his application was initially rejected because children had to be twelve years of age and Ōsugi would have been only eleven years and eleven months (according to his false, but legal, birth date) when the school year began in April 1897. He was provisionally accepted in the end. Despite his "youth," he survived well in a very competitive system: about twenty-three students advanced with Ōsugi from higher elementary school to middle school. Half dropped out before gaining full admittance in the September term. A majority of the remainder failed to enter the second year, and one or two more failed to enter the third year. [39] If this is true, only three or four of his classmates survived middle school: Ōsugi himself dropped out to enter Kadet School in April 1899.

While Ōsugi was not the best student in his classes, he may have taken honors in the "department of punishments." As early as age five, when he was still in nursery school in Tokyo, he reports being scolded by his teacher. Instead of being contrite, he spat in her face. Cryptically giving no explanation of the incident, he states that he also spat in the face of one of his elementary school teachers. When he was in an after-school cram school in Shibata, he remembers that his teacher carried and freely used a bamboo-root switch. He remembers being whipped quite often and speculates that because of such treatment he came to hate mathematics. In grade school, he recalls enjoying the variety of punishments that were handed out to him. One was that he had to stand at the front of his class, facing his schoolmates, and hold teacups full of water on the back of his hands held at arm's length. This particular punishment he quite enjoyed because he could engage in various pastimes, like sticking his tongue out at his classmates. Another punishment was to be confined to the teachers' room. A third was being confined in a small storehouse. This last was less interesting, in fact quite boring after a while, because there were only a number of rats to keep him entertained. [40] The general impression is that Ōsugi was constantly either being punished or searching out avenues that would lead to punishment. As a result, his academic standing suffered.

Only one teacher in the period prior to Kadet School made a positive impression on him. This was Ōsugi's first male teacher, a higher elementary school instructor whom Ōsugi portrays as very masculine, unrefined, and unpretentious. He was dark-complexioned, powerfully built with thick fingers, and the only male teacher in the school who referred to himself as *boku* (a rough and informal first-person-singular word used only by males). Ōsugi remembers that this teacher, whose name he forgets, was the only male teacher who taught singing and contrasts this to his strong, coarse image. He played the organ skillfully and sang in a strong, beautiful bass. He also became the model and friend to all the students. Most impressively for Ōsugi, he was the only teacher who never chastised him and who took a positive interest in him. He singled out Ōsugi and two other students, told them they should apply for middle school, and said he would guarantee the ability of these three students only.[41]

Although it is impossible to say whether Ōsugi was a successful student or not, perhaps Sakai Toshihiko summed up the situation aptly when he wrote in 1913:

> You cannot say that his education is wide. And you probably cannot call it deep. However, his comprehension is very clear. . . . [Ōsugi] has not yet sufficiently exhibited scholarly techniques; nevertheless, his writing is usually simple and plain, true and coherent, open and above-board. Then again, sometimes he writes unexpected rubbish.[42]

Ōsugi also attended special after-school classes in Shibata, not unlike many present-day Japanese students who attend "cram" schools (*juku*) in preparation for entrance examinations to university, high school, or, recently, even junior high school. He began cram school during his first year in higher elementary school (his fourth year of formal education), presumably in order to better prepare himself for the competition to enter middle school. Although the subjects certainly included mathematics and probably other such "modern" topics, it was here that Ōsugi also received his only exposure to classical Chinese learning.

Japanese socialists born earlier than Ōsugi and subjected more directly to social and educational systems imbued with traditional values often demonstrated those very values as central to their lives. Kōtoku Shūsui related that his earliest desire, the Confucian-based value placed on rendering service to one's lord, or, in modern times, to the nation, continued to be prominent throughout his life. In a similar vein, selflessness has been pointed out as the crucial element in Kawakami Hajime's thought and personality. [43]

A like conclusion cannot be drawn from Ōsugi's early years. Raised in an environment thoroughly penetrated by the values of a modern army and educated in a strictly modern curriculum, Ōsugi received no formal instruction, not even at home, about traditional or Confucian values. He remembers not a single thing he read in cram school during his brief instruction in the Confucian Classics, and he paid little attention to Japanese history or the lives of heroes of the Meiji Restoration whence such lessons might be drawn. The formal educational system gave no attention to the Confucian Classics, although Ōsugi remembers that his middle school principal, who taught logic and English, was nicknamed "Confucius-*sama*" because he insisted on lecturing on the *Analects* and constantly brought Confucius or Confucian principles into the lessons. Ōsugi recalls reading some or all of the Confucian *Analects,* Mencius's *Doctrine of the Mean* and the *Great Learning* "without getting the meaning." Tada Michitarō says that Ōsugi had no experience with the Confucian Classics and, although this is an exaggeration, it is true that the Classics and their ethical values never influenced Ōsugi as they did many socialists who were older than he. [44]

Perhaps the one exception to this rule was his attitude toward money. As a child, he received no allowance and never learned about money while growing up. In his later life, he treated money, especially money advanced to him for articles and translations or lent to him, in a cavalier manner. Samurai of the Tokugawa period were taught to despise and avoid commercial transactions. Ōsugi's attitude was similar, but there is no evidence that he learned it in a formal setting, or that he was taught this or any other traditional attitude or value at home.

Outside of school, Ōsugi relates that from a very early age he enjoyed reading. We are given little indication of what he read, but he says that he frequently went to a bookstore near his home where he was well enough known to have a charge account. This was no small blessing, since he was never given an allowance and therefore had no money of his own to spend on books. His mother willingly paid his bills, but did urge him to be reasonable. After entering higher elementary school, Ōsugi and a number of his friends formed a group devoted to writing essays and reading them. Ōsugi quickly assumed leadership of the group because his wide reading gave him the knowledge with which to interest and astound his contemporaries.[45]

In the summer of his tenth year, Ōsugi first discovered sex, something that was to be a problem and a preoccupation for years to come. His activities with his first "partner" seem to have been largely innocent, although he does mention cryptically that he and the girl sometimes went to his room for two or three hours at a time where, "without worrying about anybody [disturbing us], we played and did adult-like things." At about the same time, he had another girlfriend whom he calls Rei-chan. This relationship was perhaps a little less innocent for, at one point, the two children's parents became quite incensed by something they had done, first his mother alone and then together with Rei-chan's mother demanding an apology of him. He refused, but finally gave in to Rei-chan's pleas and allowed her to apologize for both of them.[46] Puberty did not arrive until Ōsugi was in the spring of his thirteenth year and it frightened him: he recalls attempting to pluck out the pubic hair as it grew in. He soon adjusted to adolescence and proceeded to discover and enjoy masturbating so frequently that, he says, his studies began to suffer from his sexual preoccupations.

Ōsugi was sexually precocious, especially in a strait-laced society. Since censorship has denied us explicit knowledge of what Ōsugi and his sexual partners did, it is difficult to know if much of anything happened, especially considering the possibility that Ōsugi the adult was trying to prove that promiscuous behavior was natural and that therefore his complicated affairs with women as an adult were more honest than monogamous relationships. The subject will recur throughout this study, but suffice it to say at this point that Ōsugi indicates more satisfaction with having had early sexual experiences than with any inherent emotional content. In fact, he appears to have been rather cold or even self-centered about his personal relationships at this time. He had few friends if any, only followers and sexual partners.

While sex may have been a major interest for the young Ōsugi, developing close and long-lasting friendships was not. He may have named few names in his autobiography because he did not want to focus attention on childhood friends who were leading conventional lives; certainly the notoriety of an anarchist would have reflected negatively on ordinary individuals. On the other hand, he did provide sufficiently detailed information about his girlfriends to make identification of them fairly easy for someone interested in tracking them down at the time of publication. Only one male friend is positively identified—Nishimura Torajirō, the friend to whom Ōsugi gave the lily roots. Ōsugi's sponsorship of this child went even further. Nishimura was too poor to try to attend middle school, so Ōsugi hit upon the idea of giving Nishimura his books after he had finished reading them. However, because his family still could not pay the tuition fees, Nishimura was sent to Hakodate on the northern island of Hokkaidō to become a shop boy and Ōsugi never corresponded with him or saw him again.[47] The only other friends who appear are the nameless members of the gang that Ōsugi led, and the small writing club mentioned above, none of whom are in any way identifiable. The other children who were identifiable were neighbors whom Ōsugi did not consider friends. In short, there is no evidence of any close or long-lasting friendships.

Was Ōsugi for some reason incapable of forming friendships? There is some evidence in support of such a conclusion, specifically the fact that, aside from Nishimura, the only interactions with his peers he records are those in which he is the leader and the rest are, by implication, his devoted followers. Later, in his adult life, Ōsugi seemed to have been unable to get along comfortably with equals, especially those who, like Sakai Toshihiko and Arahata Kanson, were his rivals for influence within the leftist movement. Although he may not have been able to enjoy true friendship, he had no trouble making himself attractive as a leader.

One final observation appropriate at this point concerns Ōsugi's position in Meiji Japan up through his entry into Kadet School in 1899. Although most of his contemporaries dreamed of entering the civilian bureaucracy and rising to high leadership, Ōsugi was determined on a military career, because his environment was a military one in which civilian life was looked down on and because of the inspiration provided by the Yamadas. The two careers, civilian and military, can well be equated in terms of prestige, power, importance to the nation and difficulty of entry. Japan had been opened to foreign relations by an implied military threat in 1854 and subjected to a system of unequal treaties ever since then. Clearly, modern laws and industry were necessary before the treaties could be renegotiated, but the necessity and efficacy of military power were not denied: the close connection between the civilian and military arenas was reflected in the slogan "a rich nation and a strong army" (*fukoku kyōhei*) current in the 1870s. The officer corps was, like the higher civil service, a professional organization based on the most modern principles and devoted to the same modern goals as the bureaucracy. As an elite, military officers were the equals of their civilian counterparts.

Ōsugi spent his entire childhood on the fringe of this elite and imbibed enough of its attitudes and values to wish to become a formal member of it. Through early 1899, he took the appropriate steps to ensure this by gaining a good modern education and, in April of that year, he passed into the lowest level of the military elite by entering the Nagoya Kadet School.

TWO

Military Aspirations

Ōsugi's career at Kadet School[1] seemed ill-fated from the start. In the spring of 1898, after his first year of middle school, he took the academic and physical exams for entry into Kadet School. Life as a military officer was the only model offered to the youth by his upbringing in a garrison town and by his father. However, the motivation required by the highly competitive examinations must have been absent because he "failed spectacularly" on this attempt.[2] That summer, he visited his mother's relatives, the Yamadas, and was so inspired by life in Tokyo and by their high prestige in the army that he vowed to study hard and pass the exams the following year. The second time around, he passed the written exam with ease, but almost failed the physical because of poor eyesight. However, he was examined by the army doctor assigned to Shibata who had been Ōsugi's doctor for some time and began the examination by saying, "No matter what turns up this year, we must get you admitted." After trying various glasses, he was finally able to give Ōsugi a pass.[3] Ōsugi implies that, the year before, poor eyesight combined with academic inadequacy to block his entry to Kadet School.

There were seven Kadet Schools in Japan. Six were regional schools, and a student had to attend the one that was appropriate to his legal domicile. These six schools enrolled fifty students yearly in a three-year course which was preparatory to a second required three-year course offered by the seventh school, the Chūō yōnen gakkō (Central Kadet School) in Tokyo.[4] In later times, graduates from Kadet Schools were billeted with regiments for a one-year tour of duty as ensigns before they were then eligible to enter the Rikugun daigaku (Army University). Graduation from the university brought a commission as a lieutenant. Teachers at the Kadet Schools were all active-duty army officers and noncommissioned officers. The students legally were full-fledged soldiers, subject to normal army discipline and indoctrination in addition to their ordinary academic education. Ōsugi's legal domicile was his father's old home in Uji, so he entered the Nagoya Kadet School.[5]

On the basis of his entrance examination, Ōsugi entered in the top 40 percent of his class but, after the year-end exams, he rose to seventh or eighth place out of fifty.[6] Since all his courses except French repeated his middle school studies, he did well with little effort. The only subject that he had to devote some time to was French. The regional Kadet Schools offered only French and German at this time, and German was the preferred language throughout the army: Ōsugi's father had sought to give the boy a head start by tutoring him in that language. However, nearly everyone else also wanted to have one of the twenty-five places in the German class, and a competitive test had to be given. Despite his private tutoring, or perhaps because of his father's poor teaching, Ōsugi tested so low that he was assigned to the French class instead.[7]

Sports was an area where Ōsugi clearly excelled, in his own opinion. He relates that he was second in his class in his first year in fencing and first in racing. He was so good at tug-of-war that his side won, no matter how the sides were selected: the company commander had to bench him frequently to make the outcome less predictable. Swimming was the one blemish on his record: boys from Nagoya and Ise were well accustomed to the water, but Ōsugi had never learned to swim and refused to submit to formal instruction. He did teach himself, however, well enough so that he could swim 4 kilometers and was selected as a swimming aide in his second year.[8] Like his fighting in Shibata and his relationship with his mother, Ōsugi's approach to athletics at Kadet School reveals an intense competitiveness that was exceptional in Japan because it gloried in explicit, face-to-face competition. Additionally, Ōsugi's refusal to accept swimming instruction reveals a stubborn streak that had shown up in his early childhood and would again later as an adult: he was determined to be independent not only of orthodox authority but of other leftists too.

In the course of his academic studies, only one event seems to have made a lasting impression on Ōsugi. A teacher of logic explained one day that the true meaning of the Way of the Warrior (*bushidō*) was "choosing a place to die." Ōsugi admired this sentiment and set himself to choosing the place where he would die. He also was inspired to undertake a study of former warriors, especially in terms of how they died, and was particularly struck with the idea of dying by crucifixion.[9] Before entering Kadet School, he had had passing interest in heroic warriors. He had read a biography of Saigo Takamori which portrayed Saigo, leader of the 1877 Satsuma Rebellion, not as one who attacked the Emperor, but as one who was driven from the Emperor by his evil retainers. This inspired Ōsugi to read further about Yoshida Shōin and Hirano Kuniomi, both *shishi* figures of the late Tokugawa era.[10] This is the one indelible impression that past figures made on Ōsugi, and it may be the only point at which tradition clearly influenced him. The idea that one should act without thinking, in conformity with what one knows to be right, with sincerity, is strong in samurai ethics and some schools of Confucianism. Ōsugi the adult can easily be seen as drifting happily in this stream of thought, though it is difficult to draw any firm conclusion from only one example.

Although Ōsugi had no apparent trouble adjusting to the academic and sports curriculum of his new school, life was not without difficulties. In Shibata, Ōsugi had been something of a free spirit, conscious, to be sure, of the discipline that governed the army garrison, but not subject himself to anything similar to it. As one biographer put it, the words "obedience" and "rules" were not even in Ōsugi's vocabulary.[11] Yet, when he entered Kadet School, suddenly he was completely immersed in the rigorous discipline of army life. Moreover, whereas he had previously been able to escape both school discipline in Shibata outside school hours, and his mother's discipline by disappearing from home, the discipline of his new superiors was constant—in class, in the dormitories, and on the playing fields. At first, Ōsugi found the change surprising, but soon it became overpowering and, finally, it overwhelmed him.

Each group of students was under the command of a sergeant and a sergeant major. These men directed the minutest detail of their charges' lives and were responsible for them and for making their lives either tolerable or miserable. Ōsugi's first sergeant took a liking to Ōsugi and would give him a dressing down for infractions instead of reporting him. The sergeant was soon transferred and replaced by a sergeant major who disliked Ōsugi. This man imposed restrictions and punishments on Ōsugi for minor infractions of the rules, such as wearing a pair of dirty socks.

Often, the punishments escalated, especially for Ōsugi. He relates that most of the tobacco that fell into the students' hands was pilfered from noncommissioned officers in charge of them. One night, Ōsugi was the second Kadet to execute such a foraging mission against the sergeant major who disliked him and was unfortunate enough to be caught. The sergeant major marched Ōsugi before the officer on duty and charged him with stealing not only tobacco but also some change. The punishment in either case was immediate expulsion. Demonstrating a remarkable quickness of mind, Ōsugi, who had lost a button in the course of being apprehended, explained his presence in the sergeant's quarters by saying he was searching for his lost button. The officer, who liked Ōsugi, seized upon the story to persuade the sergeant major not to file charges against Ōsugi.[12] In later years, Ōsugi was able to rely on this kind of quickness and presence of mind whenever he was arrested by the police.

The officers and noncommissioned officers could make life extremely unpleasant for their students. In his fourth term, the second one of his second year, Ōsugi again had the sergeant major who had so disliked him during his first year. He relates that, one day after dinner, this man asked if the moon were in its last quarter (*kagen* in Japanese) or in its first quarter (*jōgen*):

> My name was called, and I stood up. I knew, of course, that we were in the last quarter, but somehow the "*ka*" sound just would not come out. With my stammer, the *ka* and *ta* sounds are hardest to say, and the *ka* sound is worst of all.
> "It's not in the first quarter," I replied, with no other way around it.
> "That being so, what is it?"
> "It's not in the first quarter."
> "I said, therefore, what is it?"
> "It's not in the first quarter."
> "Therefore, what is it?"
> "It's not in the first quarter."
> "What?"
> "It's not in the first quarter." [13]

He was, of course, punished one more time. Ōsugi does not indicate that the punishments administered regularly to him and other Kadets were as extreme as they became in World War II. The mental stress, in intention and impact, however, must have been as effective and disorienting for the young Kadets in 1899–1901 as the punishments visited on conscripts shortly before World War II.[14]

Soon after his arrival at the Nagoya School, Ōsugi must have learned that homosexual behavior was one of the activities prohibited on pain of immediate expulsion. He also learned that homosexuality was present at the school in covert form. Despite the regulation, however, or perhaps in his case because of it, he was soon initiated into the group engaging in the proscribed activity by students in the upper classes who had lived in Tokyo before coming to Kadet School. Once, when the entire school was on a trip to the Nara area in 1901, the sergeant major who so disliked Ōsugi caught him in some illicit activity. The *Autobiography* says that a younger student was involved, which implies that the event was in his second year at the school and that it may have been of a homosexual nature. The sergeant roughed Ōsugi up a bit at the time; although he was not expelled, he did receive a sentence of ten days in the school stockade and thirty days' confinement to the school—an indication of the extent to which the young Kadets, aged twelve to fifteen or sixteen, were subject to army discipline.[15]

Perhaps in response to the severe discipline directed at him and certainly in accord with the tradition of fighting that he had established at Shibata, Ōsugi became renowned as a fighter at Kadet School. He was not the strongest or largest in his class, but he quickly came to a dominant role because of his willingness to be violent, audacious, and arrogant. Once when one of the larger boys in his class made some grumbling criticism of Ōsugi's homosexual escapades, Ōsugi responded by thoroughly thrashing the boy in front of all his friends, thereby challenging them and, when they failed to respond, establishing his superiority over them. Another time, he got into a scrap with his largest classmate and, instead of playing around with any preliminaries, he quickly delivered a vicious poke in the eye, one which ended the contest and left a scar that was still much in evidence in 1918 or 1919 when the same lad visited him.[16]

Together with the severe discipline, fighting was to play an important role in ruining Ōsugi's Kadet School career. After the beating administered to him on the Nara trip, he realized he had done something unacceptable, for he did feel repentant. As a result, he gave up cigarettes, which seems incongruous unless he intended to atone for his act by living a completely irreproachable life in the future. He also reflected on his future and wondered whether he could in fact expect to have a successful career in the army, since the officers had actually discussed expelling him for his offense. He even considered voluntarily withdrawing from school, contrasting the disciplined Kadet's life with the life of complete freedom he had had in Shibata. At the same time, he plummeted in the class standings, to thirty-fifth or thirty-sixth in his class; he was first in the theory of discipline, but next to last in conduct. He returned to Shibata for summer vacation in a melancholic, contemplative frame of mind.[17]

Summer vacation only deepened his depression, even though he had several discussions with his father about his future possibilities.

He returned to school so close to a mental breakdown that he sometimes sat by himself at night and cried. Finally, he attempted to compensate by becoming more ferocious than he had ever been. He threatened other students with a whip, defied officers, skipped classes, and loitered around the school. At last, a doctor diagnosed a breakdown and gave him two weeks' leave. He spent the vacation with the Yamadas and returned to school apparently recovered— only to revert to melancholy again. [18]

By November 1901, some of Ōsugi's fellow students decided to try to pound some sense into him, and a fight was arranged with his agreement. Both Ōsugi and his opponent normally carried knives, but Ōsugi decided there was a good chance that he would kill if he drew his, so he determined before the fight began not to draw it. The opponent resorted to his knife, wounding Ōsugi on the face, left shoulder, and left hand and ending the fight. The wounds were serious enough to put him in the hospital for two weeks. His father was summoned and he filled out papers withdrawing Ōsugi from school. Soon after the two returned to Shibata, they received a telegram stating that Ōsugi was denied permission to withdraw and that he was ordered expelled. [19]

The next few months were extremely difficult for Ōsugi. In addition to his knife wounds, he still had to recover from his mental breakdown. A more abstract wound was the stigma of his expulsion from Kadet School: this labeled him a failure of immense proportions in army circles. He had been expelled from school under less than honorable terms, although the administrators did him the favor of not expelling him for homosexual activity but for fighting, which was presumably slightly more acceptable to the army. Worse yet, he had been expelled from not just any school, but from that school system the army used to stock its officer corps. Ōsugi had been soundly rejected by the very organization that he aspired to and that composed his entire universe. All his relatives of any importance, in addition to his immediate family, were members of the military elite society. With perhaps the sole exception of Nishimura, all his childhood friends and certainly all his parents' acquaintances were in army circles. His rejection from

Kadet School must have also meant his rejection by all those who were in army society and who accepted its values, decisions, and authority.

The only real measure we have of Ōsugi's emotions at this time is the fact that he wrote that he received no visitors, not even members of his family, into his room and he ate all his meals in complete silence. He specifically requested that he not have to meet with anyone, a request his mother and father were probably happy to agree to, since it would prevent attention being drawn to their problem child. In addition, he went every day to the hospital at the army camp for treatment, but he does not mention whether his visits were continuing treatment for his stab wounds or some form of psychiatric or drug treatment for his breakdown. [20]

Within a few days of his return to Shibata, he began ruminating on his future, bleak though it must have seemed. He recalled that, when he had begun to dislike being a Kadet, he had often told his friends that they could go ahead and become army men; he would become a war correspondent and meet them on the battlefield. This, he had thought, would allow him to take full advantage of his affinity for language study, and would permit him to indulge his fancy for the literary romanticism popular among young men of the day. Actually, he was more interested in literature than becoming a war correspondent, but figured that he might do that too if a war happened along. He calculated that, to move on with his plan, he would have to go to Tokyo and obtain a middle and higher school education before entering the university to major in literature and French. Such a course would require his father's consent and support, so he resolved to begin his preparations surreptitiously until he could devise a method of obtaining that permission.

Before that happend, Rei-chan put in a second appearance in Ōsugi's life and coaxed him out of his silent withdrawal. Rei-chan and her mother came to the Ōsugis' home for Rei-chan's wedding (presumably they no longer lived in Shibata, but had arranged for the wedding to occur there anyway). He remembered her with fondness and even felt a little jealous that she should be marrying someone else. When she arrived, he quickly forgot his hurt and rejoiced silently at being able to live under the same roof with her, if only for a short time. Although she had probably been warned about Ōsugi's troubles, she called on him in his room shortly after arriving and encouraged him, saying that being in the army was not the only worthwhile goal in life. In return, Ōsugi blurted out the grandiose plans for his future and received her encouragement. Several days later, Ōsugi overheard Rei-chan asking his mother to approve of her son's goals.[21]

A few days after Rei-chan's wedding, Ōsugi had a conference with his father regarding his future plans. Azuma objected to his intention of studying literature at a university in Tokyo; however, he approved of the idea of further education, and urged him to consider studying engineering or medicine. The next day, the army doctor who had examined Ōsugi for entry into Kadet School visited and also encouraged him to study medicine. Soon after that, a Lieutenant Morioka, whom his father respected, stopped by for a talk. To him Ōsugi proposed the alternative of attending a language school instead of a university. At this time, language training was a means by which officers who had not graduated from the Army University could accelerate their advancement and open up the possibility of foreign travel as military observers. Ōsugi's own father had studied French and German and was beginning Russian at the time. Morioka himself had graduated from a Kadet School and then attended a language school in Tokyo. Accordingly, Ōsugi's proposal quickly gained Morioka's support, and the two of them soon obtained Azuma's approval and financial assistance.[22] At long last, Ōsugi was on the way to recovering both his purpose and his equilibrium.

THREE

Socialist Beginnings

In January 1902, seventeen-year-old Ōsugi Sakae arrived in Tokyo, an exciting place for a young man to be. The center of government, the site of the head offices of most important businesses, the embodiment of modern culture, Tokyo had excited Ōsugi when he first visited his relatives, the Yamadas, in the summer of 1898. When he arrived in 1902, though, he was at first too busy with his preparations for the middle school exams to pay attention to the city and its attractions.[1]

Immediately he entered the cram course offered by Tōkyō gakuin (Tokyo Academy) for students hoping to take exams to enter the fifth year of middle school. He devoted special attention to mathematics and physics, his weakest subjects. Around April, he also began attending a French school in the Yotsuya area, since he intended to enter one of three middle schools that offered French. Denied entrance to these schools, however, he had to set French aside and hope that he could learn enough English to pass the September entrance exams for some other middle school. In the midst of his preparations, he received a telegram from his father ordering him home because his mother was dying.[2]

By the time he reached Shibata, his mother had died. Soon after the funeral, he returned to Tokyo and continued readying himself to enter middle school. In October, he took the entrance examinations at Junten chūgakkō (Junten Middle School) and Tōkyō chūgakkō (Tokyo Middle School), both of which were private and, like many second-rate private schools, offered entrance exams nearly every semester. Ōsugi wrote of this:

> I thought I have to get into one or the other somehow. But the exams took place at nearly the same time. By then, I had confidence in my own ability. However, worrying about the worst [that could happen], I decided to take Tokyo Middle School's [exam] which started a bit earlier and to use a substitute for Junten Middle School's.[3]

Unfortunately, his confidence was misplaced: he failed to pass his exam because, he says, he did not know three of the mechanical drawing problems. The substitute did his job properly and passed the Junten exam. Junten was definitely a second-rate school, one that virtually lived off students like Ōsugi who were unable to finish their middle school careers for one reason or another. There were only 40 or 50 students in each of the first and second year classes, yet there were about 200 or 250 in the fifth year class.[4] Junten, however, served his purpose by providing him in 1903 with the required middle school diploma so that he could enter Tōkyō gaikokugo gakkō (Tokyo Foreign Langauge School) in September.

From the time Ōsugi first arrived in Tokyo to begin cram school until 1905 or 1906, he seems to have been at loose ends and unsure of what he was doing. Ostensibly, he was still determined to make a career for himself as a langauge instructor at the Army University—the reason he entered foreign language school. This was the period, however, in which he came into initial contact with the fledgling socialist movement, culminating not in employment with the army, but in an arrest for riotous behavior in March 1906.

From the very first, Ōsugi realized that he was free from any authority or discipline. Though he had to make periodic reports to his father, he was left to his own devices when it came to choosing schools and courses. Furthermore, he realized early on that the teachers at Tōkyō gakuin were indifferent to discipline. They merely taught and paid no heed to whether the students were learning or even if they missed class, arrived late for lecture, left early, slept, or talked. The situation at the French school in Yotsuya was even more removed from his previous experience. Here, most of the students were older than he, usually near the instructors in age, so that friendships between students and teachers often sprang up outside class.[5]

Ōsugi's own friends consisted mainly of young men like himself. He lived in a boarding house (*geshuku*) which was of course open to all, so that some of his fellow roomers were Waseda University students and Waseda Middle School graduates studying to take their civil service exams. Ōsugi associated not with these older youths, however, but with boys who, like Ōsugi, had been expelled from various Kadet Schools and were in Tokyo attempting to enter middle schools. Several of these ex-Kadets had been expelled for homosexuality. All of them eventually got into and through middle school: one followed Ōsugi into language school, one entered a marine products training school, one a merchant marine school, and one a higher school.[6]

Perhaps this group of friends, whom Ōsugi referred to as "fugitive warriors,"[7] insulated Ōsugi from Tokyo and the wide variety of interests it could arouse and cater to. The boys all came from similar backgrounds with the black mark of being expelled from the elite Kadet Schools and had the same determination to make the best possible alternative career become a reality through proper education. The group's determination, individually, to remove from itself the stigma of failure must have reinforced Ōsugi's own determination to work his way back into the army elite which had so recently rejected him.

Ōsugi's own determination, even reinforced by his friends, however, was recently arrived at and lacked strong foundations. In the two months between expulsion from Kadet School and arrival in Tokyo, Ōsugi had to recover from a mental breakdown as well as decide upon a profession to which he could devote himself. To expect both full recovery and absolute commitment to a course of study would be too much, especially if another stress-filled situation should arise. His mother's death must have been just such a strain.

In his *Autobiography,* published nearly twenty years later in

1921, Ōsugi attempted to belittle the effect of his mother's death by describing at great length the renewal of his easygoing friendship with Rei-chan during the two weeks he was in Shibata for the funeral. However, he made a point of mentioning the possibility that his mother may have died from her doctor's malpractice and his father's willingness to pass over the story as a case of "What's done can't be undone" (*Sunda koto wa mō shikata ga nai*).[8] Certainly the death of the only parent and one of the few adults who demonstrated affection for him and whom he loved must have shocked him more than he admitted. Speaking of the time soon after his mother's death, he wrote:

> There was, however, some dissatisfaction within me. I had almost completely forgotten such a matter as the death of my mother, yet there is no mistaking the fact that subsequently I was consciously very melancholic. Further, while I had similarly forgotten about Rei-chan, there is no mistaking the fact that, having completely turned my back on homosexual love, which I had indulged in for several years, I was very melancholic about this side [of life] too. As for friends, there was only the fugitive warriors group from Kadet Schools . . . but we only emulated each other and did not really have close, unreserved relationships.[9]

After entering Junten Middle School, Ōsugi became aware not only of his own discontent, but the world around him. His interest in literature, which had led him to propose to his father that he study it at the university level, reasserted itself about this time. He relates that he and his roommate named Tosaka, one of the "fugitive warriors," read so much that they soon exhausted the offerings of a book-rental store near their lodgings and that they frequented another one in Jimbō-chō, the used book store area in Kanda. At the latter, Ōsugi also branched out from literature and read some philosophy and religion and a little on social problems too. He does not mention what novels he read at this time, whereas he does specifically point out that in 1908–1909 he read, and was strongly impressed by, Tolstoy, Dostoevsky, Turgenev, and Gorky,[10] so we may assume that the earlier literary meanderings had no permanent influence on him. Supporting this conclusion is the fact that the only book he remembered clearly as having influenced him was Oka Asajirō's *Shinka ron kōwa* (Discourse on evolution):

> My interest in natural science was awakened first by this book. At the same time, the theory of evolution, holding that all things change, cried out for the reformation of various social systems which remained as authorities deep within my mind, and made it extremely easy to associate myself with the tenets of socialism.[11]

Evolutionary thought did not lead him to socialism directly, but it opened his mind to the authority of science, which would be an important basis on which socialism, including anarchism, would later appeal to him and other young men in the late Meiji and early Taishō periods. Evolutionary theories were, in any case, an attractive diversion that led in directions other than Ōsugi's original educational plans.

About the only other aspect of the exciting side of life in Tokyo that impinged on Ōsugi's limited interests at this time was a small demonstration. Late one night while studying, Ōsugi heard a ruckus in the street and peeked out to see a group of Waseda University students gathered under his window urging one of their colleagues, a resident in Ōsugi's boarding house, to hurry out and join them. They carried flags bearing the inscription "Oratorical Meeting on the Yanaka Village Copper Poisoning Case." Although he was not curious enough to become involved in the demonstration or anything else to do with the copper pollution case, he was sufficiently interested to pay attention to articles on Yanaka Village that appeared in the *Yorozu chōhō* newspaper.[12]

Shortly before graduating from Junten Middle School, or around the spring of 1903, Ōsugi, responding to the "deficiency" and melancholy he felt after his mother's death, began visiting various Christian churches. Eventually, he went to Ebina Danjō's Hongo Church. Though he always doubted some aspects of the religion, especially the miracles recorded in the Bible, he eventually succumbed to Ebina's argument that full understanding of doctrine and belief could come after baptism and, despite his doubts, he agreed to accept baptism.[13] One of his primary biographers, Akiyama Kiyoshi, claims that Ōsugi did finally become a believer after baptism, as Ebina had predicted, but Ōsugi's own writings make that conclusion unwarranted. In addition to disbelieving the miracles, he wrote that many of his beliefs came not from the Bible, but rather "I believed in that which is within me."[14]

Later in life, Ōsugi wrote that what drew him to Ebina's church, in addition to whatever Christianity might have done to assuage his melancholy over his mother's death, was Ebina's contention that religion was cosmopolitan, that it superseded national boundaries, and that it was libertarian in its denial of all earthly authority.[15] This must be something of an embroidery on the facts. There is no indication at this time that cosmopolitanism and internationalism should have appealed to him instead of a vague "serve-the-nation-through-the-army" nationalism. On the contrary, though he may have been at loose ends and receptive to new ideas, there is no reason to believe that he was ready to abandon the nationalism which he, as an associate of the military elite still intending to return to the good graces of that elite, had been imbued with all his life. The second part of the statement, though, has a ring of veracity. Throughout his school days in Shibata and at Kadet School and in his relations with his mother and other figures of authority, he had constantly denied and rebelled against the claims and directions of authority. Accordingly, Ebina's denial of all earthly authority met with Ōsugi's ready approval.

Perhaps the most important influence on Ōsugi's late adolescent years was the *Yorozu chōhō*. At the time, this newspaper was the most liberal published in Japan. It had attracted some of the most radical writers of the time, including Uchimura Kanzō, a social critic and Christian; Kōtoku Shūsui, a prominent socialist; and Sakai Toshihiko, also a socialist and later Ōsugi's chief rival within the leftist movement. He began subscribing to the paper soon after he arrived in Tokyo in 1902, partly because he wanted to receive any newspaper after getting out of Kadet School, where all papers were prohibited. But the main reason he subscribed was not this or the reporters' reputation or because it contained more information than most papers about events surrounding the Ashio Mine Copper Poisoning Case in which Ōsugi was vaguely interested. *Yorozu chōhō* was simply the cheapest newspaper, and that alone fit the requirements of a poor, struggling student.[16]

While the *Yorozu chōhō* was inexpensive, it served to open up more new ideas and options for Ōsugi's future. Through its columns he became familiar with the names and ideas of Kōtoku, Uchimura, Sakai, Kinoshita Naoe of the *Tōkyō mainichi shimbun* (Tokyo daily news), and Abe Isoo, another member of the socialist movement. He also became aware of, if not immediately interested and involved in, social problems like Yanaka Village and the copper poisining case. Most important, he was presented with an alternative to a military career, the possibility of abandoning a career at which he was proving himself inept. "I had flaunted before me by the *Yorozu chōhō* for the first time the various social lives existing outside of the army. Especially, I had flaunted right before my eyes their unjust and immoral aspects."[17] Rather than being upset or shocked by what he read, he was "surprised by the freedom and wildness"[18] of the newspaper in general and by Kōtoku's writings in particular.

Ōsugi might have remained a distant admirer of the radicals associated with the *Yorozu chōhō* had not the radicals themselves offered him a convenient way to get in touch with them directly. In 1903, just as it was becoming apparent that war with Russia was inevitable, the antiwar articles of Kōtoku, Sakai, and Uchimura came into opposition with the paper's official editorial position, which had changed and ceased to accept pacifism. The three were ultimately forced to resign from their positions. Sakai and Kōtoku quickly formed the Heimin-sha (Commoners' Society) in November 1903 and began publishing the *Heimin shimbun* (Commoners' newspaper) as an organ through which they could spread their antiwar ideas primarily, but also opinions on social problems and essays on socialism.[19]

Within a month or so of the founding of the Heimin-sha, Ōsugi took advantage of the opportunity to become acquainted with the men whose words he had been reading for almost two years. One snowy evening he attended a session of the Shakaishugi kenkyū–kai (Society for the Study of Socialism) at the Heimin-sha. Sakai was presiding and suggested that, since there were many new faces present that evening, they would dispense with the lecture on socialism and have the newcomers introduce themselves. Ōsugi rose in his turn and said: "I was born into an army family, raised among army men, and educated at army schools; because I feel most deeply the falsehoods and stupidity of army life, I want to devote my life to socialism." Sakai rose and said "Here we have the son of a capitalist, we have the son of a soldier, we have this man and we have that man: in fact, our ideas are now spreading into all corners under heaven. Our movement is striving to become the greatest movement in the world. The coming of the society we aim at is certainly not far off."[20]

Both men were responding to the partisan atmosphere generated by the meeting and the reinforcement of sympathetic listeners to overstate themselves. No one expected radical social change or a revolution in Japan in 1903, and Ōsugi certainly was not about to devote himself to socialism in the same year. In fact, he did not devote himself irrevocably to the socialist movement until March 1906, nearly two and a half years later, when his arrest forever sealed off his chance of making a career for himself in the army. Until that time, Ōsugi naively participated in the left-wing movement even while aiming for an army career, either not realizing or consciously minimizing the impediments to such a double life in such disparate arenas.

When Ōsugi went to visit the Heimin-sha for the first time, the socialist movment was still small and eclectic. Within the Heimin-sha itself there was a wide variety of ideas ranging from anarchism to humanism, social democratic thought, and Christianity. Christianity, in fact, was considered by most to be the most progressive idea of the period, and certainly it was better known to more radicals and a more important basis for their action than was social-ism.[21] The first socialist party, the Social Democratic Party (Shakai minshu tō), was formed on May 22, 1901, by six men, five of whom were Christians: Nishikawa Kōjirō, Abe Isoo, Kinoshita Naoe, Kawakami Kiyoshi, and Katayama Sen (the sixth was Kōtoku Shūsui). The party was banned by the government on the same day that it was established. Christian influence on the radical movement was so pervasive that Suzuki Bunji, another of Ebina Danjō's converts who later presided over the Yūaikai (Friendly Society), Japan's largest labor union from 1912 to 1921, once launched a new local union with words reminiscent of a Communion service: "'Brothers, take this wine and this bread and think of them as my blood and my flesh.'"[22]

The Heimin-sha was administered by Kōtoku Shūsui, Sakai Toshihiko, Nishikawa Kōjirō, and Ishikawa Sanshirō. Nishikawa had converted to Christianity while in middle school, but under the tutelage of Katayama Sen left the church in favor of socialism before becoming involved in the Heimin-sha. Ishikawa was a Christian and brought to the Heimin-sha the support of his fellow Christians, Abe Isoo and Kinoshita Naoe.[23] Ōsugi recalled that the influence of Christiantiy within the Heimin-sha was so strong that half the younger members were Christians, which he still considered himself to be at the time he joined.

His faith weakened, however, soon after he began frequenting the Heimin-sha, not due to any circumstance of great moment, but rather to the antireligious trend of its dominant leaders, Kōtoku and Sakai. They frequently brought up the subject of Christianity and subjected it to criticism in informal and private conversations, but basically accepted the German Social Democrats' opinion that religion was a private matter and so to be left alone.[24] Among other members, though, the debate between Christians and non-Christians was constant. Ōsugi recalled that he listened to an argument between a young Christian and an older atheist on the evening he went to the Heimin-sha for the first time. He was surprised by the statements of the Christian because, though he too was a Christian, his beliefs were quite different. The young man took a very orthodox stance, believing in the miracles and in the transcendence of God over all things, whereas Ōsugi doubted the miracles and "believed that God is something within the self." The older man argued against the very existence of God and "I rather sympathized with the cynicism of the old man who seemed an atheist."[25] Ōsugi's belief in Christianity probably was shaken by the double impact of discovering that other Christians differed from him in their interpretations of "Christianity" and hearing the attacks on Christianity made by leaders and other members of the Heimin-sha.

Nevertheless, he did not abandon Christianity for socialism at this time. During the next two years, he frequented the Heimin-sha, presumably attending the weekly meetings of the Shakaishugi kenkyūkai. In addition, he often stopped by after classes to do odd jobs like cleaning the premises, distributing the *Heimin shimbun,* and passing out handbills. Though his diary is silent on most of this period, we know that he continued attending Ebina's church until the outbreak of the Russo-Japanese War in February 1904. Of his break with Ebina at this time, Ōsugi wrote in his *Autobiography:*

> After I came to frequent the Heimin-sha, due to everyone's influence, I too began to have questions first regarding those who called themselves believers and then regarding the religion itself. Subsequently, the beginning of the Russo-Japanese War completely cut the ties between the religion and me. . . .
> . . . Primitive religion, that is real religion, I thought, is a communist movement of the first order that seeks to break loose from the social anxieties that come from the discrepancy between poverty and wealth.
> However, the attitudes of religious men toward the war, especially the attitude of Ebina Danjō whom I had believed, were altogether contrary to this belief of mine. Ebina Danjō's nationalistic Christianity, filled with the living spirit of Japan (*Yamato-damashii teki kuristokyō*) became clearly visible to me. He held prayer meetings for victory. He sang hymns that were like army songs. He preached on loyalty and patriotism.[26]

Akiyama Kiyoshi attempts to trace Ōsugi's conversion to socialism to this nationalistic period around the outbreak of the Russo-Japanese War. He points to Ōsugi's reaction to his father's departure for the front as evidence that Ōsugi was already a confirmed socialist by 1904.

Shortly after the war began, Ōsugi's father was sent to command a rear-echelon battalion, and Ōsugi went to see him off at Ueno Station in Tokyo. He was more than a little proud of the figure his father made upon his horse and was nearly moved to tears. "However, my father's appearance also seemed ridiculous to me. I thought, 'For what purpose are you stirred up by the war?' and rather than feeling distress on his behalf, I felt it all ridiculous."[27]

Akiyama writes of this incident: "It is unclear whether or not any kind of effect was imparted directly on [Ōsugi], who sympathized with pacifism, by his father's departure for the front, but I think that his socialism had matured to the extent that his ideas could not be disturbed by his father's military occupation."[28] This is not, however, a supportable conclusion. Akiyama's logic is that Ōsugi's belief in socialism and his father's military career would have been mutually antagonistic and that this antagonism would necessarily have shaken his belief in socialism or caused him to rant against his father if his socialism had not "matured" to the point that it could withstand contradiction. Such an argument ignores, however, the capability of most people to deceive themselves unconsciously and infinitely: Ōsugi might have seen no contradiction between socialism and his father's work or his pride in his father. When he saw his father at Ueno Station, he gave no indication that socialism or pacifism had anything to do with his reaction. Indeed, he seems to have thought either that a man should not be affected emotionally by uniforms and military pomp in the way his father was or that it was ridiculous for a man of his father's inadequacies to be in command of anything.

On a less speculative tack, Ōsugi may have been astounded by the articles on socialism which had appeared under the by-lines of Kōtoku and Sakai in the *Yorozu chōhō,* but there is no indication that socialism made any impact beyond surprise at this time. It certainly did not motivate him to investigate the subject on his own. Indeed, a colleague of Ōsugi's, Miyajima Sukeo, wrote that both he and Ōsugi came to socialism as "curious onlookers": "He did not understand anything about the theories of socialism, but he certainly felt a strong need to have to become an onlooker to socialism."[29] Moreover, Ōsugi's sympathy for pacifism should not be equated with a conversion to socialism: pacifism was consistent with the cosmopolitanism that he saw in Ebina's Christianity before Ebina suddenly emphasized nationalism and deemphasized cosmopolitanism.

More basically, Ōsugi's sympathy for pacifism, on which Akiyama bases his argument, is itself suspect. Ōsugi does not directly offer any reason for abandoning the *Yorozu chōhō* for the *Heimin shimbun* and the Heimin-sha, but it is possible that he felt that Kōtoku and Sakai were wrongly ousted from the *Yorozu chōhō*, and felt he should be loyal to them personally. If this was true, Ōsugi would not have been concerned about what ideas the two men espoused. The fact that he had been a reader of the *Yorozu chōhō* because it was cheap, not because of its ideas, would indicate that personalities as well as price, but not ideas, were what must have been foremost in his mind when the Russo-Japanese War began.

Akiyama presumably considers Ōsugi a pacifist at this time because he went to the trouble of joining the Heimin-sha, which was associated with pacifism by the very nature of its founding, and because of the manner in which he had introduced himself at the very first meeting that he attended: "... I feel most deeply the falsehoods and stupidity of army life [and] I want to devote my life to socialism." There is, however, only the most ambiguous material to support Akiyama's conclusion.

In July 1904, Ōsugi went to Nagoya and spent most of his time on activities associated with the *Heimin shimbun.* He wrote to Nishikawa Kōjirō on July 17 that he was passing out handbills and a few copies of the newspaper each evening and that he felt extremely proud to be able to hand passersby "the newspaper that I love to read." Later, the *Heimin shimbun* published in its July 31 issue a second letter from Ōsugi reporting on a meeting of sympathizers in Nagoya at which the discussion centered on the two questions "How does one become a socialist and how does one work on behalf of socialism today?"[30] A full year later, in August and September 1905, he published an article entitled "Shakaishugi to aikokushugi" (Socialism and patriotism) in *Hikari,* the journal established by the more radical socialists after the *Heimin shimbun* folded. This article consisted of nothing more than his translation of a series of statements by the presidents of the English, German, Italian, and French socialist parties on the problems that patriotism posed for socialism.[31]

When, then, did Ōsugi become a socialist? It is difficult to pinpoint any date because his autobiographical writings leave a gap from the time he went to the Heimin-sha in late 1903 until he was imprisoned in 1906. The police report on his life and thought notes: "In April 1905, he entered the *Heimin shimbun-sha,* joining Sakai Toshihiko, and at the request of [Ōsugi], he did some translations from French. He finally gave his approval to socialism and became a member of the Japan Socialist Party (Nihon shakai tō)."[32] The Nihon shakai tō was formed on February 24, 1906, and lasted until February 22 the following year. This report, however, summarizes the period from 1903 to 1906, despite the date at the beginning, and is therefore unreliable. According to this passage, Ōsugi professed himself a socialist by February 24, 1906, at the latest, but there is still no corroborating evidence: one may join an organization for any number of reasons other than full agreement with its philosophy. Ōsugi joined the Christian church and the Heimin-sha without completely agreeing with either. He probably was equally equivocal in signing himself into the Nihon shakai tō.[33]

In early 1906, there arose a popular movement, strongly supported by leftists, in protest against an increase in the fares of the Tokyo trolleys. The trolley company raised the one-way fare from 3 sen to 5 sen (1 yen equals 100 sen)[34] and is alleged to have passed around nearly ¥100,000 to Tokyo municipal legislators and newspaper men to insure their support. As a member of the Nihon shakai tō, Ōsugi participated in the movement.[35] He certainly had plenty of time to devote to the movement since he had graduated from the foreign language institute in July of the previous year. Shortly before then, on May 18, 1905, he wrote to Andō Chūgi, who was a French instructor in the army's educational system and had been Ōsugi's language instructor at Kadet School, seeking his aid in securing employment following graduation.[36] He hoped at this time to be employed as a French instructor at the Army University (Rikugun daigaku).[37] Ōsugi wrote in his auto-biographical *Zoku goku-chū ki* (Prison diary: continued) that he had some hope when he entered language school of becoming a general or a diplomat or a language instructor at a Kadet School as a result of his language training. But his arrest, on March 15, 1906, ended any possible career in the army. "I was imprisoned for the Trolley Incident several days before the day on which I was supposed to go hear the results of this teacher's efforts."[38]

The arrest, in fact, marked him indelibly as a radical and a socialist, a member of the Nihon shakai tō and an active demonstrator who would interfere with police. Until the time of his arrest, he could perhaps have continued to associate to some degree with radicals while carrying on a normal career in the army. The arrest ended the possibility of such a double life and forced him into socialism. Later he was to write that he was "completed" in prison and, in the sense that he became a socialist there, this was true: it was only in prison that he read for the first time the literature of socialism. Despite the fact that he had been associated with socialists for over two years, he had not become a convinced, educated socialist until the prison doors shut him off from a position in the army elite and made a position in the socialist elite his only alternative.

FOUR

Prison

In the ten-year period after his first arrest in 1906, Ōsugi Sakae became a major leader of the Japanese socialist movement. In the first half of that period, he had an opportunity to study intensively the works of writers from whom he drew many of his own ideas; like most radicals of the period, Ōsugi gained his real education through a series of prison sentences. From 1912–1916, Ōsugi emerged as the foremost activist, theoretician, and publicist of the Japanese socialist movement at the same time the movement was slowly recovering from the nearly fatal setback it had experienced after the High Treason Incident (Taigyaku jiken) of 1910–1911.

Ōsugi spent a total of more than three years in prison from his March 15, 1906, arrest for rioting until his last release in November 1910. He served prison terms for rioting in the trolley demonstrations, simultaneous terms for infractions against the press laws in connection with two articles published in late 1906 and early 1907,[1] a term for violating the Peace Police Law in the course of the Rooftop Incident (Yane-jō jiken) in early 1908, and a term for violating the Peace Police Law again for resisting a police officer during the Red Flag Incident (Akahata jiken) in the same year.

The Rooftop Incident occurred at a meeting on January 17, 1908, of the Kinyōkai (Friday Group), socialists who supported

Kōtoku's direct-action tactics following the 1907 split in the socialist movement over the question of direct action.[2] Kōtoku had gone to the United States in 1905–1906 and returned with convictions about the futility of attempting to reform society and of the tactics of a legal political movement. Revolution was necessary, and he proposed direct action to accomplish it. By this he meant unified action by workers against the existing economic system, a general strike which would destroy the capitalist economic system and the political system together. The corollary of this was that political action within current legal confines guaranteed indefinite continuation of a political system that might suppress a moderate socialist movement at any moment. This tactical theory shocked the socialist movement in 1906 when Kōtoku enunciated it. In February 1907, Kōtoku was able to get the annual meeting of the Japan Socialist Party to drop its policy of staying strictly within the limits of the law, although he was not able to make it accept his position regarding tactics. The move split the socialist movement into sharply opposed wings on the question of direct-action tactics, wings that resisted all attempts at mediation. It also caused the government to take more aggressive action against both factions.

At the Kinyōkai meeting of January 17, police ordered the meeting halted because of what they considered a radical turn in the conversation (the speaker had begun to talk about Thomas More's *Utopia*), but the order was ignored. Ōsugi, Sakai Toshihiko, and Yamakawa Hitoshi mounted the roof to avoid the police and harangued passersby until they were arrested. Ōsugi was sentenced to only a month and a half for this incident, whereas he received a year and a half for his earlier rioting charge in the trolley demonstrations. In that case, he was initially found innocent, but the public procurator appealed to higher courts and, after one more finding of innocence and a further appeal, obtained the heavy sentence.[3]

The Red Flag Incident—occasioning Ōsugi's only other arrest until 1919—brought him his heaviest sentence: two and one-half years in prison and a fine of ¥25.[4] This incident resulted from competition between members of the moderate Dōshikai faction of the socialist movement and the radical Kinyōkai. The clash with the police was precipitated by a gathering of both factions on June 22, 1908, to celebrate the release of Yamaguchi Gizō (Koken) from prison. Earlier, on the 19th, when Yamaguchi arrived in Tokyo, there was a small street demonstration, apparently by members of the Dōshikai faction, complete with red banners bearing the legends "socialism" and "revolution." At the close of the meeting on the 22nd, Ōsugi and Arahata Kanson led other members of the direct-action group in an escalated response: they carried red flags inscribed with the more radical words "anarchism" and "anarcho-communism." When they tried to leave the meeting hall, police scuffled with them for possession of the flags, but they succeeded in carrying their demonstration into the street. Sakai and Yamakawa were not involved in the fracas to begin with, but were arrested (as were Ōsugi, Arahata, and ten others) when they attempted to intervene between police and radicals. In the trial, one defendant received a suspended sentence and two were found not guilty, while everyone else received stiff sentences of one year or more; Ōsugi's sentence was the heaviest.[5]

The Red Flag Incident is significant in two respects. First, it occurred just when there was rising pressure against the first Saionji Cabinet which had refused to initiate excessively repressive action against the socialist movement. In the face of ever more outrageous actions by the socialists, this policy was criticized by Saionji's enemies. The Red Flag Incident provided Saionji's political opponents with ammunition to topple the Cabinet on July 14 when the second Katsura Cabinet was formed.[6] The stiff sentences dealt to defendants in the Red Flag Incident represented the harsher attitude of the Katsura Administration and foreshadowed even worse repression to come, namely, the High Treason Incident for which twelve radicals, including Kōtoku, were executed.

The Red Flag Incident was significant for Ōsugi too. Most important, it saved his life and the lives of Sakai, Yamakawa, and Arahata by putting them safely in jail when the High Treason conspiracy occurred. A defendant found innocent in the Red Flag Incident was later arrested, tried, and executed in the High Treason

Incident. Ōsugi, Yamakawa, and Sakai were in fact questioned about the conspiracy. The public procurators insisted that the plot had been launched four or five years previously, so that Ōsugi could have known about it. They also claimed that others had named him as a conspirator. Although he was questioned only once, his jailors treated him with a great deal of suspicion thereafter, and refused him his normal twice-monthly letters and visits. This worried him, even though Sakai, who had been sentenced to two years, was released on time without trouble.[7] Ōsugi notes that he saw the High Treason defendants in prison, but was afraid to try to speak to Kōtoku in anything but a whisper, which the partially deaf Kōtoku could not hear.

When Ōsugi was released from prison in November 1910, just two months before Kōtoku was executed, he found that all the activities of Japanese radicals, even publishing, were suspended. The series of incidents in which Ōsugi was involved, topped off by the gloom that followed the High Treason Incident, taught him a lesson he never forgot even though he never articulated it: a radical may do almost anything, but he must never directly confront and oppose a policeman or execute any violent action against the government. In the future, when he wrote about labor tactics, he always restricted himself to economic action, the formation of model future societies among workers, and the development of the individual's ego. He also lived his own life in a more subdued fashion once he learned that confrontations with the police were always losing propositions for radicals. The only time he forgot to live by these rules of behavior was in 1919 when he was irritated enough to punch an officer and was sentenced to three months, his only sentence after 1910 except for a short term in French jails in 1922.[8]

As Kadet School was necessary for a boy to become an army officer, prison was required to make Ōsugi an anarchist. It was in prison that he finally gained familiarity with radical ideas that before then he had neither the opportunity nor the inclination to acquire. The first educational step he took in prison was to study foreign languages, which were absolutely crucial tools for Japanese radicals, because "translations were treated by censors much more severely than the foreign originals (doubtless from fear of the proletarian audience which vernacular editions might reach). . . ."[9] Each time he went to prison, he arranged to do some language study, allowing himself three months to learn the basic grammar and vocabulary and three more to be able to read without a dictionary. Thus, when he entered Sugamo Prison in Tokyo on May 29, 1907, he began to study Italian and, by June 11, he wrote that he had finished 40 out of 400 pages in an Italian grammar text. On July 7, he thanked his wife, Hori Yasuko, for a better text which would let him "graduate" by the end of August. In this way, he added Esperanto, Italian, German, and Russian to his repertoire. Esperanto in particular paid a dividend: he opened Japan's first Esperanto school after he married Hori Yasuko in September 1906.[10]

Ōsugi was also able to devote considerable time to reading, although he had to work too: convicts were expected to fulfill work quotas. At Chiba Prison between 1908 and 1910, Ōsugi was assigned to make hemp straps to hold *geta* (wooden clogs) onto the foot. Eventually he was able to increase his study time by persuading prison authorities to substitute Japanese hemp for the stiffer Nanking hemp he had been using.[11] "From morning to night I pass the time looking at books . . . and counting the unavoidable bedbug bites."[12] When he entered prison, he once reported, he took with him a dictionary and five or six books, one of which he was permitted to exchange each week for a new one.[13] Sandwiching his reading in between his work hours, he began to expand his theoretical knowledge in accordance with his interests.

His investigations were sparked by the theory of biological evolution which he first encountered before entering prison in the work of Oka Asajirō: "As I read [Oka], I felt as if I were gradually growing taller and as if the limits in all directions were steadily expanding. The universe which I had not known until now was opening itself to my eyes with every page. . . . There is nothing at all which is not changing."[14] Evolutionary ideas formed the foundation for all his later thought.

In prison, Ōsugi imbibed large doses of anarchist literature and discovered that anarchism was in close agreement with evolutionary theories. Kōtoku sent him a copy of Bakunin's *Collected Works,* probably in French,[15] and on September 16, 1907, Ōsugi wrote that he was reading Bakunin, Kropotkin, Reclus,[16] and Malatesta.[17] He noted that anarchist writers commonly discussed nature and the biological world before touching on human affairs because of the strong parallels they saw between biology and sociology:

> Anarchists begin by explaining astrology in the introduction. Then, they explain the plants and animals. Finally, they discuss human society. In due course, I tire of books. I raise my head and stare into space. The first things I see are the sun, moon, and stars, the movement of the clouds, the leaves of the paulownia tree, sparrows, black kites, chickens, and then, lowering my gaze, the roof of the opposite prison building. It's exactly as if I were practicing what I was just now reading. As scant as my knowledge of nature is, I am constantly embarrassed. I think, "From now on I will seriously study nature."
>
> The more I read and think about it, nature is for some reason logical, and logic is embodied completely in nature. Further, I must admire nature greatly, for this logic must similarly be embodied entirely in human society which has been developed by nature . . . .
>
> Besides a desire to study nature, I have come to have a great taste for anthropology. And anthropology has deeply drawn my mind toward human history.[18]

Just as Marxism and Leninism later appealed to Japanese with their claims to be scientific, anarchism attracted Ōsugi with its apparent base in science or at least its attempt to emulate biology.

Kropotkin was especially appealing to Ōsugi for this reason. In the same letter quoted above, he added that he would like to translate Kropotkin's autobiography, a task he did not accomplish until 1920. While in prison, however, he did read Kropotkin's *The Conquest of Bread* and his *Mutual Aid,* which argued, in opposition to Darwin's theories, that all forms of life survive by helping members of the same species, not through a competitive system of survival of the fittest. Humans especially need not be constantly and murderously competitive, as Social Darwinists argued. Rather,

Ōsugi saw in Kropotkin a peaceful existence in which all animals could best survive by aiding each other; unfortunately, humans had abandoned mutual aid for coercion, but careful study of people living in relative freedom revealed a tendency toward mutual aid. Ōsugi in 1915 criticized Oka Asajirō for expounding Huxley's misinterpretations of Darwin's theory of the struggle for existence. [19] Kropotkin's *Mutual Aid* remained important to Ōsugi, and he translated it in 1917.

One very important aspect of Kropotkin's theory was that human society, like the biological world, was characterized by growth, evolution, and change. Although mutual aid was not a primary characteristic of current society, and especially not of the relationship between state and citizen, it could be found here and there in society. Cooperation inevitably would evolve as the single characteristic of all human interaction. Kropotkin's view of the future was, in short, far less violently revolutionary than Bakunin's. Kropotkin was less interested in the mechanics of revolution than he was in the distribution of wealth after the revolution. [20] Bakunin, on the other hand, gloried in revolutionary violence: he was perfectly willing to appeal to the baser instincts and to enlist the aid of criminals in order to further the revolutionary cause. "It was Bakunin's opinion that, the more destruction there was, the better: if only for the reason that by this destruction of the old system any return to it would be impossible or at least extremely difficult." [21] For Ōsugi, leaving prison just as the full weight of suppression broke the back of the socialist movement in 1910–1911, Kropotkin's evolutionary approach was perfect. It may have even prolonged his life, since Ōsugi might otherwise have left prison in a more radical, more violent mood than when he entered, had he come more under the influence of a revolutionary like Bakunin instead of Kropotkin. In fact, in late 1907, before his long prison term in which he read Kropotkin extensively and before the Rooftop and Red Flag Incidents, he wrote that he was anxious to get out of prison and to become active again. He said he had been thinking about what kinds of activity to pursue and planned to discuss them with other members of the socialist movement when he got out of prison.[22] The combative frame of mind that had gotten him into the two incidents was later quieted by large doses of Kropotkin.

We cannot know for certain what Ōsugi read, but we do know his reading list was broad enough to include science, anthropology, philosophy, sociology, economics, and literature in English, French, German, Russian, Italian, and Japanese.[23] We also know he read in a systematic fashion:

> Since I previously had hopes of making sociology my own specialty, I set my mind to making it a reality during the two and a half years [I had in prison]. However, were it similar to the existing sociology, it would have been worthless. I wished to pursue earnestly a very particular sociology on my own. In order, first, to understand the fundamental characteristics of the human beings who constitute society, I wanted to be well versed on the main points of biology. Next, in order to understand the course by which humanity has come to conduct social life as human beings, I wanted to proceed to anthropology, especially comparative anthropology. And finally, I wanted to achieve a sociology built on these two sciences. Thinking of this now, I am embarrassed: I was thinking the thoughts of a mere novice. When I added up all the books that I wanted to read and tried counting the days required to read them, [I realized that] two and a half years would never be enough.[24]

With typical lack of modesty, he added that "I needed at least another half year."

Even though Ōsugi did not achieve his goal of composing a major new sociological theory, his prison reading provided him with much of the material he was to write about beginning in 1912. Moreover, his prison experience was one of the most significant periods in his life. He wrote in 1919:

> Actually when I got out of [prison] at last, I felt for the first time that I had become a real person. I felt that no matter where I went in the world I could present myself without hesitation as a unique being. And I embraced a kind of religious feeling about my prison life being an ordeal, a blessing imparted by the gods (kami).[25]

This semi-religious feeling of conversion was obviously stimulated by the discovery of new ideas from many sources which seemed to fit together into a coherent philosophy. It may also have been stimulated, however, by the conditions of prison life, conditions that pushed inmates beyond their physical limits.

Food in prison was always in short supply, and Ōsugi invariably lost some weight in jail. When he was incarcerated for the longest time (1908–1910), his body reserves were depleted and he found himself constantly hungry, no matter how much he got to eat. He often dreamed of gorging himself and reported that, in contrast, Sakai dreamed of nibbling delicacies. The dreams were so realistic that Ōsugi would even suffer from diarrhea the following day. The prisons were not heated, and in winter, especially when hungry, he was cold except when briefly warmed in the Japanese-style bath. However, staying in the bath too long caused fainting or, as he put it, "cerebral anemia." While in prison, he contracted pulmonary tuberculosis and was to suffer from weak lungs for the rest of his life.[26]

The harshness of prison life was best reflected in Ōsugi's remembrance of sexual desire in prison. His first prison terms were short enough that he continued to feel desire: his energy reserves and mental balance remained essentially unaffected by the lack of food and by confinement. When he was in prison for longer, though, he was surprised to discover that after a while he felt no sexual appetite at all. He even worried when he found himself unable to respond in any way to a series of memories and fantasies that previously had been stimulating. As in modern American prisons, homosexual encounter was a common event: attractive new prisoners were sought after, and most fighting was caused by competition for exclusive access to one prisoner. One of the ordinary prisoners propositioned Ōsugi one day in the bath, but Ōsugi repulsed him, abiding by the resolution he made in Kadet School to give up homosexual activity. He and some of the other socialist prisoners who had also been propositioned by common prisoners laughed about the incident later, but he added that it was not really a laughing matter.[27] It brought him close to the undercurrent of violence in prison life.

All these physical complaints combined to place the idea of death uppermost in Ōsugi's mind. He may have been thinking of figurative death before he even entered prison and encountered literal death. He wrote his father when he entered jail, requesting two things. First, that Azuma legally disinherit him so that Ōsugi's siblings never need suffer on his account; Ōsugi suggested that this matter be taken care of by his younger brother's father-in-law, who was a lawyer. Second, he asked that Azuma support his prison education by providing ¥300 for books, even though he was, in his words, "an unfilial son."[28] Azuma turned down both requests.

In prison, however, death was real. He recalled seeing a prison employee who seemed to be considered inferior to all other guards and who was repulsive in appearance and action. Nevertheless, Ōsugi was intrigued until another prisoner told him the man was the executioner who, in truly macabre fashion, supposedly received ¥1 for a feast after every official act. Ōsugi learned later that this was the man who carried out the sentences of the High Treason conspirators, after which he retired. Ōsugi's last term in prison, his longest, when he met the executioner, was filled with what he termed "impressions" (*inshō*) of death: his father's death in November 1909, the death of a close but unnamed friend, the death of a fellow prisoner, the death of a comrade who went insane soon after his release from prison, purple rings around the necks of executed prisoners he had known, even the deaths of insects in his cell. He once captured a dragonfly and attached a leash thread to it the way Japanese children do until he realized with a shock that he was robbing the insect of its freedom and threatening its life in much the same way that the state was treating him.[29] He did not become morbid about these "impressions"—even when cold, hungry, and ill, he was too optimistic to be dragged down by them—but they showed up several years later in his philosophical writings about life.

The extent to which Ōsugi was distressed can perhaps be imagined by contrasting prison conditions as he saw them with his finicky stylishness. In a letter that probably dates from his first period in jail in 1906, he said that it was absolutely necessary for him to use a comb and a dandruff brush in the morning or else he felt everything was in a state of disorder. He also revealed that he had been given the nickname Ōhai, a diminutive of *haikara* (literally, high collar, or a dandy, a swell).[30] Bedbugs, hunger, cold, and death helped to jar this dandy irrevocably from his course and brought into question all his previous concepts and assumptions. Yet, rather than recant, as arrested radicals would do later, he used his prison years to deepen his understanding of the radical ideas he had been toying with prior to his arrest.

One man Ōsugi met in prison had a particularly strong impact on him. This was an ordinary criminal who managed to live in complete disregard for all the rules and regulations that were supposed to govern life in jail. He had accomplished this feat by making sure that he broke every rule he could and by not caring whether he was punished or not. His ability to transcend chastisement convinced the guards that punishing him was ineffective because they thought him crazy. Therefore, they stopped all punishments and the man lived in perfect freedom, aside from his physical confinement.[31] Ōsugi admired the man's approach to prison life, and the spirit with which he lived, and his admiration appeared later in his theories on the expansion of life.

Ōsugi's time in prison had a profound effect on him. He entered jail as a hotheaded, unlettered, radical youth, and exited full of ideas. Prison was a forge in which ideas were pounded together and shaped by reading, then tempered by the physical hardship of prison life. He needed now only the opportunity to display his new thoughts in print.

FIVE

Intellectual Foundations

When Ōsugi finally was released from jail in November 1910, armed with all his new-found ideas, he discovered that the socialist movement was in hibernation. News that Kōtoku and the other High Treason conspirators were accused of plotting to assassinate the Meiji Emperor had undermined the entire socialist cause: hundreds of anarchists and socialists had been arrested and questioned in connection with the incident, and for good reason they were afraid. Publishers would have nothing to do with socialists and their writings for fear of being associated in the public mind with treason. The socialists themselves had no organ of their own to speak through except for Katayama Sen's *Shakai shimbun* (Socialist news), which advocated socialist goals achieved by democratic, reformist means. Even Katayama, however, was forced to halt publication in mid-1911. Ishikawa Sanshirō and Katayama finally gave up and left the country for France and America, respectively. The mood of the times dictated caution and Ōsugi was urged to follow suit.

In December 1910, Sakai Toshihiko began his Baibunsha (literally, Purveying Literature Company), for the express purpose of providing a living for as many radicals as possible. He solicited for publication virtually any material that would sell: translations, opinions, advertisements, and announcements.[1] The intent was strictly commercial. The Baibunsha was to replace the income that radicals once were able to secure by writing for newspapers and journals. The Baibunsha paid flat rates for translations (which were just about the only thing that would still sell even if done by socialists): translations from English to Japanese paid 50 sen per page; from other languages to Japanese, 60 sen; translations from Japanese to a foreign language, 1–2 yen per double-spaced, typed page. Compositions in Japanese brought only 50 sen per 400-character page.[2] Sakai's company became the main source of income and a central gathering point for socialists when no other avenues of activity were available.

While the Baibunsha provided its beneficiaries the opportunity to hold body and soul together, it remained cautiously apolitical in response to the surrounding ocean of hostility. Ōsugi was advised to leave well enough alone and not vociferously advocate anarchism, but he was unhappy with the passive attitude that was taken by Sakai, who had become the leader of the more radical socialists after Kōtoku's execution. In August 1912, he and Arahata Kanson began planning to publish a new socialist journal. At one time, they had been convinced that they should wait until public opinion seemed more amenable. Now, growing impatient, they decided to set to work to create a climate favorable to a revival of socialism.[3] In 1958, Sakai wrote:

> At that time, I thought that, as far as the movement was concerned, there was nothing to do except wait a while for an opportunity and I said so. However, young, spirited comrades like Ōsugi and Arahata could not "wait for the [right] time," but thought they should proceed and "make the [right] time" by themselves, and they persisted in that. The realization of that persistence was, then, the monthly journal, *Kindai shisō* (Modern thought).[4]

In October, Ōsugi and Arahata began publishing *Kindai shisō*. In the first issue, Ōsugi wrote that he had contemplated publishing a journal two years earlier, while still in prison, but was delayed, owing to the High Treason Incident.[5] The journal would give equal attention to literature and literary criticism, science, sociology, and philosophy, echoing his primary areas of interest while in jail. Both Arahata and Ōsugi hoped that *Kindai shisō* would stimulate new growth in the socialist movement by being both literary and abstract, a hope that reveals the narrowly intellectual basis of the movement at that time. The journal published between 3,000 and 5,000 copies each month for twenty-three issues until September 1914, by which time Ōsugi and Arahata felt unhappy with its overwhelming literary bent.[6]

By this time, Ōsugi was known as an anarchist. Anarchism was the leading radical socialist philosophy in the world at the time, the main competitor with moderate social democracy for leadership of the socialist movement worldwide. In Japan, as elsewhere, Marxism-Leninism and other forms of socialism ultimately became more important, but anarchism provided the starting point for the socialist debate early in this century.

Anarchism defies a simple definition. George Woodcock described anarchism in the following way in his *Anarchism, A History of Libertarian Ideas and Movements:* "As a doctrine it changes constantly; as a movement it grows and disintegrates, in constant fluctuation. . . ." (page 18). There are as many theories of anarchism as there are anarchists. Nevertheless, a degree of definition is necessary and possible.

Anarchism as it developed in Europe rejects authority and rigid organization, especially as found in government. Anarchists, however, differ regarding the nature of their ideal society and the degree to which post-revolutionary society will be structured. Anarchism developed out of classical liberalism, taking liberalism's assumptions about individualism and the role of government to a logical extreme and arguing that the individual and his full development were of first importance. Although the individual is the central concern of nearly all anarchists, the range of approaches to his liberation is extremely wide, stretching from absolute individualism to syndicalism. Individualist anarchists see men living as hermits in nearly complete isolation, whereas anarcho-syndicalists envision men living in voluntary, highly complex, and constantly changing social organizations. The same spectrum of opinion is present on the question of how to revolutionize society. The individualist would have anarchism achieved through assertion of self or will, while the syndicalist would organize a union within which an anarchistic lifestyle could exist while, simultaneously, the union members worked together to form the foundation of an anarchistic society.

All anarchists hew to a naturalistic view of man and society. The essence of man and the essence of society are contained one within the other. Man is by nature social and good; the anarchist must somehow discover that nature and help others discover it in themselves. Society is a natural growth and good as long as it is free from laws and institutions imposed on it by man: imposed institutions render society unnatural and bad. Anarchists therefore reject Utopian thought because it seeks to create an artificial society rather than allowing society to evolve naturally. Moreover, a Utopian's society is a perfected one which cannot change except to become imperfect. In their natural states, man and society are, anarchists hold, free to change constantly. Although anarchists disagree on the question of the progressive nature of evolution, man and society may both grow better, but there is no perfect state that either will achieve. This fact in part prevents anarchists from describing in detail (and often in general, too) what men or society will be like after the revolution overthrows authority. Their visions of the future are frequently expressed through studies of the past or of primitive peoples in which men can be found living naturally in society. Rather than rejecting the past as dictated by progressivism, anarchists appear to revivify the past for use in the future, thereby suspending themselves between the two.

Since the anarchists spring from the fountain of romantic naturalism, there is a strong tendency to reject the industrial economy and modern society in favor of a more bucolic and pastoral setting for the anarchist future. Even syndicalists who seek to develop new ways of organizing industrial relations are susceptible to the call of the farm—so close to nature, so simple.

Anarchism should not be confused with nihilism and terrorism, as it so often is in the popular mind. Nihilism as a philosophy denies moral truth and natural law. Even further afield are the Russian Nihilists who formed a political organization dedicated to establishing constitutional government by means of assassination; the Nihilists, however, were philosophically neither anarchists nor nihilists. Terrorism is a tactic that few anarchists deny, but no anarchist advocates it as a primary tool of revolution.

Ōsugi had a steady concern for discovering truth and natural law through the study of man and society and cannot, therefore, be identified as a nihilist. His stance on the question of violence was more ambiguous. He frequently voiced his support for the tactics of "direct action," which became a code word for the general strike and for industrial sabotage, but he never advocated using terrorism against the state or against individuals and certainly never saw terror and violence as the sole means to effect the change to anarchism. He might have been hesitant to print statements supporting industrial sabotage because of fear of censorship, preferring instead to praise the inexplicit concept of "direct action," but there is no evidence that he spoke even in private in favor of violence.

The first anarchist who attracted Ōsugi strongly was Kropotkin, whose collectivistic anarchism appealed to Ōsugi on the basis of its scientific approach; his influence on Ōsugi has already been mentioned. During the period from late 1912 through early 1916, Ōsugi drew heavily on his reading of Kropotkin and other European writers to introduce the new ideas he had picked up in prison and soon after his release. Other important influences were Henri Bergson, Friedrich Nietzsche, Max Stirner, and Georges Sorel.

Much of Ōsugi's revolutionary and syndicalist thought came from Georges Sorel, who in the late nineteenth and early twentieth centuries reacted violently against the European rationalist and positivist traditions. Sorel disagreed with the prevailing assumption that human experience was progressive, an assumption that was not seriously doubted until the Great War destroyed it. The war

was a hideous embarrassment to the prevailing Meliorist myth which had dominated the public consciousness for a century. It reversed the Idea of Progress. The day after the British entered the war Henry James wrote a friend: "The plunge of civilization into this abyss of blood and darkness . . . is a thing that so gives away the whole long age during which we have supposed the world to be, with whatever abatement, gradually bettering, that to have to take it all now for what the treacherous years were all the while really making for and meaning is too tragic for any words."[7]

Sorel had rejected rationalism and progress long before, seeking instead an intuitively knowable, "non-rational basis of thought." In the words of one scholar, Sorel "framed a political philosophy of active radicalism based on the assumptions of irrationalism—on the superiority of the myth of projective impressions over critical judgment."[8] Irrationalism led Sorel to glorify violence, which he distinguished from force:

> Basically an act of force is said to represent an act of officialdom—of established authority. Force is that which is employed by the state to defeat its only potent adversary—those able to employ counter force. Now counter force, the force not of established authority but of producers in capitalist society (and by inference, the middle class in feudal society, the industrialists in mercantile society, etc.), is given the designation—violence. "A terminology which would give rise to no ambiguity" would be one in which "the term violence should be employed only for acts of revolt," while "the object of force is to impose a certain social order in which the minority governs."[9]

Sorel insisted that, although malice was inappropriate in the workers' revolution because it made them blind to their task while subjecting them to demagogues, economic and political changes were mere palliatives which prevented workers from developing direct violence to the fullest. Violence was an absolute necessity to achieve freedom: "Violence in Sorel's scheme is not an accidental aspect of social existence, an agency for eliciting changes. Violence forms the warp and woof of social structure."[10] To reduce violence artificially was ultimately counterproductive, because the system became more oppressive as the middle class became less violent. Oppression increased worker violence which led to more middle-class violence. Sorel's irrational violence was action in which thought and act were simultaneous, a simultaneity of motive force and act that Ōsugi was to incorporate into the beginning of his essay, "Sei no kakujū" (The expansion of life), where he pointed out that "the existence of energy and of movement are synonymous."[11]

At first glance, Kropotkin's emphasis on cooperation in the evolutionary process and Sorel's glorification of violence as the means of social change seem contradictory. Kropotkin had accepted violence as an unavoidable but temporary aspect of the revolutionary movement only, not as a constant of human existence. Similarly, cooperation among men and Sorel's class competition appear in opposition. Ōsugi never successfully eliminated these tensions, but he did find a link between Kropotkin and Sorel in Henri Bergson, the French philosopher (1859–1941), who strongly influenced such writers as Marcel Proust and George Bernard Shaw at the turn of the century, as well as Sorel and, of course, Ōsugi, who was one of the first to introduce Bergson to the Japanese reading public.[12]

Bergson was one of the leaders of the anti-positivist, anti-rational, anti-mechanistic school of thought which Sorel was attracted to and so forcefully espoused. He championed humanistic and spiritual values, much to the delight of Ōsugi, who, under the combined influence of Bergson and Sorel, later penned "Boku wa seishin ga suki da" (I like spirit) in 1918. Bergson strongly defended the idea of human liberty from the pessimism of scientific determinism. He held that the mind and the spirit were independent of all physiological factors of the body and that thought, accordingly, was independent of the limitations and controls of the material world. He also held that there was a vital impulse in the evolutionary process which constantly changes and gives rise to new forms. Unlike Hegel's Idea in History, this vital impulse does not control and guide evolution in an inexorable, progressive direction, but allows for change in all possible directions: one development may lead to either a much lower one or a higher one without favoring either one. Bergson also divided thought into two categories: analytic thought which can only conceive of things as opaque and discontinuous, and intuitive thought which sympathetically grasps the innermost reality of a thing and knows it absolutely.[13]

Bergson's ideas made it possible for Ōsugi, in considering the evolutionary process, to allow for the vagaries of the free human mind and the will (Bergson's vital impulse) in either an individual or a class. With Bergson, he emphasized the limitations of science and the limitless possibilities of intuition, emotion, and instinct. He also argued at length for the necessity of the full development of the individual as the independent entity it deserved to be. This was to be done by applying intuitively grasped knowledge to the self by means of the force of the will. Ōsugi never rejected science; rather he hailed science as humanity's genius, arguing only that it should not be assumed to be superior to intuition.[14] In short, Bergson provided Ōsugi with a way to reconcile his twin concerns of science and the intuitive spirit and also with a way to bridge the gap between Kropotkin and Sorel.

The last two Europeans who exerted major influence on Ōsugi were Max Stirner and Neitzsche, whom Stirner influenced. Stirner, the pen name of Johann Kaspar Schmidt (1806–1856), stressed the efficacy of the will and instincts as opposed to rational elements, which he regarded as useless at best and certain to lead the individual toward servility.[15] He held that each person must become his own master at any cost. Ōsugi summed up Stirner's extreme individualism: "There is no necessity for people to conform to anything outside themselves, not to God and not to morality. Outside of individual rights there are no rights whatever."[16] Ōsugi refused to agree completely with Stirner's individualism, since it so isolated the individual from society.

Neitzsche's ideas of the "superman" and "will to power" also affected Ōsugi. Ultimately he rejected the idea of a "superman" who would command the obedience of the masses: he rejected even the possibility of the intellectual class leading the workers. He did accept, most strongly, the "superman" who transcended his limitations through his own will power.

Ōsugi was a foremost exponent of individualism in both his thought and life style. However, he also reflected the cautious attitude that most Japanese have toward individualism, which so often seems to them to border on selfishness. He therefore took pains to note, in late 1915, that individualism and selfishness were not identical, since selfishness was a willingness to sacrifice anything, including other people, their belongings, and their interests, in order to force a way into and up in the world.[17] Ōsugi was careful to set himself at a distance from the extreme individualism of Stirner and Neitzsche, even while he praised them.

Ōsugi accomplished this by arguing that true individualism, especially in the Japanese context, was still in the process of developing. He saw two main schools of individualist thought. The first was "psychological individualism," which was introspective, subjective, and pessimistic. It denied the reality of social organizations. The other school, "social individualism . . . lacks subjective sensitivity regarding all social organizations and, accordingly, quickly falls into optimism which approves today's social organization." Since neither of these satisfactorily allow for both the individual and society to develop equally, a third form of individualism will emerge which "will be, if viewed on a plane, a fusion of psychological individualism and social individualism, or, if viewed three-dimensionally, a harmonization of early individualism and later individualism."[18]

The question of the isolation of the individual from society, which Ōsugi saw and rejected in Stirner, is an interesting one. Most Japanese socialists found themselves unable to resist the influence and power of social and family ties. Often, when their Western-based, modern ideas came into conflict with society or family, they were unable to reconcile the two or to reject social traditions in favor of ideological truths. Kōtoku Shūsui was buffeted by familial pressure and criticism from colleagues when he became extramaritally involved with Kanno Sugako, and he was unable to withstand either. Later, in the 1930s, when police were pressuring Communists to recant (*tenkō*) international revolution, one of the most effective tactics was a series of visits by influential family members, friends, and former teachers, all pleading for recantation; few could resist a mother's tears.

Ōsugi, however, discovered individualism early and made it one of his major concerns. He was able to provide the individual, at least himself, with a fully developed theory of individualism. His individual, however, was linked to society through syndicalism. Syndicalism brought together individuals in labor unions in which they could construct small liberated societies within society in general. The unions, or syndicates, sustained the liberated individual and provided him a base from which he could work to change the rest of society. This integration of individualism with a social structure provided Ōsugi with immunity from the traditional pressures of society.

Although *Kindai shisō* eventually proved too moderate and literary for Ōsugi's pleasure, its pages included articles that remained basic to all of his thought, whether on the nature of man, revolution, revolutionary methods, or the labor movement. These articles concentrated on life (*sei*) in the broadest possible meaning of that word, and reflected, in its most literal sense, a subject that had been of crucial concern to him in prison. Perhaps not coincidentally, his health was poor when he wrote some of these articles. In November 1913, he complained that bronchitis prevented him from writing or editing, and Arahata, substituting for him, noted the next month that his partner was much worse. In January, he was still restricted to bed, and in February he moved to Kamakura where the milder climate eventually proved healing. His tuberculosis also recurred. This bothered him and his wife through the middle of 1914 and was compounded by an intestinal disorder in the spring.[19] Thus life in even the most elemental sense was a great worry to him.

Ōsugi began a series of three articles on the history of human society and the life of the individual in the middle of 1913, a series that closely paralleled his own development in prison. They were his most important writings prior to his love affairs. Jail had by brute force made him realize that he was subject to society's wishes as expressed through the established institutions of his society, especially the legal system. His first article, "Seifuku no jijitsu" (The reality of conquest), echoed Kropotkin and reflected his interest in uncovering the origins of subjugation. The fact of conquest, or subjugation, was important, not merely to him as an individual, but to society, for "Society, or at least what people now call society, began with conquest." Presocial humans lived in romantically free bands, much like beasts. When over-crowding occurred, however, friction arose and "the previous life of peaceful, semi-beastly freedom was lost and civilization, so-called, was born. History had begun."[20] Friction led to war in which one band achieved victory through the accident of technological superiority. The victor subjugated the loser, and a society of two classes, the conqueror and the conquered, was established.

Although the superior class had come to power because of military technological strength alone, it attempted to make real the inferiority of the conquered class by asserting the inferiority of the conquered class's gods, language, customs, and traditions. Eventually, this discrimination became institutionalized in a coherent government which promulgated regulations touching all facets of human activity in such a way as to insure continuation of the two-class system. Educational systems were established "to implant fully in the hearts of the conquered class the concept that in all ways the conquering class was the superior race." Often, however, the conquerors were only militarily superior and were forced, therefore, to obtain the assistance of some members of the culturally superior conquered class. Recruits quickly appeared: "Intellectuals among the conquered people entered the ranks of the conquerors, cooperating with the enterprise of conquest." Society always has been and always will be divided into two classes, whether they be, as the *Communist Manifesto* put it, "Grecian freeman and slave, Roman patrician and plebian, Middle Ages lord and serf, guild member and journeyman."[21]

In recent society, there still were only two main classes: the conqueror and the conquered, capitalist and worker. The worker was kept subjugated through ever more refined tools: "Government! Laws! Religion! Education! Morality! Armies! Police! Courts! Parliament! Science! Philosophy! Literature! All the other social systems!" All other classes either consciously or unconsciously acted like intellectuals in earlier periods and became collaborators with the ruling class. "This fact of conquest is the basic fact of human society through tens of thousands of years, past, present, and near future. As long as one is not clearly aware of this fact of subjugation, one cannot properly understand anything about social matters."[22]

Ōsugi concluded the essay with a blast at most of the readers of *Kindai shisō*, readers who were mainly writers, critics, or connoisseurs of the literary arts:

> Along with boasting of superiority and wisdom, you literati proclaim the supremacy of individual rights. As long as your sensitivity and wisdom touch not on the reality of subjugation or on opposition to it, your writings are jokes. They are submissions which try to forget the weight of this reality that presses in even on our daily lives. They are a potent element of constitutional deception.
>
> Static beauty which spellbinds us with vanity has no relation to us now. We yearn for dynamic beauty which gives rise to ecstacy and enthusiasm. The literature we cry for is a creative art of malicious and rebellious beauty in opposition to that reality.[23]

This attack presaged, in its Sorelian orientation, the Japanese school of proletarian literature which took the life of the worker as its primary focus and sought to demonstrate the Marxist truths of life in a capitalist society while instructing the worker-reader and inspiring him to revolutionary activity.

The role of malice or hatred in literature or art in general was a topic Ōsugi later expanded on when he translated Romain Rolland's *The People's Theater* in June 1917, and in an article based on the ideas of *Theater*, "Atarashiki sekai no tame no atarashiki geijutsu" (A new art for a new world) in October 1916.[24] According to Ōsugi, art of all kinds epitomized the ideas and emotions of the class from which it derived: it propagated that class's ideas. In a society in which two classes are necessarily struggling against each other, the oppressed class needs its own art as an expression of its ideas, as a revelation of its "life power" (*seimeiryoku*), and as a tool with which it can fight against the conqueror class. When the classes are struggling, "it is the purpose of art to support and fight together with the people, to arouse the people, to destroy the ignorance that obscures the way the people should take, and to drive back ignorance."[25]

According to Ōsugi, violence, as defined by Sorel, was a significant part of the daily life of the oppressed class. It was not to be minimized, for this would allow the lower classes to rest content in their subjugation.[26] Rather, it had to be harnessed and directed against the ruling class in order to prevent advanced elements of the working class from being enticed to collaborate with the rulers. As Sorel wrote:

> The bourgeoisie tries to annihilate [the abject poor] and assimilate [the rising poor]. But it is our political and artistic ideal to bring together these two peoples and give them a collective sense of their party. And in this respect we agree with the aims of syndicalism. Not that we are endeavoring to set one class against the other, but because we wish to establish the greatest harmony among the various forces of the nation; to this end, we would have each of the constituent elements—above all, those in which strength is greatest—preserve intact its individuality.[27]

In July 1913, the month after "Seifuku no jijitsu" appeared, Ōsugi continued his argument in "Sei no kakujū" (The expansion of life), the second of his three important articles on human existence and life. He had established that the primary condition of man in society was subjugation, which was an unnatural state that resulted from civilization. Life (*sei*) and the expansion of life or of the ego were a single force and were the opposite of subjugation: "Life and the expansion of life are, it goes without saying, the keynotes of modern thought. They are the alpha and omega of modern thought." Life, in the narrowest sense, was the ego, comparable to energy:

> After all, the ego essentially has one kind of energy. This kind of energy conforms to the principles of energy in energy dynamics.
> Energy must appear at the instant of movement, for the existence of energy and of movement are synonymous. Consequently, the action of energy is not something that can be averted. Action itself is the entirety of energy. Action is the sole aspect of energy.
> Thus, the inevitable logic of life commands us to action and to the

expansion of life. And what we call action is nothing but causing the spatial expansion of whatever exists.

However, the expansion of life must also be accompanied by the fulfillment of life. Indeed, fulfillment is forced by expansion, and, accordingly, fulfillment and expansion must be the same thing.

Thus, expansion of life becomes the sole duty of our lives. That which causes satisfaction of the tenacious demands of our lives is only the most effective action. Also, the inevitable logic of life directs that we remove and destroy all things that try to impede the expansion of life. When we defy these orders, our lives, our egos, are retarded, corrupted, and destroyed.[28]

Ōsugi continued to define the expansion of life and of the ego. In discussing deeds or practice (*jikkō*), which he defined as "the direct action of life," he stated that practice is a deed in which

the background of the primary event is activity quite amply reflected in our heads. There is contemplation as a consequence of this activity. And there is fascination as a consequence of this contemplation. As a result of the fascination there is emotion. And this emotion calls forth further activity. Therein is no simple subjectivity or objectivity. Subjectivity and objectivity are congruent. This is my ecstatic frontier as a revolutionary . . . .

While in this ecstasy, my consciousness of the reality of subjugation is at its highest and clearest point. My ego, my life, are then reliably established. Every time I experience this frontier, my consciousness and my ego become more and more clear, more and more reliable. The joy of living begins to overflow.

This perfection of my life is at the same time the extension of my life. And at the same time, the expansion of the life of mankind.[29]

All people who are self-conscious, expanded, know what must be done and how. They know and therefore act in concert with their knowledge.

Reflecting the influence of Kropotkin, Ōsugi noted that competition with other men, or the expansion of one's own ego over the egos of other men, might hinder the development of others; that is, expansion of the self in a class society resulted in conquerors and conquered. The conquered were prevented from developing and, since that which is not evolving is devolving, their egos were degraded and corrupted. However, "if there was a slavish depravity among the slaves, there was a masterly depravity among the masters." The servility of one excited the arrogance of the other. He added, "Further, the struggles and exploitations among humanity conspicuously hinder humanity's struggle with and exploitation of the environment."[30] When the morals of members of both classes became too corrupt, a middle class revolted and established itself as the new conqueror, only to repeat the cycle again. No one ever imagined the consequences of simply getting rid of all masters and slaves; people throughout history kept repeating the process. No one "presumed to put at last the ax to the fundamental reality of conquest itself. This is the greatest error of human history. We must end the repetition of history."[31]

Ōsugi believed that, in his own lifetime, subjugation had again reached an apex. "The master class has begun to agonize over the excessive and singular expansion of life. The subject class has begun to suffer asphyxiation in its oppressed life. The middle class also has been infected by the agonies of both these classes. This is the primary cause of the afflictions of modern life."[32] When men came to hate the reality of conquest, they would rebel and their rebellion would free them to enjoy the "expansion of life":

> Seeing the supreme beauty of life in the expansion of life, I see the supreme beauty of life today only in this rebellion and destruction. Today, when the reality of conquest is developed to its utmost, harmony is not beauty. Beauty exists only in discord. Harmony is a lie. Truth exists only in discord.
>
> Now the expansion of life can only be gained through rebellion. Only through rebellion is there creation of new life, creation of a new society.[33]

In his final article in the series, entitled "Sei no sōzō" (The creativity of life) and published in January 1914, six months after "Seifuku no jijitsu" and "Sei no kakujū," Ōsugi drew heavily from Sorel to study the consequences of the freeing of the ego: "A life rapidly progressing from necessity to freedom! A creative life [moving] from external compulsion to internal initiative! This is surely the final goal regarded as the ideal of socialism."[34]

Although Ōsugi equated his philosophical goals with the ideal of socialism, he departed from the socialists, in his own estimate, in two ways. All socialists, himself included, agreed on public ownership of the means of production, but socialism, he felt, so emphasized the social environment that the spiritual dimensions of the individual were ignored:

> Socialism is based on the materialistic view of history, but, as a result of its excessive concern for economic progress and industrial technological progress as the elements of social evolution, it has forgotten that, while it emphasizes the leap from necessity to freedom, the creation of internal initiative out of external compulsion must be not only the point of arrival, but the point of departure. [35]

In short, Ōsugi believed that an economic revolution could not occur unless the workers were mentally, spiritually, psychologically, and morally prepared for it. Efforts were required in the present society to create new ideas which would simultaneously bring into existence and fit the new society. Both the post-capitalist technology and the post-capitalist mentality had to evolve under the present capitalist system:

> When the workers have completed these preparations themselves, that is to say, when they are able to administer their own society, then for the first time will come the social revolution.
> Thus the workers' spiritual education is the essential thing. You must teach the workers what they themselves will, you must discipline them by action, you must reveal to them their own abilities. This is the entire mystery of socialist education. [36]

Syndicalism was preferable to socialism insofar as it concentrated on this educational process, striving to prepare each worker to perfect his ego and to work together with other workers as if in their future society.

Also, unlike the Japanese socialists, Ōsugi remained skeptical of the final goal of the social revolution and refused to state explicitly what the final goal was; instead, he implied that a parallel existed between a movement and its goals, energy and action, thought and act:

In a movement there is direction. However, there is no "ultimate purpose." The ideal of a movement is not something that discovers itself in its "ultimate purpose." Ideals usually accompany the movement and advance with it. Ideals are not things that precede the movement. They are in the movement itself. They cut their pattern in the movement itself. [37]

On the individual level, much the same thing is true. The perfected ego will not spring suddenly from the ideal economic system: the ego and economy must be simultaneously constructed out of the present and the materials it offers:

Freedom and creativity are not ideals that we should yearn for only in the future. We must seize them now from reality. We must derive them from within ourselves.

Deriving freedom and creativity from within ourselves is nothing but knowing that these things are one's own self, knowing that they arise from this self by virtue of the self. [38]

Ultimately, the individual is by himself responsible for his own development toward freedom and creativity. This the individual accomplishes by both the rational and irrational exercise of his will:

We know that we evaluate various social trends and select from them those that are close to our inner aspirations, that are close to our individual purpose of life. We also know that sometimes we repudiate and transcend the trends. In other words, we see our will for authority [*kenryoku ishi*] bestir itself. Thus, when we consider the freedom and creativity of the individual initiative of the ego, we feel that we must let it be the basis for individual and social progress.

As Neitzsche says, the self, meditating and acting freely, is an eager arrow speeding to the target. We must seize and develop, then, the mysterious impulse which contains this self and the entire future.

Freedom and creativity are not outside of us nor in the future. They are within us now. [39]

The ego must continually strive to assert itself against a hostile environment. It changes or develops only with struggle and cannot even be discerned when it does not struggle. The social environment, continually threatened by the development of the ego, oppresses life and tries to destroy it. The few individuals who best carry on this struggle are anarchists and syndicalists. "On the one hand, [syndicalists] have affinities of intellect and feeling and ties of interest, and, on the other hand, they have observed a resolute struggle against their environment. Their watchwords are union and revolt." The creativity of life is achieved, then, through the destruction of present society and the development of "elements of the new society amid the organizations of the old." When the elements are sufficiently developed, "a last great struggle" will overthrow the old system and erect the new one.[40]

These three articles form the basis for Ōsugi's ideas, a foundation that can be found beneath most of his subsequent writing. The theory of the expansion of life is particularly important to an understanding of his anarchism because upon it he built not merely his radical philosophy but his personal lifestyle: he became his own best example. His anarchism, however, eludes facile description. There is no single work or series of works in which he offers a definition of his version of anarchism. In part, this is due to the medium in which he expressed himself. Ōsugi was a free-lance journalist and received most of his earned income by writing articles which usually appeared in one of the journals that he published consecutively. He therefore expressed himself mainly in short articles eight to twelve pages long. Some of these he must have written merely because he had a bill to pay or he had to flesh out that month's issue: many articles were cannon fodder and contained nothing new or significant. The rest of his articles were so short that each contained, at best, one complete idea that was not directly related to any other idea or series of ideas: the three articles on the expansion of life were a unique and closely related series. It is difficult, then, to piece all his published work together into a coherent whole. The matter is made more complex by the fact that Ōsugi relied on a variety of European sources for most of his ideas. He borrowed material from across the entire spectrum of anarchist opinion; many of his most important articles were mutually exclusive if not antagonistic. Even his theory of life, carefully constructed as it was, was not without contradiction.

The contradiction was contained in the idea of the expansion of the ego. Ōsugi argued that expansion of the ego in all social systems experienced by man heretofore injured the egos of others. Therefore, the only possibility of ego expansion was at the cost of others; on the class level, it caused one class to rise to dominance at the expense of another class. Ōsugi described men as forced into either egocentric behavior or annihilation of the ego through submission to the fact of subjugation. Exactly how the individual could "properly" expand his ego without impinging on others was not explained. The reader is forced to assume that a total revolution, one that would eliminate subjugation altogether, would put an end to the cycle of ruling classes. Presumably, a society without subjugation would also be one in which each individual's ego could expand infinitely, but it is not clear why such expansion would not continue to cause harm to the egos of other people.

Ōsugi's thought bears a resemblance to Marxist thought. His commitment to a socialist society, whatever its definition, and his European sources, are within the socialist spectrum. Nevertheless, there are major differences between Marx and Ōsugi that make the resemblance superficial. Like Marx, Ōsugi assumes classes to be irreconcilably antagonistic and seems to accept an economic definition of class. Ōsugi, however, does not assume that classes are based strictly on their relation to the means of production. Instead, he theorizes that classes originally were established by force of conquest and that the subsequent rise and fall of a class relates to its ability to employ violence to overthrow the ruling class, then to use the organs of government and institutions of culture in addition to force to subjugate other classes. This process has no specific relation to the economy except that the ruling class is able to appropriate the fruits of the economy for itself. The ability of a class to bully its way to superiority depends solely on whether it has sufficient will to achieve its goal and whether other classes lack the will to oppose it.

In this emphasis on human will, Ōsugi was similar to other Japanese socialists. Reflecting the Confucian influence in their backgrounds, Japanese socialists were often uncomfortable with starkly materialistic interpretations of Marxism because these failed to allow any role for the spiritual side of man. Ōsugi differed from the socialists, however, even while mirroring their concern with the spiritual side of existence in his emphasis on ego expansion. Here was an idea completely un-Japanese in its promotion of individualism and self-assertion, rather than altruism and the achievement of self-fulfillment through service to society.

SIX

Ōsugi and the Police[1]

Although Ōsugi's three articles on life formed the basis for highly revolutionary statements and conclusions, he was unable to put his radical views into practice. In "Sei no sōzō," the last of the three, he voiced his discontent, saying, "At present we do not have the freedom to theorize here on the details of [the syndicalists'] movement."[2] A few months later, Arahata Kanson expressed the same kind of discontent. In the April 1914 issue of *Kindai shisō*, he said he was bored because he and everyone else had to write continually with an eye to what the police would or would not allow to be published. Writing for the police in this manner resulted in a magazine containing diluted theories. Indeed, Ōsugi had to act as an in-house censor in order to avoid police censorship, and once he had to suppress two of Arahata's articles. This provoked Arahata to observe that Ōsugi exercised more rigorous censorship than the police.[3]

Censorship was a constant problem that all Taishō radicals had to come to terms with. There were basically two varieties of censorship: before or after publication. In the case of censorship prior to publication, articles were seldom rejected, but would appear in the published version with either an "X" or an "O" in place of any word deemed objectionable by the police. If the editors decided not to submit to prior censorship, then the only form of post-publication censorship was a prohibition on sales and distribution and, usually, confiscation of the entire issue. Since virtually none of Ōsugi's manuscripts exist today, those of his articles submitted for prior censorship are often found only in their published, mutilated form, while those that were in banned magazines exist in their entirety, since libraries and the authorities carefully filed them away.

Ōsugi published, edited, or was in the background of nine different magazines and newspapers. He submitted none of them for prior censorship, so he had to live more often with the consequences of post-publication censorship. While this was a decision consistent with his anarchist ideas, it engaged him in a running battle against the censors and police who had to watch him trying to circumvent their surveillance.

Ōsugi's first magazine, *Katei zasshi* (Home journal), was no more radical than the name suggests and was not censored. The second one, *Kindai shisō* (Modernism), was published from October 1912 to September 1914 by Ōsugi and Arahata. This journal was dedicated primarily to literature, science, and philosophy for young intellectuals and did not directly challenge the censors.[4] By 1913, however, the magazine had begun to change. Arahata was summoned to the Metropolitan Police Headquarters and informed that it was becoming more and more a "frankly ideological" journal that was in danger of suppression if it did not limit itself to literature. Arahata was warned that he and Ōsugi should return the journal to primarily literary activities or face confiscations and bans on sales and distribution.[5] It was for this reason that Ōsugi exercised rigorous censorship himself throughout the magazine's tenure and noted Arahata's complaint that the in-house censor was much more severe than the official censor.[6]

Tiring of such a tame publishing endeavor, Ōsugi and Arahata stopped *Kindai shisō* and began *Heimin shimbun* (Commoners' newspaper), which lasted for only six issues, from October 1914 to March 1915. The new journal was intended to reach a new audience, the workers, who were encouraged to struggle for their own best interests. This more radical position was also reflected in the tone of Arahata's proletarian literature and Ōsugi's expositions

on anarchist theories.[7] The title itself called to mind the paper of
the same name published by Kōtoku Shūsui and indirectly evoked
memories of the High Treason Incident. All of these were
essentially challenges directed at the police; the censors responded
by prohibiting the sale and distribution of all issues but one.

Ōsugi reacted to the censors in a spirit of confrontation. In
issue No. 4, he bent a bit by publishing only articles that had
already been published elsewhere,[8] but later he, Arahata, and
six others walked around downtown Tokyo wearing sandwich
signs explaining their problem with the censors and passing out free
copies of the fourth issue. The police report notes dryly that "this
action appears to be in retaliation for the banning and confiscation
of the newspaper's fifth issue."[9] After the sixth and last issue was
banned, Ōsugi went to the Metropolitan Police Headquarters and
reportedly threatened to publish and distribute surreptitiously if
the censors persisted. He also warned that publishing bans and
police surveillance should not continue because ideology would
simply spread underground, as had religion in other periods of
Japanese history.[10] Apparently, the police were not very impressed; Ōsugi had to give up his radical publication for lack of
money and return to more moderate activities. His difficulties
bore out the policies of Okuma Shigenobu, who became Prime
Minister in April 1914: rather than create martyrs by oppressing
socialism, he urged the police to disrupt their publications, continually forcing them into financial difficulty, then collapse.[11]

The name of Ōsugi's next journal, *Kindai shisō*, was intended to
reflect the moderation of its namesake, the first *Kindai shisō*.
Ōsugi hoped that the name alone would alter the police attitude
toward his publication by bringing to mind the moderate image of
the first *Kindai shisō* and diverting attention from the content
which remained unchanged from the *Heimin shimbun*. Unfortunately, this plan was bound to fail, and all issues after the first
were banned. The journal ceased publication in January 1916, after
four months of existence, unable to survive the double burden of
external pressure from the police and internal conflicts that arose
between Ōsugi and his colleagues. The other participants in the

publishing venture refused to continue futilely beating their heads
against the wall of police suppression and were angry, in part, with
Ōsugi's behavior in a much-publicized love affair (see Chapter 7
below). They felt that Ōsugi was too dictatorial in his management
of the magazine,[12] and that his personal finances in relation to
those of the magazine were questionable. Specifically, they worried
that the financial demands of his love affair might make him spend
Kindai shisō money for his private concerns.[13] Ultimately, they
removed him from dominant editorial control after the third issue
was banned. When the fourth issue was also censored, the endeavor
collapsed from lack of income, lack of unity, and failure to avoid
the censor's wrath.

Ōsugi did not publish a magazine of his own again until *Bummei
hihyō* (Cultural review) appeared for three issues from January to
April 1918. Although short lived, *Bummei hihyō* suffered no
problems with the police. Ōsugi chose to stop publishing it in favor
of establishing a new journal that would be directed at the working class rather than to maintain an abstract, theoretical level of
writing.

This new publishing effort was *Rōdō shimbun* (Labor news), of
which four issues were printed from April to July 1918. Officially,
Ōsugi had no position on the editorial staff, a fact that saved him
from serving a term in jail. Two of his young followers, Wada
Kyūtarō and Hisaita Unosuke, served as editor and office manager,
respectively. No copies of the monthly newspaper are known to be
in existence, but it apparently strove to be inflammatory, encouraging the workers toward class antagonism, a general strike, and
disruption of the public order. The young men were able to keep
several thousand copies of issue number four out of the hands of
the police and distributed them to workers. They, but not Ōsugi,
were convicted of violating the Newspaper Law.[14]

Ōsugi's next publication came in October 1919, when he
brought out the first of his three journals named *Rōdō undō* (The
labor movement). The first *Rōdō undō* lasted for six issues
between October 1919 and June 1920. Although none of these
were banned, Ōsugi halted publication for lack of money. The

police seem to have left the journal alone because, rather than being a theoretical journal that condoned revolution and advocated the tactics of the *Rōdō shimbun,* it acted as an organ for educating workers and as a clearing house for their writings.[15]

The second *Rōdō undō* was published from January to June 1921 with money from the Communist International which was given to Ōsugi at the Conference of Far Eastern Socialists held in Shanghai in October 1920 (see Chapter 9 below). This was Ōsugi's first and only weekly magazine and, partly out of deference to the Comintern's wishes and partly because he believed in a united front of all revolutionaries, Ōsugi included both anarchists and bolsheviks[16] on his staff. Editorially, it favored both groups. Ōsugi thought that they could work together successfully, but he gradually realized that their theories were incompatible and felt that the bolsheviks on the staff were plotting ways to eliminate the anarchists from the magazine. The feud grew until Ōsugi halted publication in June 1921.[17] Again, there was no problem with censorship, perhaps because the articles, despite the forecast by both anarchists and bolsheviks of an early revolution, were more concerned with providing information on the Russian Revolution than promoting one in Japan.

The third *Rōdō undō,* Ōsugi's last publishing endeavor, began six months later in December 1921 and lasted until July 1923. Ōsugi was careful this time to include only like-minded anarchists and dedicated the journal to battle against the bolsheviks. Although absent in France for the last eight months of the journal's life, Ōsugi apparently kept the censors happy by concentrating on criticism of the Russian Revolution and its Japanese supporters. Again, not one issue is recorded as being banned.

Thus, Ōsugi was able to distribute his publications providing he was discreet, and he learned lessons sufficiently from *Heimin shimbun,* the second *Kindai shisō,* and *Rōdō shimbun* to know exactly what he could not print. According to a definition of thought control which stipulates, among other things, that it "may be directed . . . toward . . . external expressions of thought. . . ," any form of censorship amounts to thought control.[18] On the other hand, there is no indication that Ōsugi changed his thinking on account of censorship or that censorship was intended to have that effect. Moreover, by choosing to submit his journals only to post-publication censorship, he was quite clearly betting that he could publish his articles unchanged. Whenever he lost, he had not just a word or sentence suppressed, but a whole issue. He was able to publish in his own and other journals enough material so that anyone who read a sufficient amount would have little question of what he thought. In this sense, whatever semblance of thought control there was, was so desultory that it might just as well not have existed.

More troublesome than censorship was physical surveillance. Like most other socialists from late Meiji through Taishō, Ōsugi was continually followed by police detectives.[19] We do not know when the police began shadowing him; the first few entries on his record simply note the incidents for which he was arrested and tried, beginning with his conviction for rioting on March 15, 1906, during the strike against an increase in the Tokyo street car fares. The first definite indication that he may have been shadowed is an entry in the police record dated December 1910, when he is noted to have said to an unidentified person: "Though I am an anarchist, I believe neither in adopting direct action as Kōtoku [Shūsui] has nor in engaging in a movement like parliamentary politics; rather, the only solution will come through education of the workers. Things like his general strike and assassinations are only exceptional measures of last resort. . . ."[20] Though it is not clear when surveillance began, it continued daily until his death in 1923.

Much of the information produced by the shadows was of only marginal value and interest, but it does indicate the intensity with which surveillance was undertaken. Many entries in the police record, like the one quoted above, consist of fragments of Ōsugi's conversations with other, often unidentified, people or his remarks at study groups which he often organized or attended. The record, which includes quotations of half a page or more, does not indicate whether the police agents were openly attending the meetings or whether they were listening secretly. Other quotations were probably overheard through open windows or in public places.

It seems likely that Ōsugi's daily shadows were usually uniformed policemen. Unlike the later Shōwa period, when there was a special Thought Control Bureau within the Metropolitan Police Headquarters assigned to keep track of Communists and other radicals, surveillance during the Taishō period was the responsibility of local police stations. After Ōsugi moved from Sugamo to Kameido in December 1917, he quoted an article in the *Jiji shimpō* (News of the times) which said that the Sugamo police were much relieved by his departure while the Kameido police were reported at their wits' end. [21]

The quality of the surveillance, therefore, varied according to the practice of the police station involved. When Ōsugi went to live in Kamakura for a few months in early 1914, the Kamakura police kept a record of who came to visit him and for how long. These facts were not kept track of by other police stations except as background for the record of an overheard conversation. Similarly, recorded surveillance on study and oratory groups that Ōsugi was involved with varied. The recorders always noted the place and time of meeting, usually the number of people who attended, and sometimes the names of the more renowned radicals present, but only in the case of one organization, the Sanjikarizumu kenkyūkai (Society for the Study of Syndicalism), did the reports go so far as to note also the number of attendees who were not socialists or anarchists. [22]

Police seldom interfered directly with these groups. One exception was a meeting of the Heimin kōenkai, which was interrupted because unconfiscated but banned copies of the *Heimin shimbun* (Commoners' newspaper) were distributed. The police pressed no charges but merely cautioned the group for this and for trying to make speeches outdoors. They also objected to public meetings of the Sanjikarizumu kenkyūkai; so, instead, meetings were held at Ōsugi's home. [23] As long as rules of this nature were not broken by the radicals, however, the police did no more than listen to what was said, noting only the more radical comments, but taking no action.

The police were also expected to obey certain rules in their surveillance activities. For instance, when an organization held its first meeting in a police station's jurisdiction, the police always made a brief investigation. Thereafter, the meetings were not disrupted except for good reason, such as a speaker explicitly advocating assassination of an official or other revolutionary activity. At a meeting of the Heimin kōenkai on February 1, 1916, police dispatched from the Ueno police station attempted to ask questions about the nature and purpose of the meeting, even though it was not the first within their area. Ōsugi and the other radicals verbally abused the police and were consequently placed in custody but released. Two days later, Ōsugi went to the Metropolitan Police Headquarters to object to the interference and threatened some unspecified retaliation, which apparently never occurred or was never recorded. [24]

Police also maintained watch on Ōsugi's mail, although it is impossible to determine exactly how thoroughly this was done. The police record includes the text of a post card he sent on September 10, 1911. Later, in early 1918, Ōsugi complained that, after a move from Sugamo to Kameido, he was able to ascertain that five or six letters had not been forwarded. He wrote that the Sugamo post office was slovenly, but there is also the possibility of police interference. The only time this kind of surveillance led to an arrest was when a sympathizer in Niigata wrote to Ōsugi and included some comment of a lese majesty nature. The sympathizer was tried and convicted. [25] This is the extent of information on mail surveillance.

Ōsugi's attitude toward police shadows demonstrates that both he and the police worked within limits. When he was in Osaka at the time of the Rice Riots, he heard that a riot had developed at a particular rice shop so, together with a group of friends, he decided to inspect the location. Since most of the men present, including Ōsugi, were being shadowed, the tour group consisted of about twenty uniformed policemen and their radicals. After the radicals, surrounded by the phalanx of police, inspected the riot, the officer in charge begged Ōsugi and his friends to leave the area because, "if anything happens, I will get in trouble: if headquarters finds out about this, I will be held responsible."[26] Ōsugi complied and discussed the Rice Riots with the policemen until they arrived at a colleague's home. The policemen appeared about to enter and continue the discussion until Ōsugi sharply reminded them that their place was outside.

Several years later, Itō Noe, who was Ōsugi's second wife, described an incident in which three policemen followed Ōsugi, Yoshida Hajime, and herself. She complained that they were following much too closely and reminded them to obey the "shadowing rules." When they began arguing with her, Ōsugi grabbed one by the collar and marched off to their station where he was threatened with arrest. Itō finally found the station chief and explained the situation. He ended up admitting that the shadows had acted improperly and assigned new shadows to them with his apologies.[27]

Usually, however, relations between Ōsugi and his shadows seem to have been relaxed, even friendly. He and other radicals often had their shadows run errands for them. Itō relates that she sent her shadow to a labor union meeting in 1919, when she became worried about not receiving any message from Ōsugi; he was eventually arrested but not charged. Again, when Ōsugi was being questioned about defrauding his landlords, she relates that he sent his shadow to tell her that he might not be home that night and again later to tell her that there was still no decision on whether he would be charged or not. In the same essay, she notes that Ōsugi had not returned by seven o'clock that night and that there was no word from the shadow either.[28]

Ōsugi frequently felt the need to slip off without his shadows. In 1920, his wife and children pretended he was sick so that he could arrive in Shanghai before the police discovered his absence. Later, in 1922, when he was trying to borrow money to go to Europe, he slipped away from his shadow, presumably to conceal the identity of his benefactor. When he actually did leave for Europe, his family again pretended that he was sick, and for ten days the shadow was sent to a nearby shop to buy ice for him before his absence was discovered.[29]

However often Ōsugi might have used his shadows as errand boys or escaped from them so that he could go somewhere alone, he was careful to follow certain rules, just as he expected the police to follow certain rules. Kondō Kenji, a close colleague during Ōsugi's later years, recalled an incident demonstrating this. When the Shin'yūkai, a typesetters' union under strong anarchist influence, went on strike in 1919, Ōsugi's faction held a secret meeting to lay plans for inducing all printers in the Tokyo area to join the strike. Kondō was a bit late so, instead of taking the time to lose his shadow, he merely sent the man off to buy some cigarettes, then disappeared in the opposite direction. Later, Kondō related his deception to Ōsugi and Wada Kyūtarō. Osugi said, "That's contrary to *bushidō* (the Way of the Warrior)." Wada asked, "What kind of connection is there between deceiving a shadow and missing an important meeting? How is it different from giving the shadow the slip and sending him to do some shopping after you return?" "They are different!" maintained Ōsugi. Wada retorted with "According to historical materialism . . ." when Ōsugi cut in with "Historical materialism? Don't talk rot! This is a spiritual matter!"[30]

What Ōsugi called a "spiritual matter" could well be called a matter of principle too. Subterfuge in order to escape the prying eyes of a shadow was acceptable, provided that he and his fellow radicals did not take advantage of the shadow's trust and good will. Ōsugi made no objection if the police watched him and managed to overhear his conversations, but he repulsed them if they became overbearing or imposed themselves too much. Ōsugi used the shadow as an errand boy, but only when the errand would not prevent the officer from performing his duties. Conversely, Ōsugi was friendly with officers, but would not let that relationship interfere with his own activities.

Even on the subject of arrests and imprisonment, it is possible to argue that the authorities exercised moderation. Between 1910 and

1923, Ōsugi went to prison only once, serving a short sentence in the winter of 1919–1920. He was arrested several other times, but always released. In light of police and judicial action against radicals in the late 1920s and early 1930s, and in view of Ōsugi's own violent death at the hands of the military police (*kempeitai*) in 1923, it is significant that, in the late Meiji and Taishō periods, there was no pattern of repeated arrests and trials that might indicate an intent to imprison Ōsugi for long periods or of sentences intended to pressure him to change his opinions. Moreover, his single prison sentence during the period under consideration was for assaulting a police officer, and his punishment—three months in jail—can hardly be considered excessive.

Two writers, Ōsawa Masamichi and Morinaga Eisaburō, allege that the police tried for several months in 1919 to put Ōsugi in prison.[31] Ōsawa even goes so far as to say that police attempts to imprison Ōsugi dated from March 1918. A review of his arrests, however, and an examination of the disposition of his case in each event reveals that this was not the case.

Ōsugi's first arrest during this time was on March 1, 1918, when the police detained him for nine days for allegedly interfering with an officer performing his duties. Ōsugi had tried to mediate between some disputatious drunks and hoodlums and persisted in trying to solve the problem even after police arrived to handle it. On this occasion, he was released because of insufficient evidence.[32]

In late 1918, he was accused of being the editor of an issue of a magazine in which one of his articles appeared. To edit a magazine or other publication without being registered with the authorities as an editor was contrary to the Law on Newspapers and Journals (Shimbunshi hō). On December 20, he was summarily ordered to pay a fine of ¥100, then formally tried and sentenced to fifty days in prison. He appealed this sentence and was found innocent on March 14, 1919.[33] Another entry in the police reports states that he was found guilty of disrupting the public order with his article "Minshū no geijitsu" and fined ¥100 on January 20, 1919, but exonerated on appeal on March 17. Except for the charges, the circumstances and dates are so similar that the entries must be

confused and actually refer to the same incident.[34] Regardless of
the dates, the incident is close enough in time to the period Ōsawa
and Morinaga refer to that one wonders why neither they nor
Ōsugi nor his second wife, Itō Noe, ever brought it up when they
wrote accusing the police of trying to incarcerate him. Perhaps the
fact that he was found innocent would, when considered along
with other instances when he was arrested but not charged, reduce
the impact of their charges of persecution.

When Ōsugi was finally arrested, tried, and imprisoned, it was for
a crime only indirectly related to his political activities. According
to his biographers' accounts, on the evening of May 23, 1919, he
told the police officer assigned to shadow him to go away and stop
bothering the neighbors by standing around keeping an eye on him.
When the officer, Andō Kiyoshi, refused, Ōsugi grabbed the man
and struck him. Ōsugi was then arrested, questioned at the police
station, and released the same day. According to the police reports,
the officer was not Ōsugi's shadow, but an ordinary officer on his
rounds who had merely stopped to inquire about the price of some
fruit when Ōsugi assaulted him, causing injury requiring ten days'
treatment.[35] The paper-work was not forwarded to the procurator's
office until July 21, and Ōsugi was arrested on July 23 to face trial.
At Ōsugi's first trial, he was found guilty and fined ¥50, but the
procurator appealed and in the second trial demanded and received
a sentence of three months, which Ōsugi served.

A series of events that occurred between May 23 and July 23
superficially supports the charge of police harrassment made by
Ōsawa and Morinaga. On July 15, Ōsugi attended a meeting of the
Nihon rōdō rengokai (Japan Labor Federation), a conservative
union being founded on that date to promote the harmony of
capital and labor. The audience of about eight hundred people
consisted mainly of workers plus a few radicals. Police officers
dispersed the meeting and arrested Ōsugi after he attempted to
take over the podium without being a scheduled speaker. He was,
however, released the same day.[36]

Two days later, on July 17, 1919, he and several friends attended
a meeting of the Rōdō mondai enzetsukai (Oratorical Society on

Labor Problems) and attempted to speak illegally in the street after the meeting was ordered halted by the police. He was arrested and released the following morning. Again, no charges were pressed, even though he allegedly resisted arrest. The very next day, July 19, the police questioned him and determined that he had defrauded seven different landlords of a total of ¥415.67.[37] Once again, however, no charges were pressed.

Itō Noe wrote in August 1919, while Ōsugi was undergoing trial for assaulting Andō, that she and Ōsugi had jokingly expected his arrest and incarceration for up to six months because he had insisted on addressing numerous labor meetings. She wrote that the police wanted to prevent her husband from speaking because anything he said would create a disturbance.[38] This is essentially the argument that his biographers make. The fact remains, however, that he was charged in only the assault case and not in any of the others.

To return to the May 23 assault incident, charges were pressed, but only because a blatant physical attack on an officer had occurred, an attack attested to by both sides. The final sentence of three months can hardly be considered excessive. Moreover, Ōsugi actually helped the procurator secure the prison sentence rather than the original fine during the second trial. At the first trial, Ōsugi refused to stand for the procurator's argument as was traditional, though not required by the court rules. The procurator made an issue of this at the second trial. The judge explained that it was customary to stand for the procurator, agreeing with the procurator that prisoners did so as a means of showing respect to the Emperor by deferring to the Emperor's prosecutorial representative. When Ōsugi refused to rise even after the judge ordered him to conform, the judge, it was reported, turned livid over what he considered to be an insult to the Throne.[39] Under these circumstances, it is surprising that Ōsugi did not receive a heavier sentence.

If the authorities were striving to put Ōsugi in prison or to pressure him to abandon anarchism, their failure to prosecute him for the other incidents is inexplicable. Even if they had been forced to manufacture charges that could not be proven in court, they could have prosecuted him in hopes of increasing the pressure on him or of obtaining a conviction by chance. They had ample opportunity to lodge charges against him in at least four incidents in which his actions were on the very edge of being criminal, his arrests of March 1, May 23, July 15, and July 17. The charge resulting from the March 1 incident might have been interfering with an officer in the performance of his duties, while the July incidents involved creating a public disturbance and speaking out of doors without a police permit. There is one circumstance that appears to support the contention that the authorities were persecuting Ōsugi; the quick succession of arrests on July 15 and 17 and the questioning on July 19 on the fraud charge, followed by his arrest on July 23 for prosecution in the May 23 Andō Incident suggest that the police and procurators were searching for the one best charge that would guarantee Ōsugi's trial and conviction. Ōsugi's own challenging behavior, however, adequately accounts for his arrests on July 15 and 17; there is no need to infer a police conspiracy. Furthermore, a period of two months between the May 23 and July 23 arrests does not seem to be an excessive one for conducting a thorough investigation, turning the results over to the procurators for their study, and drawing up the papers necessary to schedule and begin a trial. Indeed, it is evident that the only time authorities pressed charges was for an assault on a uniformed policeman, an offense too serious to ignore. At the same time, by arresting or questioning him regarding other offenses, they warned Ōsugi, in effect, not to go too far in his activities. Given Ōsugi's contentious behavior toward them, the police may be said to have bent over backward not to prosecute him.

Ōsugi was arrested several other times after he was released from jail in 1910, but these arrests, although unconnected with the series of arrests in 1918–1919, reinforce the conclusion that the police were not harassing him. Mentioned before was the instance in which Ōsugi and some of his companions harangued policemen from the Ueno police station for asking questions about a meeting of the Heimin kōenkai: Ōsugi was arrested, but released the following day with no charges being pressed.[40] Much later, on December

19, 1920, Ōsugi was arrested at a meeting to announce and establish the Nihon shakaishugi dōmei (Japanese Socialist League). On that day, several thousand socialists, workers and students, filled the meeting hall to overflowing. Outside with the overflow and the curious were members of a right-wing group shouting "Kill the traitorous socialists!" Police, apparently worried by the crowd in the street, halted and dispersed the meeting. Ōsugi arrived about this time and tried to enter the auditorium. When police blocked his way, he announced his identity, assuming a combative pose while standing in a confused, angry crowd that was near to rioting. He was immediately arrested and removed from the scene. Police did not file a charge against him. Although it is not known exactly when he was released, two days later Kondō Eizō, who later joined Ōsugi in publishing the second *Rōdō undō* (The labor movement), met Ōsugi at his home in Kamakura.[41]

In addition to being placed in custody for criminal or fraudulent action, Ōsugi was also placed under protective detention a number of times. During the Rice Riots in 1918, he was arrested and detained for a total of ten days, from August 16 to 26. He was not kept in a cell during the day, however, but was allowed to keep the station chief company in his office. After a few days, the police invited his wife, Itō, to reside at the police station too if she wished to be with him.[42] Ōsawa makes the point that protective detention was designed to keep the socialists separated from the masses and adds it to the varieties of harassment visited upon them.[43] This, however, ignores the fact that the Rice Riots began in late July and continued until the middle of September, while Ōsugi was detained for only ten days. It also ignores the fact that the police in Osaka made absolutely no attempt to prevent him and a large group of radicals and sympathizers from wandering around Osaka at night watching a riot in progress. Ōsugi sarcastically wrote that the police often detained him out of kindness so that he would not be mistaken for a rioter and end up on a soldier's saber. In any case, he only mentioned this one specific instance of preventive detention, so we may assume that other detentions were never more than annoyances to him, and minor ones at that.

From Ōsugi's point of view, then, there was a clear set of rules governing his activities, boundaries beyond which he ventured at a risk. The risk, however, was limited and was a known quantity; a sentence of up to a certain length for each crime and the suppression of a word, sentence, or journal were meted out on a strict one-for-one equivalency. At no time was the risk awesomely unlimited: Ōsugi was never held forever awaiting trial and he was never given an interminable sentence as forms of psychological torture or pressure. His notoriety may have served the paradoxical function of centering police attention on him while preventing them from being excessively oppressive. His experience indicates, however, that the police and procurators had only a few tools at their disposal, which could be used against specific actions, but not against a state of mind or a thought. This was known by Ōsugi and the authorities; there were rules by which the game of cops and crazies was played, and they were effective rules.

SEVEN

Scandal and Eclipse

In December 1915, Ōsugi began a complex love triangle that sub-
stantially changed his personal life, his relations with fellow socialists, his radical ideas, and his methods of attaining his ideological
goals. From December through the following November, he
attempted to carry on affairs with Kamichika Ichiko and Itō Noe
while continuing his first marraige to Hori Yasuko. This complex
affair was backed up with a theory of free love, a subject Ōsugi
had been interested in at least since 1906, but it may also be seen
in terms of an experiment by him to apply his theory of the expansion of the ego to a real situation.

Kamichika Ichiko was a twenty-six-year-old reporter for the
Tōkyō nichinichi shimbun (Tokyo daily newspaper) when she first
met Ōsugi in April 1914, at a meeting of his Sanjikarizumu kenkyūkai (Syndicalism Study Society). She was born in 1888 in
Nagasaki prefecture, on the southern island of Kyushu, the daughter of a Chinese herb doctor. After grade school, she attended an
American missionary school for girls and in 1909 entered Tsuda
eigo juku (Tsuda English School), where she had to be careful to
behave well toward the other middle- and upper-class girls: "I
covered up the cat and did not bare my claws."[1] At Tsuda, she
met Aoyama Kikue (who later married Yamakawa Hitoshi) with
whom she became a regular participant in meetings of the Seitō-
sha (Bluestockings), an early feminist organization run by Hiratsuka

Raichō, in which could be seen "the awakening of educated young women to social consciousness and fuller awareness of their own dilemma."[2] After finishing Tsuda, she taught at a girls' school in Hirosaki, Aomori prefecture, a job arranged for her by a teacher who thought it would be good for Kamichika to remove herself from contact with the radical *Seitō* group. Unfortunately, she was forced to resign when her connection with the Seitō-sha was discovered again. Returning to Tokyo, she worked for a year as secretary to the head of a Friends school for girls before joining the *Tōkyō nichinichi shimbun*.[3]

Kamichika met Ōsugi through Miyajima Sukeo and his wife, Reiko, two of Ōsugi's fellow anarchists. At first, Ōsugi did not take enough notice of her to write about her but, in the middle of 1915, they began to know each other better when she also began attending his Furansu bungaku kenkyūkai (French Literature Study Society) classes.[4] By the time Ōsugi and his wife had moved from Tokyo to Zushi, Kanagawa prefecture, in order to begin publishing the second *Kindai shisō* in December, he and Ichiko knew each other well enough for him to spend the nights with her when he came to Tokyo on Sundays to teach French.[5] Kamichika, writing fifty years later, recalled that he suddenly appeared at her apartment one day in the early spring of 1915 saying: "I've lost my shadow today. It's all right if I stop in."[6] By December, their affair was an open secret in radical circles and had provoked the antipathy of their professional and political associates. Ōsugi recalled in June 1916 that a writer for the *Yorozu chōhō* called Kamichika "the first adultress."[7]

In the meantime, Ōsugi began seeing Itō Noe. Itō was also born on Kyushu, near the city of Fukuoka in Fukuoka prefecture, on January 21, 1895. Since her parents were poor, she received only an elementary education before going to work for the Post Office in 1909 for a year.[8] In April 1910, she moved to Tokyo and managed to enter Ueno jogakkō (Ueno Girls' School). Soon after graduating in March 1912, she became the mistress of one of her teachers, Tsuji Jun,[9] who was immediately fired. By Tsuji, Itō had a son, Makoto, on January 20, 1914, and a second, Ryūji, on

August 10, 1915. The couple registered their marriage with the authorities in the summer of 1915. Perhaps because of the infamous affair with Ōsugi, authors find it difficult to resist commenting on Itō's looks. Hiratsuka Raichō described her as "wild," with a nose and nostrils that were much too active, tending to spread when she was animated, and unusual eyes that made people uncomfortable when peered at too long. Ide Fumiko notes that hers was a "southern beauty" (meaning tropical, almost overripe), with the sort of looks that were not in style at the time, but which men found attractive even if women did not. [10]

As her love affair with her teacher suggests, Itō was eccentric and precocious from an early age. Such nonconformity led Itō to choose increasingly independent paths during her life. In November 1912, only ten months after the first issue of *Seitō* was published, she began helping with the administration of the magazine. On November 17, 1914, she became editor and publisher in charge of all administrative affairs, editing the magazine and running all the auxiliary discussion and study groups. By January 1915, she had virtually taken over control of the entire organization. Hiratsuka Raichō, founder and owner of *Seitō* and editor until Itō succeeded her, explained that Itō had written her twice requesting to be made editor, causing Hiratsuka to think that she would split ownership of *Seitō* from editorial control. Itō claimed that she had in mind no particular rules or regulations for the magazine, no set policy, and no doctrine, yet her own name and her anarchist opinions came to be synonymous with *Seitō*. When her affair with Ōsugi led her to leave Tsuji's home and left her with a besmirched reputation, *Seitō* suffered too: no one was willing to take it over, and the last issue appeared in February 1916. [11]

Ōsugi was familiar with the *Seitō* circle because their concern with the liberation of women coincided with his own concern with the general liberation of mankind. For this reason, Ōsugi and Itō moved in the same general circles for some time before meeting. In February 1913, Itō spoke at a Seitō-sha kōenkai (Seitō-sha lecture meeting) which Ōsugi attended, but he made no mention of her speech when he wrote about the meeting in *Kindai shisō*. In

September of that year, Itō published a translation of an article by Emma Goldman, the Russo-American anarchist, in *Seitō*. Ōsugi had thought of doing the same translation, and then Arahata Kanson had taken over the translation project from him, but, before Arahata had done much work on it, Itō's translation appeared. Ōsugi noted Itō's translation in *Kindai shisō* and praised it highly. In May of the following year in a review of articles about women's liberation and its Japanese proponents, he recalled writing over two pages in appreciation of Itō's translation and added some very complimentary comments on her other writings.[12]

Although Ōsugi and Itō knew of and appreciated each other's journalistic efforts, they did not meet until September 1914, when Watanabe Masatarō introduced them in the Tsuji-Itō home. The initial attraction between the two seems to have been strictly platonic. They shared both an interest in anarchism and a bold, enthusiastic approach to life. When an issue of *Heimin shimbun* was banned by the police, Itō's *Seitō* was the only journal to criticize the police. Ōsugi was heartened by this gesture of solidarity and had Arahata repay it with a thank-you piece in the next issue of *Heimin shimbun* in November 1914. In January 1915, Ōsugi sent her a picture of Rosa Luxemburg. According to Ōsawa, he was captivated by Itō's zeal while she appreciated his manliness and contrasted his high esteem for her efforts with Tsuji's tendency to laugh at her enthusiasm. Ōsugi visited the Tsuji-Itō home three times in February 1915. His affair with Itō probably did not begin, however, until the following February at the earliest, or possibly the following May when they definitely began sleeping together.[13]

For Itō, the period extending back to November 1914 was one of both personal growth and great frustration. She was not only the editor of *Seitō*, controlling and guiding the content of the journal along increasingly anarchistic lines, but, at about the same time, she was expecting her second child, who was born in August 1915.[14] The pregnancy must have hindered her career with *Seitō*, if only by making intense activity increasingly difficult. She could not count on financial or emotional support from Tsuji, who maintained a cold and critical attitude toward her passionate devotion to *Seitō*.[15] Tsuji also seemed insensitive to Itō's feelings about motherhood. During her first pregnancy, she had felt incapable of caring for a child, viewing motherhood as nothing but "acts of sacrifice." After Makoto's birth, however, her love for the child overcame her revulsion and her daily life centered on the baby. At the same time, she felt that a father could not be as self-sacrificing as a mother. Tsuji was an individualist who hated to have other people interfere in his life and accordingly refrained from interfering in other people's lives. This attitude extended even to his own wife. Thus, when Itō wanted to speak frankly about her discontent with him which was precipitated by the presence of the child, he was entirely unsympathetic.[16]

The tension between her own wider horizons at the Seitō-sha and pregnancy without support from Tsuji gradually intensified. Exactly when her relationship with Tsuji soured is nearly impossible to pinpoint. They registered their marriage in July 1915. Conflict might have arisen soon thereafter as the pregnancy neared term. On the other hand, difficulties might have predated the registration of the marriage, which could have been an attempt at reconciliation. Itō wrote that Tsuji had always been a refuge for her when she was unhappy with the family (in addition to the child, Makoto, Itō also took care of Tsuji's mother and siblings). Around mid-1915, she felt no longer able to seek refuge in him and her declining faith in him, together with her realization that her feelings toward Ōsugi were growing stronger, gave her the determination to leave Tsuji. Instead, in July 1915, Itō and Tsuji went to her home in Kyushu where she had her baby in August and did not return until the following January; in that interval, Ōsugi's affair with Kamichika began.[17] In February 1916, Ōsugi called on Itō while Tsuji was not at home and they exchanged their first kiss while strolling in Hibiya Park. That same night Ōsugi visited Kamichika and told her of the kiss; after they parted the next morning, she mailed him a letter breaking off their relationship.

Ōsugi's response was to try to persuade Kamichika, Itō, and Hori to accept the situation as it was. One day, while he and Kamichika

were together, Itō appeared and Ōsugi announced his rules of love
to both of them: first, each individual was to maintain an independent, self-sufficient economic existence; second, each was to live
in his or her own apartment or house; and third, each must accord
everyone else complete freedom of action, in sexual as well as
other matters.[18]

In part, this may have been a spur-of-the-moment way of avoiding an inherently unpleasant crisis but, in larger part, the rules
were well founded on general principles that Ōsugi had been concerned with for a long time. He had first addressed himself to the
question of love in November 1906, when he wrote on "Dōbutsu
no ren'ai" (Love among the animals). Since he was writing for the
first time in his non-radical, women's magazine, *Katei zasshi*, he
mainly restricted himself to tracing the sex lives, or lack thereof,
of animals from protozoa up through the higher mammals, taking
care to point out that many birds and mammals are monogamous.
With regard to humans, he noted two parallels with animals: humans too pay close attention to the process of selecting a proper
mate and they unite with ardent intimacy.[19] This was the same
glorification of passion and emotion over rationalism that was
characteristic of Ōsugi's own thoughts about life. In the next
month's issue, he published a stronger statement in which he condemned capitalism for perverting love and marriage. Capitalism
makes love absolutely impossible in existing society: love "is
trampled under foot," and marriage is either an accident or the
result and victim of greed. If capital were destroyed, love would
blossom forth and "release its high scent." In a communal system
(*kyōsan seidō*), love would be more perfect and relationships
would be long-lasting ones in which each person would evolve,
grow, and help the other(s) do the same. Divorce would be easier
because, although long-lasting unions are more desirable, the
refusal to recognize divorce would deny the truth that "love is
something that necessarily demands freedom."[20] Since most relationships will be permanent, children would benefit even if divorce
were easier because "I do not think that a home where the parents

are always fighting with each other every day [screaming] 'Get out!' 'I'm going!' is a moral home that ought to be prized."[21]

In March 1913, in an article entitled "Shūchi to teisō" (Shame and chastity), Ōsugi described sexual practices in Polynesia and Melanesia, emphasizing the freedom with which sex was treated. He noted early sexual intercourse, indiscriminate pairings regardless of blood relationship, clubs devoted to satisfaction of sexual passion, and the rapid changing of partners. He also noted, regretfully, that, when marriage became an institution, women became the possessions of their husbands and thereafter needed their permission to have an affair or do anything else. At the same time, men could not only have affairs as they pleased but could lend or even sell their wives. This occurred because society moved away from "a system of free communism" (*jiyū kyōsan no seidō*). Men learned also the concepts of morality, shame, and chastity when the free communist system was replaced by private property. In June 1913, he quoted Engels's *The Origin of Family, Property and State:* as with all freedoms "True free love cannot become a reality except under a communist system."[22]

With all this intellectual baggage in hand, Ōsugi tried to convince his wife and his two lovers to live by his three rules of love. Hori might have had the best chance of understanding the rules since she had known Ōsugi for over ten years and had cooperated with him when he was publishing on the subject of free love in their jointly edited *Katei zasshi.* Instead, she was uncooperative and unyielding, though willing to put up with her husband's antics for a while. Ōsugi told himself that Hori, educated by common customs, was essentially unschooled and, therefore, not able to understand difficult matters quickly. Through habit, she was used to his unreasonable acts, but she was adamant when it came to his love affairs: these were an affront to her and to her expectations that the institution of marriage should conform to customary monogamous standards. Because her idea of marriage and her entire existence were based on hundreds of years of custom, she felt hatred, jealousy, and malice toward Itō, Kamichika, and even

Ōsugi. He claimed he was very sympathetic to her plight, even when he seemed to be cruel to her, and implied that what he was doing would be for her own good because it would slowly force her into a period of personal growth, broadening her horizons and expanding her ego.[23] Aside from a few sharp comments directed at Itō and Kamichika and her refusal to agree to the three rules, Hori seems to have taken little action against the other women. Her entire reaction was probably summed up in a comment she allegedly made to Ōsugi. Once, she referred to Itō as "that fox" (*ano kitsune-san*),[24] imputing to her not only great sexual appetite, but also an ability to cast spells on her quarry, Ōsugi. In any case, he gave her little opportunity for personal growth or accommodation to the affair, because when they returned to Tokyo from Zushi in March 1916, following relentlessly his second rule of love, he established Hori in a house near Yotsuya and rented lodgings for himself a short distance away in Kōjimachi.[25]

Itō tried a little harder to accommodate herself both to Ōsugi's theory and to his other women. In a letter to him, dated June 1, 1916, she wrote: "I think only that my 'you' and Yasuko's 'you' are different. Now, I appreciate and respect you in contrast to Yasuko. If Yasuko, however, would be sure of herself with respect to you and could understand you, I think I probably could sincerely respect Yasuko."[26] She added that he should explain her feelings to Hori so that the two women could arrive at a mutual understanding and respect. She also complimented herself on her ability to advance to such a progressive position under Ōsugi's guidance, implying that Hori had not made a similar advance. In the same letter, she stated:

> I believe that I can love and respect Kamichika properly. I think that I want to have the same affections for Yasuko. I don't suppose that Yasuko would meet with me? For some reason, I strongly feel I want to meet her. As you said the other day, I feel I want to try to understand her as much as I am able. I think that I probably don't know Yasuko and that she probably doesn't know very well the person I am.[27]

Ōsugi, while proud of Itō's effort to get along with the other two women, was not always so pleased with her reaction to the affair. He complained that she found it difficult to tolerate the sexual freedom of his rules. He objected that, around May 1916, in her first considered opinion on the affair, she posited an exclusive husband-wife relationship.[28] Earlier, he stated that there was no distinction between friends and lovers. With friends, and by extension lovers, there would be differences in his feeling about their relative value, differences in his respect and love of them. Despite that, he continued, one would not compare the two friends and discard the one who fell short of the other.[29] In their own affair, he argued, his love for Itō was not reduced or extinguished by his love for Kamichika or Hori. Likewise, a decrease in his love for Kamichika would not mean a corresponding and equivalent increase in his love for Itō. Quite coldly, he warned her of the possibility that yet another woman might appear, becoming his newest lover and taking him away from Itō in the same way that Itō had partially taken him away from Kamichika. Would she, he wondered, threaten to kill him as Kamichika had?[30] At this point, Itō seems to have stopped trying to arrive at her own rationalization of the affair.

Kamichika's initial reaction to Ōsugi's first kiss with Itō boded ill for the possibility of her accepting the three rules of love that he presented to her later. She wrote him, "If you are really considerate of [my feelings], try not to see me hereafter. Goodbye forever." Shortly after Ōsugi appeared at the Miyajima house the next day, Kamichika arrived and explained herself more precisely: she threatened to kill him.[31] They were reconciled, however, that same day and, after two months of reflection, Ōsugi reported, she was able to put into perspective the fact that she had stolen a woman's husband who had then been stolen by yet another woman.[32] Never, however, was Kamichika able to persuade herself of the three rules: in fact, she probably made little attempt to. She later wrote that Ōsugi's free-love theory was to her only a rationalization of the existing situation and modestly added that she was then too immature to go along with such an advanced theory.[33] In fact, though, Ōsugi knew she had a better-trained mind than either of the other women, and he played on her vanity by convincing her of her intellectual superiority and getting her to act as their older sister (even though she was younger than Hori and even though she would have nothing to do with the theory). This proved impossible as his stronger love for Itō grew increasingly evident to Kamichika.[34]

Soon, however, complications arose which put increasing strains on all four. These strains caused contradictions between Ōsugi's three rules and his actions, creating even more tension and anger that built toward an explosive resolution. In January 1916, the second *Kindai shisō* folded, and Ōsugi had no income except for occasional articles published elsewhere. *Kindai shisō* actually only appeared once, all issues after the first being banned by the police. Ōsugi received considerable criticism for allowing the second issue to be banned, and on November 26, at a meeting of all persons associated with the journal, he was stripped of primary responsibility for the journal, although he was allowed to remain one of three editors along with Arahata and Momose Susumu.[35] Apparently all of the criticism directed at Ōsugi at this time centered on his mishandling of the journal. Kamichika, however, mentioned feeling responsible for the disruption of a *kenkyū-kai* (study group), possibly meaning the directors of the journal, because of her affair with Ōsugi.[36]

In February, Itō published the last issue of *Seitō*. Thereafter, she had no regular income. She finally left Tsuji in April, taking with her their second son, the ten-month-old Ryūji, and, after staying briefly with Ōsugi, moved into an apartment in Chiba prefecture at Onjuku, about 85 kilometers southeast of Tokyo.[37] In May, their affair began to be criticized in newspapers and magazines. In a letter to Itō on May 6, Ōsugi mentioned articles in the *Tōkyō asahi shimbun* (Tokyo morning news), *Yorozu chōhō*, and *Yomiuri shimbun* (Yomiuri news),[38] presumably about the affair and, later, he noted three magazines that ran special editions in December 1916 on the love affair and his theory of free love. Ōsugi's name was so thoroughly associated in the popular mind with sexual license that, in March 1917, he was blamed for the love affair between Yoshikawa Kaneko, wife of Count Yoshikawa Akimasa, and her chauffeur, even though there was no indication that she advocated free love.[39] As a direct result of this publicity, Kamichika was fired from the *Tōkyō nichinichi shimbun*. Fortunately, her superior gave her an introduction to Yūki Reiichirō of the Gembun-sha (literally, "Profound Writings Company") who liked her work and gave her enough part-time work to survive. She knew that the affair was making laughing stocks of all four of them and felt "I could not stand the derision of our colleagues (*nakama no hitobito*)."[40]

Ōsugi's love affairs soon exacted a toll from all four persons involved, especially a financial one that complicated the psychological toll. Kamichika was left with the only regular income. Hori had not been an earner since *Katei zasshi* stopped publication. Itō had little income after February and Ōsugi none after January. Ryūji was turned over to a foster family primarily because of financial problems, but, even so, Itō had to rely on Ōsugi for some support.[41] Ōsugi himself was very hard-pressed. In a letter to Itō dated April 30, he mentioned the necessity of paying his landlord ¥30 immediately, but by May 1 managed to put the matter off until May 15.[42] Kamichika always seemed forlorn and pitiable, and his comments about her to Itō indicate he found her presence disagreeable. At the same time, he often complained to Kamichika not only about how short of money he was but also about what difficult straits Itō was in. This led to a series of loans from Kamichika to Ōsugi. Some of the money went for rent,[43] but sometimes Ōsugi asked her to send money to him, for instance when he was stranded at Itō's apartment in Onjuku with no way to return to Tokyo.[44] She did not inquire how he spent the money, knowing well that he spent some of it on Itō and perhaps gave her cash outright. Although he promised to repay these loans by translating and selling Darwin's *Theory of Evolution,* he felt no remorse over accepting money from her.[45] These loans reached a large total, perhaps ¥200 altogether. In "Buta ni nageta shinju" (Pearls cast before swine), she listed ¥120 in loans lent on three occasions plus five other loans of unspecified size, including emergency funds sent to Ōsugi on two trips to Osaka.[46]

Some biographers argue that Kamichika tried to use the loans to

manipulate and control Ōsugi.[47] Ōsugi encouraged this interpretation, especially when he claimed that Kamichika brought up money
matters when the affair came to its ugly climax.[48] Kamichika
denied pressuring him about the money and wrote that he finally
volunteered to repay it all, adding that their affair was over.[49] There
is no simple way of determining who was more concerned about
money "flow." In later years, Kamichika divorced a husband who
had turned to expensive degeneracy.[50] This might demonstrate the
same great concern for money that she allegedly had when she was
with Ōsugi. On the other hand, it might only show that, after he
gave her so much trouble over money, she became very cautious
about money and men in combination, or it might have been the
final defense that anyone might resort to when threatened by a
mate's incurable excesses. Ōsugi's own carelessness about money
was lifelong. Even during the affair, he borrowed ¥300 from
Gotō Shimpei, who was Home Minister at the time, in order to
begin publishing a new journal.[51] He returned ¥1 to Kamichika
and used about ¥200 for the journal, but gave ¥50 to Hori and
¥30 to Itō, while appropriating ¥20 for his November working
vacation at Hayama near Kamakura.[52] On this occasion, as Ōsugi
reported it, his method of borrowing was high-handed. He called
at Gotō's residence during a dinner party and demanded money
of Gotō, saying he was very hard up. Gotō said, "I've heard that
actually you have a good head and strong arms. Why are you in
such difficulties?"

Ōsugi: It's because the government obstructs our business.
Gotō: And why have you come begging to me in particular?
Ōsugi: Since the government is obstructing us, I figured it a matter of
course to come begging to the government. Further, I thought that you
would understand such talk.
Gotō: Ah, I see. How much do you want?[53]

In contrast to this brashness, when Ōsugi borrowed from
sympathizers, he seems to have been quite uncomfortable. Often
he would send a restaurant waiter to the "mark" with a written
request for a loan or an advance on an article. He would then
have a meal while waiting for the money. He did this even when

borrowing from a close business acquaintance such as a man named Kitahara of Ars (Arusu) Publishing Company, which printed several collections of his articles during his life and an edition of his collected works after his death.[54] Ōsugi's personality was so appealing and powerful that his creditors, even though they might criticize him when making a loan on promised writings, could not hold a grudge against him for borrowing or for not repaying.[55]

In view of all this, it seems fair to conclude that Kamichika was probably no more or less concerned about money matters than anyone with a steady, middle-level income and that she probably did not use the loans to attempt to control Ōsugi or pull him away from Itō. Similarly, Ōsugi's carelessness and cavalier attitude toward those he borrowed from was much to blame, *if* money was in fact a major point of disagreement between them and the reason for Kamichika's later violent behavior. Ōsugi's free-love rules were another important bone of contention. Also, Kamichika could not help but be increasingly jealous of Itō, and angry with Ōsugi, after Itō moved in with him in September.

In November, Ōsugi set off for Hayama so that he could be alone to work on a translation and two articles that he wanted to finish in order to augment the money he received from Gotō Shimpei. Before departing, he told Kamichika of his plans and assured her that he was going by himself, without Itō. Itō, in fact, had a piece to write for the *Ōsaka mainichi shimbun* (Osaka daily news) and needed to remain behind. He also told Kamichika that he and Itō were going to rent separate lodgings after his trip, a gesture toward his free-love rules that cheered Kamichika, if only because it meant he and Itō would not be as close as before. Nevertheless, Kamichika pressured Ōsugi to allow her to come for one day to Hayama and he grudgingly agreed. The day before Ōsugi was to depart for Hayama, Itō announced she had decided to visit Hiratsuka Raichō who lived in Chigasaki, about 25 kilometers to the west of Hayama. Ōsugi suggested, then, that he accompany her to Chigasaki and that she spend a night with him in Hayama before returning to Tokyo.[56] That evening, after visiting with

Hiratsuka they spent some time on the beach, strolling and boat-
ing a little.

Kamichika, meanwhile, had heard rumors of Itō's and Ōsugi's
joint departure[57] and naturally felt she had been played for a fool.
Sometime previously, she had bought herself a short sword, thinking in a vague way about suicide, and she brought this along without considering why when she too left for Hayama.[58] She arrived
at Ōsugi's room just after the other two had bathed and found
Itō grooming in front of a mirror, cooling off and bared to the
waist. The three shared an uncomfortable meal after which Itō
suddenly departed for Tokyo. Ōsugi and Kamichika conversed
sullenly for a while, even though he had come to "dislike looking
at her face" now that she had seen Itō half naked. Soon, there was
a phone call from Itō saying she had forgotten the key to Ōsugi's
lodgings so she returned to the inn on his insistence to spend the
night. Kamichika by now so suspected the other two of collusion
that she figured this was another ruse, one calculated by Itō to
keep herself between Ōsugi and Kamichika. Ōsugi, susceptible to
colds because of his earlier bout with tuberculosis, was the only
one to sleep that night, due to a slight cold and fatigue from the
day on the beach.[59]

The following day, November 8, Itō returned to Tokyo, Kamichika occupied herself on the beach, and Ōsugi, disturbed by the
whole situation, failed to do any work, although he was left with
the day to himself. That night, they went to bed without talking
about their affair but, according to him, she woke him up to talk
three times. The first time he ended the conversation by bluntly
saying they should end their liaison; the second time he angrily
swore he would return the money he owed her the next day,
money being a subject she brought up, he claimed; the last time,
she was trying to enter his bedding, an advance he quickly rejected, even though he had previously found her extremely physically attractive. He also had a premonition that she would kill
him with a knife.[60] Shortly after three a.m., she did slash him on
the throat.[61] A wild chase through the hotel ended in her capture
and arrest; Ōsugi was taken to the hospital in Zushi where he

underwent ten days' treatment. He recalled hearing a wheezing noise in his throat when he breathed, and later he heard a doctor say that his trachea had been punctured.[62]

Kamichika's version of the stabbing was briefer, less detailed, and shifted much of the blame onto Ōsugi. According to her, she tried to make him talk about their relationship, realizing that it could not continue as it was. He, however, immediately assumed she was worried about her money and this assumption hurt her feelings.[63] She also stated that Ōsugi's story of her attempt to go to bed with him was a half-sleeping, half-waking hallucination. His continued promise to repay her money was the final straw: "I had gone beyond sorrow and anger and stared at him in a daze. Surely there was more between us than the exchange of a little money. He had made me throw away decency, family, friends, and job. Was the result going to be a few scraps of paper thrown at me along with the words 'I am returning the money'?" After she stabbed him and presumably mortally wounded him, she said, "Forgive me. I'm going to die too."[64]

The versions put forth by Ōsugi and Kamichika are understandably different. He published his first, and it was, of course, an attempt to justify both his actions and his theories. Kamichika's versions are of a much later date and, in addition to justifying herself, were written with an eye to his story. It really matters little who brought up the loans first. The fact that both felt money was foremost in the mind of the other is sufficient evidence of a complete breakdown of emotional attachment. To that may be added Kamichika's emotional response to everything about the affair and Ōsugi's total disregard for her feelings after his affair with Itō began. The whole affair was in part an attempt by Ōsugi to put into practice some of his theories on love and social organization, to make theory real. Whether or not the theory was correct, the attempt failed because of his own insensitivity.

The reaction to this stabbing was immediate among the participants of the love affair and in the socialist movement as a whole. The stabbing caused permanent changes in Ōsugi's personal life and affected his professional life in the short run, by casting him into the depths of isolation, as well as in the long run, by paradoxically confirming him in his theories while ironically turning him away from theory as his primary concern.

Kamichika went on trial. Her lawyer attempted to call for Ōsugi, Itō, and Miyajima Sukeo to testify, in order to make a plea for a reduced sentence on the basis of passion, but the judge refused to permit their testimony. The prosecutor presented the case mainly from the point of view of the antisocial nature of the whole affair. On March 7, 1917, Kamichika was sentenced to four years in prison. The judge pronounced himself sympathetic to her, saying that Ōsugi's actions invited death by her hand, but added that the episode could not be condoned morally or socially since she had not ended her relationship with Ōsugi when Itō began her affair with him. On appeal, the sentence was reduced to two years, which she served from October 3, 1917, to October 3, 1919, after a final appeal to the Supreme Court was rejected.[65]

Hori wasted no more time on Ōsugi, but published a statement in the January issue of *Shin shakai* (The new society), announcing she had at last ended all connection with him.[66]

Itō remained with Ōsugi until their premature deaths in 1923. Police spies reported overhearing Ōsugi tell a visitor that he had now been stabbed twice, once by a schoolmate and once by Kamichika. He added that he might be destined to be stabbed next by a policeman or a member of the military police (*kempeitai*) or possibly hanged,[67] speaking more prophetically than he could have then imagined for both himself and Itō.

Criticism of Ōsugi, and, to a lesser degree, Itō, was universal, even among socialists who tripped over each other putting distance between Ōsugi and themselves. Miyajima Sukeo spoke his mind clearly. He accused Ōsugi of forcing Kamichika to loan him money and said she had even pawned her clothes to raise the cash. He also threatened to duel with Ōsugi if he attempted to seek revenge against Kamichika. Outside the hospital, Miyajima met Itō and attacked her with an umbrella.[68] Miyajima remained so emotionally opposed to Ōsugi that his anger was one reason he established a journal, *Rōdōsha* (The worker), in opposition to Ōsugi's second *Rōdō undō* (The labor movement).[69]

Other socialists restricted themselves to written criticism, often vicious in nature. The most important criticism came from Sakai Toshihiko, the grand old man of the socialist movement at the time and Hori's brother-in-law, with whom Ōsugi was never again reconciled. Sakai wrote calmly enough for one whose relative was involved in a catastrophic public scandal. He had earlier cautioned people against hasty judgment of Ōsugi's morals. Now, however, he remarked that Ōsugi's behavior "has not a few bad points. Specifically, I think he caused people too much trouble." He continued:

> It is problematic whether one-husband-one-wife will be strictly adhered to. What about the inconvenience and discomforts arising from children, jealousy, and so on, if it is not strictly observed? What do you do with problems like those arising from differences of beauty? These can probably be considered the major problems of the future. If Ōsugi proceeded with a daring experiment in order to solve these major fundamental problems, that could be said to be an action of some significance: but in present-day male-female relationships, where economic requirements occupy a leading position, I quickly surmise that such idealistic experiments are completely unreasonable.[70]

Takabatake Motoyuki, who later became a national socialist (*kokka shakaishugisha*) and was a major thorn in Ōsugi's side, was more vituperative in his attack on Ōsugi. He wrote that the affair represented no more than blind love, the rejection of reason and was a case of "foolishly disturbing society. Why didn't Ōsugi find as good a way to distribute goods as he did to distribute spermatozoa? Ōsugi might reply to this that it is impossible in the present world. Why is the practice of free love not [also] an impossibility in the present world?"[71]

Yamakawa Hitoshi was most concerned for the effect that Ōsugi's escapades would have on socialism. He worried that the affair would reflect badly on socialism because the actions of Ōsugi and Kamichika might imply that socialists were too full of passion, sexual and otherwise.[72] He was careful to point out that the affair had occurred because Ōsugi was human, not because he was a socialist.

With the exception of Itō and a few loyal followers, Ōsugi became isolated after he was released from the hospital. No one sought him out as a speaker or a writer, even after the furor over the Hayama stabbing died down. He was, however, able to cash in on the scandal in an article published in January 1917, in which he tried to respond to some of the criticism leveled at him. He was not unaware of the trouble he had caused his colleagues: "All this [past] year . . . I have done nothing but surprise people, and I apologize sincerely to everyone. As might be expected, I have been reprimanded by various quarters and I apologize from the bottom of my heart."[73] He then proceeded to comment on criticism of himself. Some of his comments were theoretical in nature. Yamada Waka, for instance, had complained that sexual morality had evolved to its present state, but that Ōsugi and his women had tried to make it regress. Ōsugi responded that Yamada could not know the direction of future evolution in this field. Other critics were quoted and then rudely dismissed with as little as a simple "nonsensical scoundrel."[74]

More significantly, he related his experiences with newsmen while in the hospital and after his release. They had asked him in the hospital if there had been any changes in his ideas since he was stabbed but, "because they were annoying, I replied there have not been changes in anything." After he returned to Tokyo and was asked the same questions, he felt like replying that there were no changes in ideas but that perhaps he might make some changes in his methods for putting his ideas into action. Instead he said that, had he been an ordinary man, without a theory or a self-conscious attitude, an incident like being stabbed would have plunged him into thorough reconsideration of his situation, but that he was not such a fool as that.[75] The implication is that the stabbing was strictly incidental to the theory and neither it nor the collapse of the affair negated the validity of that theory.

Having developed a theory, he saw no reason to change it merely because its implementation proved unsuccessful.

Although Ōsugi was referring to his theory of free love, he might have been thinking of his theory of the expansion of the ego too. The entire affair was, in a sense, an attempt by Ōsugi to impose his ego, his self, and a new system of relationships between the sexes which grew out of that self, on his immediate society. However, just as the original theory of ego expansion did not resolve the fundamental question of how expansion could occur without incurring the subjugation of others, the execution of the love affair did not reveal how Ōsugi's ego expansion (as the implementation of the theory of free love can be seen) could be reconciled with the way it forced Hori, Kamichika, and Itō to conform or have nothing further to do with him. One is tempted to conclude that both free love and expansion of the ego could occur without subjugation only if the rest of society chose to convert to Ōsugi's theories.

Ōsugi's treatment by his comrades after the stabbing at Hayama brings to mind the way in which, as a last resort, troublemakers could be subjected to *mura hachibu,* or ostracism, by villagers in modern as well as traditional times. *Mura hachibu* meant that no villager would communicate with the troublemaker, and would pretend he did not exist. In addition, the village as a whole would refuse to continue sharing tools and pooling labor and water works with the ostracized individual. Ostracism was the ultimate sanction that could be brought against an individual or a family, subjecting them to the psychological stresses of absolute social isolation as well as the economic disaster which would soon follow the villagers' refusal to include the troublemaker in the cooperative system that was crucial to rice cultivation on which most villagers relied. In an urban setting in Taishō Japan, however, *mura hachibu* was probably impossible.

Neither crushing psychological strain nor economic failure could be forced on a Tokyo resident. First of all, it was impossible to enforce isolation in a metropolis of millions; if an individual was ostracized by some, other acquaintances and friends could be found. Furthermore, there did not exist in Tokyo, or even in the socialist movement, the high degree of unanimity necessary to initiate ostracism and make it effective. The movement was so factionalized that one group or more could be relied on to disagree with the general consensus, and that would be enough to destroy the psychological impact of the tactic.

Second, economic disaster could not be guaranteed. Unlike a village which was based on rice cultivation and the intense cooperation demanded by that cultivation, Tokyo offered an individual unnumbered alternative means of making a living.[76] Although Ōsugi wrote little in the months after the stabbing at Hayama, thus making us wonder how he provided for his family (Itō had a baby girl, Mako, in September 1917), he did not starve, nor was he forced to work in a factory, nor was he forced to leave town (which was, after all, the object of *mura hachibu*). In some way he made ends meet.

Indeed, the whole situation was more like a purge than *mura hachibu*. Those who disagreed with Ōsugi's conduct refused to have anything further to do with him, partly in order to defend their movement from the social opprobrium they expected to be directed at him and, through him, at themselves. He was not included in any of the normal activities—study groups, publishing, speech-making and so on—but no overt action to harm him and drive him away forever was undertaken. In short, Ōsugi was placed at a distance from the movement, not driven irrevocably away, until such time as all danger to the movement had passed and it was safe to associate with the renegade again.

EIGHT

Theories on the Labor Movement and Art

After the public furor over the love affair subsided, Ōsugi went through a period of forced withdrawal. Most of his comrades were personally affronted by the scandal and fearful of damage to the socialist movement. Consequently, they avoided contact with Ōsugi as much as possible. Except for a few comments on the affair itself, Ōsugi published few articles and only two translations in the year after he was stabbed and until he began publishing *Bummei hihyō* (Cultural review) with Itō's help in January 1918.[1] He was able to maintain contact with only a few of the young workers he had been cultivating in the Heimin kōenkai.

While the stabbing drained him of the desire to live according to the tenents of free love, however, it did not cause him to abandon altogether his efforts to put theory into practice. Instead, during 1917, he strove to become more familiar with the life of the working population and, to a lesser extent, to create an anarchist lifestyle. He encouraged his young worker friends to live permanently or temporarily with Itō and himself and made no distinction between his belongings and theirs. Although Ōsugi did not seem to mind living in close proximity to physical laborers, who were largely uneducated and often dirty, Itō found herself irritated by their lack of consideration. She noted unhappily that one of them became uncouth when he relaxed, spitting into the *hibachi* (brazier) and walking on the veranda with mud-caked feet.[2]

In late 1917, they moved to a working-class area in the Tokyo suburb of Kameido to continue their proletarian lifestyle.

These experiences made Ōsugi more skeptical of abstract theorizing. Often he would refuse to state full-blown theories or draw conclusions himself unless he was certain they were accepted by workers. He seldom indulged in the kind of abstract essays like "Seifuku no jijitsu" (The reality of conquest), "Sei no kakujū" (The expansion of life), and "Sei no sōzō" (The creation of life) that had appeared in 1913 and 1914; nor could he any longer write expansive essays like the one he had published in June 1916, "Danjo kankei ni tsuite" (On the relations between the sexes), in which he had traced the development of the institution of marriage from the time of primitive man to the future ideal. He was also distrustful of leaders and thinkers who were not workers. How could people who did not live as workers understand them, their lives and their hopes? he asked, answering in the same breath that they could not. This was his own reason for trying to live in a working-class area.

Ōsugi's attempt to make contact with workers was in 1917 not a unique effort; leaders of varying ideological persuasions were turning to the masses as the old elite style of leadership proved incapable of solving Japan's problems. Early in the Meiji period, the central government had taken the initiative in reform efforts, and the rest of the country had followed its lead. By the end of the period, however, the goals of the Meiji leaders had been achieved, and there was a new set of problems to be solved. Environmental pollution, class antagonisms, and continuing economic instability eluded solution by the oligarchs. National unity, the watchword of the Meiji period, gave way to divisiveness, and pluralism came to characterize the nation that could not agree with itself. Toward the end of the Meiji period, this loss of a sense of common purpose and of confidence in the government marked the beginning of the breakdown of the leaders' ability to retain unchallenged control of the nation.

During the Meiji era, ideas, like politics, had been restricted to members of the elite, especially ideas that were complex or significant. As part of the process of modernizing Japan from the top down, prominent thinkers addressed each other and other members of the elite, but never the people in general. Identification of problems of national concern and their solutions was accomplished within the elite. Reform of the political, economic, and social systems implied accepting new ideological premises, but involving the masses in national affairs was one aspect of modernization that was repugnant to the venerable Meiji oligarchs. Indeed, only the conscription and educational systems directly and implacably involved the people, but in each of these cases special imperial rescripts enjoined the masses' docility, thus securing their loyalty without promoting their political participation.

In the Taishō period, however, the masses began to be viewed as new political actors who either already were or would have to be included in the political process. This was one of the unforeseen consequences of the modernization process itself: the compulsory educational system gave the people a patriotic interest in national affairs, the development of urban industry produced a new class whose importance to the modernization of Japan and potential power were as undeniable as the poor conditions in which it existed. Many Western ideas, especially political philosophy, gained acceptance by greater numbers of people, thereby presenting the Japanese elite with the need to assimilate new groups of people into the political process.

Members of the elite attempted to integrate the people into the social system by organizing them into groups controlled from the top. These attempts were not coordinated or even related to each other, but included organizations like the military reserve organizations, the youth groups (*seinendan*) and labor organizations designed to promote the harmony of labor and capital (*kyōchōkai*). Through each of these, members of the governing elite sought to cultivate the loyalty of the masses to the central structures of the state.

Left-wing activists also recognized the potential power of newly emerging classes and sought to contact and organize them; however, they wanted to use the workers, their masses, as a vehicle for overthrowing the government. Arahata and Yamakawa were distributing a pamphlet in 1917 entitled *Aofuku* (Blue uniform) among workers; Watanabe Masatarō, a worker who had made himself familiar with socialist ideas, began his Rōdō mondai kenkyūkai (Association for the Study of Labor Problems); Ariyoshi San-kichi[3] had a similar Rōdō mondai zadankai (Symposium on Labor Problems); and Sakai, Arahata, and Takabatake were all trying to reach the working class.[4] Indeed, Ōsugi expressly attended meetings of Watanabe's Kenkyūkai and Ariyoshi's Zadankai in order to widen his circle of worker acquaintances and to promote his syndicalist ideas.

Ōsugi eventually established as his base of support the Hoku-fūkai (North Wind Group), the Shin'yūkai (literally, "Sincere Friends' Society"), and the Seishinkai (literally, "Righteously Advancing Society"). The Hokufūkai was simply Watanabe's former Kenkyūkai renamed after his death in June, 1918. The Shin'yūkai was a union primarily of Western language typesetters, who were generally well educated and more receptive to ideas than were manual laborers.[5] The Shin'yūkai was founded on November 3, 1916, but was the successor to the Ōyūkai (literally, "European Friends' Society"), founded in 1907. The Seishinkai was composed of newspaper employees and led by some of Ōsugi's protégés from the Hokufūkai. It was formed in December 1919, after a strike against the Tokyo newspapers failed and the Seishinkai's predecessor was dissolved.[6] Even though these groups were generally recognized as being under Ōsugi's influence, there were factions opposed to him, especially in the Shin'yūkai, which was least of all Ōsugi's own creation.[7] As late as September 1919, opposition to him within the Shin'yūkai was sufficiently strong to reject an anarchist as the Shin'yūkai's representative to a conference to choose Japan's delegate to the International Labor Organization, even though Ōsugi and his faction had contributed ¥60–70 to defray the expenses of the September meeting.[8] Ōsugi was probably involved to a greater or lesser degree in numerous other labor groups and unions such as the Rōdōsha sōdanjo (Laborers' Consultation Office) founded in January 1919 by one of his followers, Mizunuma

Tatsuo, who was a member of both the Hokufūkai and the Shin'yū-kai.[9]

No minutes of any of these groups exist to reveal the nature of Ōsugi's control over the workers. That he preferred to be final arbiter and highest authority in any group is clear, but at least in his theoretical writings he denied himself a position of total control. An essay entitled "Shoshinshi teki kanjō" (Petit bourgeois sentiments) and published in August 1918 reveals his feelings about his relationship to the working class at that time. Frankly self-critical, he admitted his own petit bourgeois background and complained that because of it he was unable to know what was in the hearts of the workers even though he and his socialist friends often talked as if they did. How could one know the extent of oppression suffered by the workers, he wondered, if one did not experience it first-hand? Unity with the workers was possible only by getting rid of petit bourgeois sentiments, which could be done only by living as they did. Ōsugi had the grace to admit he had difficulty doing this: he was able to live in a working-class area and achieve a "good feeling" (*ii kimochi*) amid the noise and filth of the surrounding factories, but he could not bring himself to rent a tenement, instead living in the middle-class house he could afford.[10]

Ōsugi contended that an unbridgeable gap existed between workers and all intellectuals. As early as 1913, he had identified intellectuals as being responsible for the continued subjugation of one class by another: "In order to maintain inequality between two classes, the conquering class had to implant fully in the hearts of the conquered class the concept that in all ways the conquering class was the superior race."[11] Intellectuals were the tools and educational systems were the institutions that insured perpetuation of class differences. Again, in "Rōdō undō to puragumatizumu" (The labor movement and pragmatism), which he wrote in 1915, he argued that it was in the interest of scholars and scientists to help and defend the oppressing class of which they were a part. Intellectuals therefore spew forth fallacies of which members of the oppressed class must be aware.[12] By 1920, he had softened this harsh opinion, if only because he now saw himself as one of the intellectuals. In "Chishiki kaikyū ni attau" (Appealing to the intellectual class) in January, he wrote:

> The labor movement in essence is a movement for acquiring the strengths and qualities of the workers. Before anything else, the intellectual class that wants to participate in the labor movement must be consistent with this essence of the labor movement. Then, it must thoroughly reflect on the fact that the historical responsibility of the intellectual class was defense of the ruling class and the deception of the oppressed classes, and must make a new resolution to become the true friend of the oppressed classes.
>
> Idle complaining and conceit stem from the incompleteness of this reflection and resolution. [13]

In late 1921, he gave an example from literature of what he meant. In a review, "Rōdō undō to rōdō bungaku" (The labor movement and workers' literature), he criticized most novels about workers because the authors' lifestyles were not the same as that of a worker. He offered as an example of what he would consider good literature a novel about Korea by Nakanishi Inosuke, an official of a streetcar workers union whom Ōsugi disliked because he was a labor boss instead of a true union man. Nakanishi had resided in Korea for a long time and had written a novel in which he treated a Korean very sympathetically. Ōsugi emphasized the coincidence of Nakanishi's long residence in Korea and the quality of the book, but marveled at Nakanishi's inability, and the inability of all writers of workers' novels, to do the same for the Japanese working man. [14]

In this manner, Ōsugi rationalized his way around the barriers that his analysis of society's class structure threw up against his own participation in the labor movement. This rationalization also allowed for full penetration of the labor movement by the rest of the socialist movement, which was overwhelmingly composed of intellectuals. Nevertheless, he remained ambivalent about the role of intellectuals in the labor unions. He warned that intellectuals always have an ideal to which they desire the unions to conform, whereas they are the ones who should be conforming. Intellectuals try to force upon the workers many things they do not need while preventing them from striving for things they do need. Similarly, he was quick to criticize, in January 1920, articles that had appeared the preceding November and December which glorified the role of the intellectuals and implied that workers did not have the introspective consciousness required for a successful union.[15]

In this broad debate on the role of the intellectuals, Yamakawa Kikue, Yamakawa Hotishi's wife, and one of Kamichika's associates, attempted to argue that workers could manage the movement without the stimulus and leadership of the intellectuals, but that they would arrive by themselves after a greater length of time at the same conclusions that they would have reached more quickly with assistance from the intellectuals.[16] Thus, independence from the intellectuals would only result in unnecessary delays. Ōsugi said that, on the contrary, "There is no reason that [workers] should not know of the progress of ideas about the labor movement through the development of the real movement itself rather than through the intellectual aid of the intellectuals."[17] He continued by repeating that, while the assistance of intellectuals is perhaps desirable and important, they must first understand the workers' spirit and emotions, lest they be scorned by the workers.

Much of this reflected Ōsugi's earlier exposure to Georges Sorel's anti-rationalism. In "Boku wa seishin ga suki da" (I like spirit), a very short article published in February 1918, only a month after he was able to begin publishing voluminously again, he gave full vent to his feelings on the subject:

> I like spirit. However, when spirit is put into theory I generally come to detest it. I do that because, along the route to the theory, by and large it becomes harmonious with social realities and toadishly cooperative. Because it is a deceit.
>
> Thought as spirit itself is rare. The action of spirit as such is even rarer.
>
> In this sense I like the nebulous democracy and humanism of the literati. They are at least charming. I hate, however, what the legal and political scientists call democracy and humanism. It makes me ill just listening to them.
>
> I hate socialism too. For some reason, I hate anarchism a bit.
>
> What I most like is humanity's blind action: the explosion of spirit itself.

> In thought there is freedom. However, in action too there is free-
> dom. And also in incentive (*dōki*) there is freedom.[18]

Ōsugi claimed to find the same kind of irrational, emotional
response among workers. Many of the phrases that he used in an
essay in January 1920 criticizing the Christian labor leader, Kagawa
Toyohiko, echo his writings on life and growth or expansion of
the individual ego by the power of his own will:

> We are often defeated [in a strike]. However, no matter how often
> beaten, we cannot forget the joy we felt during the dispute. The plea-
> sure of stretching our will power. The pleasure of trying out our own
> strength. The pleasure of seeing a manifestation of real comradely emo-
> tions among comrades. The pleasure of seeing the world clearly split
> [into camps of friends and foes]. And above all these various pleasures,
> the pleasure of seeing faintly and gradually our own future and society's
> future. The pleasure of seeing an improvement in our own person-
> alities.[19]

A total defeat would have pleased Ōsugi if it had no more than a
cathartic effect. He valued the strike for the opportunity it offered workers to discover and develop independently the power
that potentially was within themselves, their own instinct to expand
the ego to the greatest extent possible. However, he also demonstrated syndicalist tendencies in this passage. A syndicate was first
a device for economic action, whether it be a strike or the establishing of a loan fund for each unionist's benefit. It was also a
microcosm in which the lifestyle that would typify the ideal future
society could develop. In the syndicate or in its strikes the ideal
society might momentarily reveal itself according to the needs of
the workers as they discovered them. In this framework, there was
no place for intellectuals to add anything, at least not until they
came to have the same insights and needs the workers did by living
as the workers did.

In another essay published in January, "Rōdō undō to chishiki
kaikyū" (The labor movement and the intellectual class), Ōsugi
made clear the point that present enemies were potential allies if
only they would submit to the workers and their ideas:

Workers do not take as their purpose struggle itself, nor do they try to eradicate people strongly opposed to them. They fight for the sake of their own growth. They will eradicate obstacles to that growth. At the same time that they will be rescued by this eradication of obstacles, so too their opponents who are representatives of the obstacles will be rescued. [20]

In June, 1920, in "Shakaiteki risōron" (On social idealism), Ōsugi expressed concern about the role workers would play in the revolution. Although he was not yet familiar with the progress of the Russian Revolution, he recognized that

workers who do not take a firm hold of [their conception of the future society] will become tools of the revolution, but cannot become its masters. . . . Most do not realize that when they have destroyed [the old society] by their own power, when that is over with, they leave everything to others; then the so-called new society becomes one [belonging to] others just like the old society.

Even here, though, he was less concerned with the details of the workers' plan of the future than with the manner they approached the problem, for he added: "Rather than saying, however, that this is because workers do not have a firm grasp on the conception of the future of the new society, it should be said that it is because they lack a really firm grasp on an autonomous spirit which does for itself everything to the bitter end." [21] Thus, workers with the proper spirit can master the revolution, even if they have no clear idea of the desired results. This spirit they must develop for themselves, by themselves. This last point echoed one he made in "Bokura no shugi" (Our ideology) in August of the previous year when he said that, not only is "doing for yourself . . . the best feeling," but that to ask or accept someone else's help is to stifle the growth of the ego. [22]

In 1919 and 1920 Ōsugi made numerous attempts to extend his influence into moderate and conservative labor unions by attending their meetings and heckling the speakers. His purpose in heckling was to disrupt a meeting's order, which he saw as an extension of the present class society, so as to allow workers the opportunity to enlarge their egos while they experimented with a new order that would reflect the nature of the new society. He maintained that "my heckling is not for the purpose of simply destroying [order] : it is not for the purpose of mere propaganda. It is a real movement (*jissai undō*) for the purpose of constructing at all times and all places the new lifestyle and the new order step by step."[23]

While heckling seemed to Ōsugi to be an opportunity to expand his ego and one which proved the validity of the expansion theory, his experiences led him to develop theories about heckling which he tied to some of his other ideas about man, society, and the labor movement. He saw heckling as a tool that would eliminate class-based, structured meetings designed to promote an order advantageous to a particular class. Lectures should not be gatherings at which people would be induced to dance to a new tune. They were opportunities for workers to experiment with their freedom and they should freely advance and argue their ideas. As he wrote in the context of new forms in the burgeoning people's theater:

> Long speeches are the special characteristic of old plays; in the new plays, short dialogues will succeed. The arts are the mirror of society. The world is reflected in the mirror of the arts.
>
> Listening silently to a person's long speech is only to be swept up in a marching song: it is what is done vis-à-vis upper-class people. Among people of the same class, long speeches will disappear and short dialogues will succeed. From long monologues to short dialogues: this is the evolution of conversation. This is the evolution of humanity.[24]

Moreover, heckling was one way workers could cooperate with each other for their mutual benefit as they would in a future anarchist society. Heckling, and the dialogue it would produce, was a way for workers gradually to create the perfect society.

Ōsugi summed up his opinions on the way the future society would evolve in "Shakaiteki risōron":

> ... humanity is not a book complete and fixed once and for all. It is a book of blank pages on which each and every person writes letter by letter. Humanity is merely people living.
>
> Even with the question of what is this thing called the labor movement, the answer is the same. Labor problems are human problems

having regard to the laborers. Workers are continuously writing in the big book of blank pages called *Labor Problems* word by word, line by line, page by page.[25]

The actual configuration of the new society depended upon the particular set of circumstances, values, and conditions that had shaped the immediately previous society:

> The conceptions and ideals of anarchism, social democracy, syndicalism or guild socialism may possibly be the strength and light that the workers of Europe and America have constructed. It is best for them to proceed under that strength and light. There is, however, a great distance between those conceptions and ideals and the reality Japanese workers have constructed to date.
>
> Nonetheless, for us there is nothing but to seek appropriate conceptions and ideals for ourselves by continuing to strive to raise up our own reality.[26]

Also in June 1920, Ōsugi wrote articles criticizing theories of the labor movement put forth by Arahata and Sakai and hinting at a point that would become a major one separating him irrevocably from the Japanese bolsheviks. In Ōsugi's opinion, Arahata viewed the gradual development of labor unions as constituting a revolution in Japan. "The result of day-by-day struggle of labor unions with the capitalist system will gradually but inevitably accomplish the constructive development of the future society among us."[27] Sakai held a somewhat similar view, saying that unions would gradually come to control the means of production, a theory, Ōsugi pointed out, that covertly involved centralization of power and authority. Later on, this question of centralized power and authority strongly affected Ōsugi's opinion of the Russian Revolution and became a major focus of debate between the Japanese anarchists and bolsheviks competing for control of a national labor organization.

The labor movement was not Ōsugi's sole concern during the years after he resumed publishing in January 1918. In fact, his return to acceptability in the socialist and publishing worlds was tied to his expertise on three subjects that were of wide concern in Japan after World War I. First, the sudden growth of the labor movement made his comments, as an analyst and as a leader, of great interest. Second, the Russian Revolution left all observers puzzled, as we shall see from the next chapter, but Ōsugi's opinions were considered valuable since he supposedly was familiar with left-wing theories of revolution. The last subject, though, is surprising—art. Ōsugi had written on art in 1916 and had added his translation of Romain Rolland's *The People's Theater* in 1917, calling it *Minshū geijutsu ron* (The people's art). In 1920–1921 these contributions helped fuel a major debate on the nature and purpose of art and, having already established himself as an authority on the subject, he was called on to join the debate.

Ōsugi needed little urging, since he had willingly entered the debate on art even when he was talking about the role of intellectuals in the labor movement. One of his early protégés who became known as a writer, Eguchi Kan,[28] remembered that when Kume Masao and Uno Koji, both writers, got together with Ōsugi, he was never interested in talking about revolution or socialism but about literature, movies, and art. Eguchi recalled that Ōsugi was especially fond of Rolland's idea that "art is that which displays the grandeur of man's soul."[29] Indeed, Ōsugi's theory of art was taken directly from Rolland, not independently developed from his earlier writings on the ego, although these melded well with his art theory.[30]

However much he was interested in art, Ōsugi considered the art of the masses (*minshū geijutsu*) to be the only art that need truly be of concern. In July 1917, though, he attached a narrow meaning to "the masses." The masses were the common workers (*heimin rōdōsha*), but not just any workers. The masses included only those common workers who had become conscious of their position in society, their fate, and their strength. They would be the central figures in the construction of the new society. In short, the revolution would not be a purely political and economic one: "It is a revolution in social life (*shakai seikatsu*) itself. It is a revolution in human life (*ningen seikatsu*) itself. It is also a revolution in the thoughts and emotions of mankind and in the methods of their expression."[31]

Ōsugi did not return to the subject until he wrote "Shakai mondai ka geijutsu mondai ka" (Is it a social question or an artistic question?) in September 1921. He argued first that the title of his essay was imprecise. Mass art, properly speaking, must concern itself with artistic questions and with social questions at the same time: the one implies the other. Art that is concerned only with art or only with society is not the art of the masses: "If you completely separate these two properties, the topic of mass art will be snuffed out just as is water if you separate the oxygen and the hydrogen."[32] Mass art is both for the masses and for art itself: it is also by, of, and for the masses.

In attempting to explain what he meant when he said art must be born of the people, Ōsugi avoided the problem of ambiguity he had faced earlier when he had attempted to define the role of the intellectual in the labor movement, by eliminating all intellectuals from the category of mass artists:

> There are two meanings to art born of the masses: that the artists are born among the masses; and that art using the masses as its raw material comes into existence. The former takes as its criterion the class origin of the artist, while the latter is determined by the class attached to the lifestyle and sentiments adopted as the artistic material.[33]

Mass art would serve a function not unlike a good labor union: it would educate the people, entertain them, and improve their lifestyle. At a glance, this appears to be exactly what Ōsugi objected to when he wrote critically about intellectuals who propped up the ruling class and themselves by feeding deceptions to the lower class. But, since mass art is art performed by worker-artists, using material drawn from the life of the masses, there is no possibility that it might lead the masses astray.

In an article the following month, Ōsugi tied together his most recent thoughts on the labor and literary movements in "Rōdō undō to rōdō bungaku" (The labor movement and workers' literature). Here it becomes clear that mass art and the labor movement are simply two forms of activity based on the same assumptions and have the same purpose. He complained that he felt unable to write effectively about the "reality of the labor movement" (*rōdō undō no jissai*), but conlcuded that this was true, as a matter of course, because he was not living the life of a worker anymore.[34] In fact, he had moved to Kamakura a year and a half earlier in April 1920 and, since Kamakura was then, as now, a health and relaxation spa for better-off Tokyo executives, his residence was indeed a far cry from a worker's tenement. He recalled that the articles he wrote in 1918 and 1919 were good because he was so much nearer to living the worker's life.

He also criticized others who, like himself, were not living as workers, yet aspired to be leaders of the labor movement. He warned in general about hoping to join either the literary or labor movement as some kind of a vanguard pulling the ignorant masses along toward their liberation. Rather, he said, those who wished to become leaders should join the movement as rank-and-file soldiers in order to be united in all ways with the workers. "To be accepted as a worker, it is sufficient to have the sincerity to want to be united with the workers, and to want to have the same class consciousness as the workers." He specifically singled out for criticism the Shinjinkai (New Men's Society), composed mainly of elite Tokyo Imperial University students who were trying then to join the Yūaikai in order to capture leadership of the bulk of the labor movement. He also condemned Yamakawa Hitoshi and the Japanese bolsheviks for their plans to "try to make the workers slaves of [Soviet] Bolshevism."[35] It was in this context that Ōsugi was able to praise Nakanishi Inosuke's novel about Korea, even though he found Nakanishi a despicable labor leader. Nakanishi had in fact made himself one with the Korean people by long residence in Korea and had written the novel in the same spirit as a Korean might have written.

These views completely contradicted Ōsugi's lifelong emphasis on the absolute necessity of expanding the ego through exercise of the power of the will. The contradiction can only be explained through his writings of 1917–1921, in which he added a restriction of class to the idea. Only if the individual was a worker would expansion of the ego result in personal growth of the kind that would be in accord with the ideal society. Individuals of other higher classes would only perpetuate the existing class society if they were to expand their egos without first assuming the identity of the working class by sincerely wanting "to be united with the workers."

His view of intellectuals as ideologues for the state, and his view of the state, in turn, as an oppressive force, led him to counsel passivity on the part of the Taishō-period intelligentsia. He insisted that intellectuals and other members of the elite should wait for ideas and initiatives to come to them from the workers. Intellectuals should seek to emulate the lifestyle of the workers so that they could rationally and intuitively know the workers' experiences through which the workers' ideas were developed. He urged intellectuals not to organize the masses, but rather to be passively receptive to trends rising out of the workers; only when they were able to identify with the working class could they be trusted to act in a manner that would not help the conquerer class further subjugate the workers. In this manner, Ōsugi contributed to a process which ultimately undermined the intellectual and moral foundations of the elite's approach to the masses at the same time that he contributed to the weakening of the intellectuals' self-confidence.

NINE

The Russian Revolution and the Anarchist-Bolshevik Split[1]

In the years following the Russian Revolution of 1917, the Japanese socialist movement split into two main factions which became increasingly opposed. One was composed of pro-bolsheviks such as Sakai Toshihiko, Yamakawa Hitoshi, Arahata Kanson, and Takabatake Motoyuki. The other was the anarchist group led by Ōsugi. Eventually the bolshevik group won out and dominated the leftist movement. Since all these men, especially Yamakawa, Arahata, and Ōsugi, had called themselves anarchists or anarcho-syndicalists before the Revolution, a question arises: Why did Ōsugi refuse to switch to Marxism-Leninism?

The question assumes importance because Ōsugi was one of the few Japanese socialists who came to oppose Marxism-Leninism. Whereas Marxism-Leninism led many Japanese into excessive speculation about doctrine and domination by the Comintern, Ōsugi retained a concrete sense of the goals and tactics that were essential to the Revolution and also maintained a critical stance toward Russia's revolutionary experiment. This is not to imply, however, that Ōsugi was more likely than the Japanese bolsheviks to accomplish a revolution in Japan.

Western scholars describing the split between the anarchists and the bolsheviks usually explain it solely in terms of general philosophical differences between anarcho-syndicalism and Marxism-Leninism.[2] There are, however, at least three reasons why Ōsugi resisted Marxism-Leninism. First there were personal factors. His private relations with other radicals interfered with his ability to cooperate with them. His love affair had already earned him Sakai's enmity. Other socialists also disapproved of him or openly disliked him. Second, Ōsugi was by nature anti-authoritarian and rebellious. He believed very strongly in absolute personal freedom, as his love affair indicated. Hence, he refused to recognize the authority of an outside group such as the Comintern. Finally, he made a number of empirical studies of political conditions in Russia and found there a general loss of political and personal freedom. This he could not condone intellectually.

The Russian Revolution took the Japanese by surprise. Yoshino Sakuzō wrote in the *Chūō kōron* (Central review) in October 1917: "Chaos flourishes in Russia, but the Bolsheviks probably will not seize power. The Kerensky government is doing fine."[3] Socialists were no less confused. Years later, Yamakawa recalled that, when Lenin's name first appeared, it was so unfamiliar to the Japanese that some thought it might be the name of a medicine.[4] Sakai wrote two years after the first Revolution, after the founding of the Communist International (Comintern):

> Marxism has given birth to many factions based on doctrine and policy, and it is difficult to state clearly to which of the various factions I now belong. The reason is that changes which began to appear in time of war will complete their diverse developments in time of peace, and it is difficult to discern accurately where the trend of the times will finally conclude.[5]

Yamakawa Hitoshi, in a debate with Takabatake in *Shin shakai* (The new society) tried to follow more carefully "the trend of the times." Between the Revolutions of February and October 1917, he argued that political action before the Revolution was permissible, but limited to syndicalism's direct action. Takabatake responded that syndicalism was not the only alternative to bourgeois politics and that political action should be considered to be within the realm of the direct action of a self-conscious worker. Yamakawa took a stronger syndicalist position, then, arguing that the direct action of syndicalism explicitly excluded legal political action. However, following the Bolshevik Revolution in October, and the establishment of the Hara Cabinet in September 1918, Yamakawa began arguing that direct action and political action were two sides of the same coin, that workers should be concerned with social reform and with political confrontation and competition with the bourgeoisie.[6]

A large part of the difficulty the Japanese had in coming to grips with the nature of Russian communism was that they were not immediately exposed to Leninist ideas. Takabatake finally, in February 1918, wrote "The Political Movement and the Economic Movement" in *Shin shakai* (The new society) wherein Lenin's theories were discussed for the first time in Japan. The influence of the Revolution, however, was delayed even well beyond that date and probably had little intellectual or theoretical influence until 1920–1922.[7]

Ōsugi's initial reaction to the Revolution is difficult to discover, since he does not even refer to the event in either letter or article until October 1919, two years after the Bolshevik Revolution. Was he prepared for a revolution, much less the Revolution? In 1914, he twice states that he expected socialists to be hostile to the nations involved in the Great War.[8] This attitude paralleled the declared policy of the Second International which, since 1907, had theorized that socialists must declare a war against war whenever war might break out, meaning that they should foment revolution in reaction to capitalist wars, not just to protest the wars but because conditions would be ripe for success. But thereafter, Ōsugi was silent on the subject. If he had seriously believed this argument, he should have continued to expound it, especially as the horrors and casualties of the war became known. Instead, he failed to mention the theoretical connection again in the two years of activity that remained before his love affair precipitated his 1916–1917 eclipse. In fact, the article he should have written between 1914 and 1916, "Kakumei wa itsu kuru ka" (When is the revolution coming?), in which he predicted a revolution in Japan in the next two or three years, was not written until February

1921.[9] Thus, Ōsugi in no way expected or hoped for a revolution in 1917 and, accordingly, was taken by surprise when it did occur.

Nevertheless, or perhaps consequently, he was enthusiastic in supporting the Revolution. It appeared with the spontaneity he so valued as the basis of human action. His first recorded reaction to it was his remarks at the April 1918 Roshia kakumei kinenkai (Meeting to Commemorate the Russian Revolution), which was attended by about forty radicals of all persuasions. Ōsugi gave a rambling speech eulogizing the Revolution until Takabatake Moto-yuki urged him to come to the point. Ōsugi thereupon ended up lamely, stating that Bolshevik tactics were essentially the same as those of the anarchists. Takabatake derisively asked about the dictatorship of the proletariat, which brought Ōsugi's response that some early anarchists had proposed a dictatorship too.[10] Apparently, this exchange silenced him, for we find no further reaction to the Revolution until October 1919.

At that time, he finally wrote referring to the Revolution, but it was only a passing reference: "Bolshevization (*kagekiha-ka*) is, speaking in the widest sense, the negation of capitalism: it is putting socialism into effect (*shakaishugi-ka*). England is where they most fear this change to socialism among the workers."[11] The next reference was made about a year later, perhaps in late 1920. In a survey of the Japanese labor and socialist movements, Ōsugi related how a democratic fervor rose in Japan under the stimulus of "the war of democracy against militarism," the first Russian Revolution, and the Wilsonian principles for ending the war. He continued:

> The second Russian Revolution imparted an enormously deep impression to the masses. The dispatches that appeared in the daily newspapers were read avidly and with great interest. However, the capitalists and government were confident that revolution was a foreign, not Japanese, thing.
>
> Then suddenly, but occurring naturally, there erupted the Rice Riots of the summer of '18, two years ago.[12]

The Rice Riots of 1918 made less of an impression on Ōsugi at the time than this implies. He had been traveling in Kyushu trying to promote capital for a new publishing venture, *Rōdō shimbun* (Labor news) but, on his return to Tokyo, he stopped off in Osaka to visit colleagues and to solicit more money there and in Kyoto. This was when he and a large group of colleagues, together with the police assigned to maintain surveillance over them, toured the scene of a riot in progress until the police nervously asked Ōsugi to depart from the area so that the police, not the radicals, could avoid getting into trouble with higher police officials. [13] The next day, he hurried off to Kyoto to search for money, a task more important to him at that moment than his tourist's fascination with the spectacle of the Rice Riots. For all the attention he paid to the riots, he too must have been "confident that revolutions were foreign, not Japanese, things."

Why did Ōsugi, like most Japanese socialists, pay no attention to the Rice Riots as the possible beginning of the revolution in Japan? In part, it was because German Marxist theories led the Japanese, including Ōsugi, to expect socialism to arise from among the proletariat and to expect a slow, evolutionary approach to socialism instead of a violent revolution, expectations which continued to blind the Japanese to the lessons of the Russian Revolution and Lenin's theory on imperialism long after the fact. [14] If Ōsugi still believed what he had written in 1914 in line with the doctrines of the Second International, though, he might have been ready to view any civil disturbance, especially one on the scale of the Rice Riots, in terms of a revolution. That he did not would indicate that he had stopped thinking about the possibility of a revolution in 1918, despite the Great War, despite the Russian Revolution which was not yet understood by him or any other Japanese socialist, and despite German Marxism. In this context, appropriately, he wrote two and a half years later that he expected revolution to make a steady progress from Central Europe to Western Europe to North America and finally to Japan, where it would break out in the next two or three years. [15]

Although Ōsugi's first recorded reaction to the Russian Revolution was based on ignorance and although he remained insensitive to the possibility of revolution in Japan, he was not immune to influence from the Revolution. One of the first impressions the Japanese had of the Revolution was the efficacy of a united front among revolutionary and reformist elements. This conclusion was warranted in the aftermath of the Revolution when the revolutionary government was open to Bolshevik, Menshevik, and anarchist alike. Not until Lenin began attacking the anarchists in March 1921 was the full meaning of dictatorship of the proletariat made evident. Thus, Ōsugi concluded that cooperation with other leftists could lead to mutual benefit, and he pursued this goal for a year, from the middle of 1920 to late spring 1921.

Ōsugi demonstrated his willingness to cooperate with non-syndicalists when he traveled to Shanghai to meet a representative of the Comintern in October 1920. In August, the Comintern tried to make contact with the Japanese radicals, apparently in an attempt to initiate a Communist Party in Japan. A Korean, Yi Ch'un-suk, arrived in Japan with a verbal invitation for Sakai and Yamakawa to attend the Kyokutō shakaishugisha kaigi (Conference of Far Eastern Socialists), knowing that they were tending to favor communism over anarchism, even though they still were not clear about the differences and basic incompatibility of the two ideologies.[16] They refused to make the trip, however, and suggested that Ōsugi be invited instead. Yamakawa, in his autobiography, complained that he and Sakai were uncertain whether a representative from the Comintern really was in the Far East and hence doubted Yi's authority as well as the legitimacy of the conference. He went on to say that they did not know what kind of formal organ existed in Shanghai, that there was no formal, written invitation directed to them from a certifiable Comintern source, and that, even after Ōsugi met the representative in Shanghai, Yamakawa still knew nothing of the man's personality or qualifications.[17] Takatsu Seidō later recalled that Yamakawa also felt it was dangerous to accept money from foreign agents since it could result in criminal accusations of insurrection, punishable by execution.[18]

Ōsugi was a little less formal and accepted the invitation readily, with the intention, he claimed, of establishing communications with socialists and anarchists in China and Korea. He also hoped to learn more about the Russian Revolution and, perhaps, to arrange to visit Russia at some future date. Although he asked for their approval, neither Sakai, Yamakawa, nor Arahata would give it. Sakai and Ōsugi actually got into a private argument, and there was a general coolness between Ōsugi and the other three regarding the projected trip to Shanghai.[19]

On the evening on which Ōsugi was to depart secretly from his house in Kamakura for Shanghai via Shimonoseki, a young printer from the Shin'yūkai, Kuwabara Rentarō, suddenly appeared, threatening the secrecy of Ōsugi's departure. The other strongly anarchist printers' union, the Seishinkai, was striking against the fifteen major Tokyo newspapers and required a well-phrased handbill, one of the services Ōsugi routinely provided to his followers in the labor movement. Ōsugi, without batting an eye, dashed off a quick text and then had Kuwabara carry his suitcase to the train station for him, a spontaneous but effective way of further disguising his departure from the police.[20] Ōsugi's three-year-old daughter, Mako, also had a role in confusing the police. After his return from Shanghai, a policeman described to him how he had tried to pry information from Mako about her father's whereabouts, since the police had not seen Ōsugi for a few days. The policeman said:

> I'm no match for Mako, you know. When I asked her, "Is your papa in?" she said, "Um." Thinking it odd, the next time I asked "Is your papa not in?" and sure enough she said "Um." Thinking "Aha," I asked her "Is your papa not in or in?" and she nodded saying "Um, um" twice and ran off. Thus, for something like ten days, I did not know exactly where you were.[21]

Although he had shaved off his beard, he was still worried that one of the numerous policemen in the Shimonoseki harbor area would recognize him as he transferred from train to boat. He therefore befriended a child and its mother and made the transfer with the child in his arms, giving the appearance of being a part of an ordinary family instead of a prowling revolutionary.[22]

The circumstances of the conference's meetings remain obscure. The Comintern's probable intention was to establish Communist parties or committees in China, Korea, and Japan. The meetings themselves were attended by only ten or eleven people, including Ōsugi who was in Shanghai for about ten days, Ch'en Tu-hsiu from China, and Yu Un-huong and Yi Tong-him from Korea, plus a representative of the Comintern.[23] At the time of the meeting, a number of Communist "parties" had been formed in both China and Korea, although the time of formation and the programs of the "parties" remain obscure, and none are recognized as the legitimate predecessors of the Chinese and Korean Communist Parties. Ch'en was the first secretary-general and co-founder of the Chinese Communist Party, while Yu was a "long-time leader of the left-nationalist cause and frequently . . . associated with the Communists."[24] The meetings were held in Shanghai, at least once in the home of Ch'en, over a period of two or three days. Ōsugi was not allowed status as a delegate, since he was least under the influence of Marxism-Leninism, but was allowed to sit on a committee that would coordinate future exchanges of information and communications among socialists in the three nations and the Comintern.[25]

At the end of the conference, the Comintern's representative, having sized up Ōsugi, took him aside for a private talk:

> That conversation was essentially about money. He said, we can probably put up some money if you need it for the movement: what plans do you have now and how much money is needed? I replied that at present I really had no specific plans, but I had been thinking of publishing a weekly newspaper. If I had ¥10,000, that would probably support it for a half a year and, thereafter, we [in the movement in Japan] would probably manage by ourselves.
>
> It was decided I could have this money immediately. At each of the many times we met, however, T began the usual picayune meddling concerning the contents of the newspaper. Neither my innate personality nor my ideology could excuse this meddling. Finally, I said, as I had at the earlier meeting, enough talk, I'm going back [to Japan]: I don't want to receive one penny. I didn't come here originally to receive money. I came having no such expectation. I came to devise [means of]

communicating with comrades of the various Asian nations. If only that is accomplished, each country will carry on the movement in its own way. Japan is Japan: even though no money has come from anywhere, we have continued our movement by ourselves up until now; from here on, it will be the same. I don't want a single penny of any money that tries to attach conditions. I expressly wrote down things to this effect in English, which we had so far been speaking, and gave it to him.

T agreed with this. Then he even promised that money needed for the general movement would be sent whenever [needed]. However, when I finally returned, I only received ¥2,000, since, he said, things are a bit bad just now. [26]

In late 1920, shortly after Ōsugi's return from Shanghai, radicals of all persuasions joined to form the Nihon shakaishugi dōmei (Japanese Socialist League). The Dōmei was an attempt to unite the socialist and labor-union movements and, although all leftists were welcomed, it was dominated by anarcho-syndicalists. Of the thirty members of the governing board, seven including Ōsugi came from the Hokufūkai and one each from the Seishinkai and Shin'yūkai, all of which were under Ōsugi's control. By comparison, the Yūaikai had only one seat, and no other group had more than two. [27] The Dōmei was established in August and had about 1,000 members nationwide by its formal date of inauguration, December 10. On the previous night, a meeting preparatory to founding the Dōmei was dispersed by police. On the 10th, the police dispersed the inaugural meeting as soon as the first speaker began. They also arrested Ōsugi in order to remove a possibly incendiary element from a combustible area, although they did not later press any charges. [28]

The Dōmei declined quickly after this inauspicious beginning. It tried to hold its second national meeting on May 9, 1921, but was prevented from doing so by the police. On May 28, the police ordered the Dōmei to disband, which it did without resistance.

The Dōmei offered an opportunity for cooperation by all factions, an opportunity that was accepted but not exercised to any great extent. Some speakers traveled through the country spreading the good word, but no coordinated strategy was worked out that would tie together the labor union and socialist movements and benefit both. One author concludes that the Dōmei collapsed not because of police actions but because its leadership was already beginning to factionalize. Competition and antagonism between the anarchist and bolshevik groups had already begun and grew much worse when the factions were brought together in the Dōmei. By May, the dispute would have caused the Dōmei to collapse soon, even if the police had not acted.[29] This seems to be a correct conclusion in light of the failure of Ōsugi to cooperate successfully on the joint publishing effort, the second *Rōdō undō*, which he attempted with the bolsheviks beginning in January 1921.

Following his trip to Shanghai, Ōsugi began to experience serious trouble cooperating with other socialists who were inclining toward Marxism-Leninism. The origin of this conflict dated back to his love affair of 1915–1916. The comments and criticisms of him made by Sakai, Yamakawa, Takabatake, and others exacerbated a natural competition between Ōsugi and the other leaders for paramountcy within the socialist movement. Since the High Treason Incident of 1910, the movement had been led primarily by Sakai with Yamakawa, Arahata, Takabatake, and Ōsugi in an equal rank beneath him. Yamakawa and Arahata were cool to Ōsugi after the love affair, but the three could get along. Between Ōsugi and Takabatake, though, there seems to have been an intense competition to be the most important next to Sakai, as shown in Takabatake's propensity at the time of the love affair and at the Roshia kakumei kinenkai to be excessively derogatory toward Ōsugi.

These criticisms must have come to Ōsugi's mind in mid-1921 when he became suspicious of the Japanese bolsheviks he was working with. Ōsugi had used the ¥2,000 from the Comintern to begin publishing the second *Rōdō undō* (The labor movement) journal, which lasted from January to June 1921. The hoped-for cooperation, however, did not last long. He had included two bolsheviks, Kondō Eizō and Takatsu Seidō, on the editorial staff and allowed them a special page on which they explained communism. He also published articles by them and other bolsheviks.

Ōsugi soon came to feel that these bolsheviks were secretly trying to cut off the syndicalists from contact with the Comintern and to oust them from *Rōdō undō* when Kondō Eizō went to Shanghai to talk with the Comintern representative. Kondō was arrested on his return to Japan, and Ōsugi used the event as an excuse to stop publishing the paper.[30]

Perhaps these personality clashes encouraged Ōsugi to look deeper into the nature of political developments in Russia after the Revolution, although by this time enough was known about the Revolution that it was an unavoidably important topic to all leftists. His studies uncovered troubling aspects that led him to criticize the Bolshevik regime there. In the maiden issue of the third *Rōdō undō,* which he began publishing in December 1921, he made his first critical evaluation of the Russian Revolution. He noted first that many anarchists and socialists had been imprisoned, charged with counterrevolutionary activities and supporting the restoration of the Czarist Government. He quoted the British anarchist journal, *Freedom,* which stated that anarchists from all over the world had gone to Russia to aid the Revolution, only to find that the Bolsheviks fought to establish their dictatorship, whereas the anarchists fought to gain freedom. After quoting the argument that opposition to the Bolshevik dictatorship did not mean support for the return of the old regime, Ōsugi concluded the article with his own observation: "If you win, you are the imperial army (*kangun*). If you lose, you are the rebel army (*zokugun*). Further, those who do not conform to the victors are all counterrevolutionaries and back-stabbers of the workers. What's the use?"[31]

In February and March 1922, relying mainly on a message from the Russian Social Revolutionary Party (Shakai kakumei tō), he fired a brief broadside against the Russian Bolsheviks, accusing them of establishing a dictatorship and insisting that the internal government and the economic policy must be changed, the soviets re-elected, and political freedoms restored. He then provided some details on the socialists and anarchists who had been arrested and systematically mistreated, according to various Russian sources, and concluded with the protest of three anarchist organizations in Moscow against Lenin's speech at the Tenth Party Congress in March 1921, in which Lenin issued a declaration of "merciless war" against anarchists and, especially, anarcho-syndicalists.[32]

Throughout the remainder of 1922, Ōsugi continued to publish a series of articles which criticized the treatment of anarchists by Bolsheviks.[33] All these articles were generally similar in protesting arbitrary political arrests and mistreatment in prison. Ōsugi protested not only on behalf of anarchists, but also for others who were genuinely revolutionary, like the Kronstadt naval rebels, who were labeled counterrevolutionary and ruthlessly stamped out because they opposed the Bolshevik Government. All these articles were based on communications from Emma Goldman and, more frequently, Alexander Berkman, two Russian exiles who went to aid the Revolution in 1919 after being deported from the United States. Occasionally, Ōsugi would add his own comments as when he wrote in July 1922: "The 'policies' of the Bolsheviks towards the peasants sound the death bell for the Revolution. How right are the words that Kropotkin explained time and again in his letters and to visiting Americans that "the Bolsheviks have shown the world how the Revolution should not be done.'"[34]

In late 1922, the antagonism that had existed between Ōsugi and those Japanese socialists who had become Communists changed tenor. Sakai had criticized Ōsugi roughly, saying that the anarcho-syndicalists were "totally ignorant of the 'necessary steps' required by 'social realities,'"[35] but the two groups still had sufficient mutual interests to allow Sakai and Yamakawa to continue to publish in Ōsugi's third *Rōdō undō*. In September, however, there was an attempt to form a nationwide labor union in Osaka. The effort climaxed in the so-called anarchist-bolshevik dispute (*ana-boru ronsō*). Ōsugi attended the conference as an observer. His followers wanted the organization to be founded on the syndicalist principles of local union autonomy and self-government, in contrast to the Japanese bolsheviks who wanted a more disciplined, centralized body. The anarchists failed to carry the day, walked out of the meeting, and the proposed union died before it was born.[36]

The Osaka Conference was the visible peak of the anarcho-bolshevik dispute. The dispute itself can probably be traced back to the clash Ōsugi had with Takabatake at the Roshia kakumei kinenkai in 1918, although fundamental personality conflicts date from Ōsugi's love affair. Anarcho-syndicalism reached its height in 1920–1922,[37] yet even then it was being challenged by the bolsheviks and weakened in its relationship with the labor unions because the depression beginning earlier in 1920 gradually weakened the unions and, over the next two years, demonstrated the futility of anarchism's direct-action tactics. Nevertheless, Ōsugi's influence, and that of anarcho-syndicalism, did not collapse and disappear at the conclusion of the Osaka Conference. Indeed, Yamakawa especially remained influenced by anarcho-syndicalism even after the conference, and the influence of the syndicalists in the labor movement was even slower to give way.[38]

In preparation for the Osaka Conference, Ōsugi published two articles which were allegedly about the situation in Russia, but which ended up with strong attacks on the Japanese bolshevik faction. In the first, he outlined Trotsky's recent writings on the idea of the united front, showing that Trotsky himself considered the real goal of a united front to be Communist control over the mass of the workers.[39] One of Trotsky's three methods was to infiltrate an existing labor organization which the Communists could use as a base of operations: this, noted Ōsugi, was what the Communist faction in Japan was trying to do within the Yūaikai (which had been renamed the Sōdōmei), Japan's largest labor union. He believed that the labor union soon to be founded in Osaka would be different from this kind of united front because it would reject leadership from above, but this contention remained unfulfilled with the Osaka debacle.

In the second article, he detailed his reasons, without relying explicitly on the writing of any Russian anarchists, for refusing to support the Russian Revolution. He rejected all attempts to justify a period of dictatorship and emphasized that the freedom to criticize and the freedom to act must be preserved at all times. He also warned of the dangers of betrayal when trying to cooperate with Communists, an experience he himself had endured in his attempts to form labor unions in cooperation with the bolshevik faction. "Now I know that the bolshevik gang, for instance, Yamakawa, Sakai, [Kondō Eizō], and Arahata are all a bunch of crooks."[40]

In November 1922, two more articles appeared, one an impassioned criticism of the Japanese Communist faction, the other a critique of Trotsky's united-front theory and an analysis of how the Communist faction was putting those theories into effect by infiltrating the Yūaikai.[41] In the first, he noted charges printed in *Zen'ei* (Vanguard), published by the Communist faction (which had secretly formed the Japanese Communist Party in July) that prominent anarchists had been paid by Imperial Russia to live abroad in luxury. He then quoted an anonymous post card dated September 26, and circulated just before the Osaka meeting, accusing the anarchists in Japan of being dilatory, of accepting bribes from the government, and of spending money received from the Comintern on food and wine. He next recounted a list of attacks made on him and the underhanded tactics employed against him by the Communist faction: charges that he obstructed the seating of hostile delegates to the Osaka meeting, that he destroyed the united front, that he was the center of an anti-Yūaikai movement, that he dominated and manipulated other anarchists, and that he made off with the wife of a comrade (a reference to Itō Noe and her former husband, Tsuji Jun). That all these charges were probably true, he conveniently passed over without comment.[42] Ōsugi even resorted to name-calling in this article, using the names Yamakan Hitoshi (Speculator Hitoshi), Batabata Kyanson (Flapper Kanson) and Sakai Bokehiko (Sakai the feeble-minded) for Yamakawa Hitoshi, Arahata Kanson, and Sakai Toshihiko.

What Ōsugi discovered in these studies of the fruits of the Russian Revolution conflicted directly with his own rebellious, independent temperament and with his political philosophy, which placed the utmost value on freedom. Ōsugi had never submitted to any authority—not of his father, his mother, his school teachers, or the officers of the military preparatory school from which he was expelled.[43] In addition, his commitment to anarcho-syndicalism was based on two main philosophical points. First, life, or the ego, was, he said, synonymous with action and expansion. If life is not expanding it is contracting and dying: ". . . The inevitable logic of life directs that we remove and destroy all things that try to impede the expansion of life. When we defy this imperative, our lives and our egos stagnate and are corrupted and destroyed."[44]

The second point was drawn from his understanding of syndicalism. He argued that men, like labor unions, must organize themselves on the principles of autonomy, self-government, and an absolute right to join or withdraw from an association at any time. These were the principles on which he insisted in opposing the bolshevik faction in the Nihon shakaishugi dōmei and at the Osaka meeting. These were also the principles he saw violated in the Russian system in which all facets of life were highly centralized and totally compulsory.

TEN

Ōsugi in Europe

On November 20, 1922, Ōsugi received a letter from a French anarchist, soliciting his presence at the International Congress of Anarchists that was to be held in Berlin the following January or February. Although this was the first knowledge he had of the meeting, he immediately decided to attend. His most immediate problem was to finance the trip, which he estimated would cost ¥1,000. Although he had already borrowed as much as he could on the security of unwritten manuscripts, he finally remembered a friend who was able to produce a lump-sum loan.[1] While Ōsugi did not mention any names, other sources identify the novelist Arishima Takeo[2] as the source.[3]

In order to confuse the police about his departure, Ōsugi pretended to be sick and ostentatiously sent Mako to spend eight days with a friend while ice was ordered daily for his comfort during his "illness." On the night of December 11, he departed by train to Kobe where he boarded a British boat bound for Shanghai on December 13.[4] In Shanghai, Ōsugi enlisted the aid of Yamaga Taiji in securing a passport to continue his trip. Yamaga, who had contacts with Ching Mei-chin of the secret Chinese anarchist group, the "F.A.," was unable to obtain a passport and Yamaga had to turn to Cheng Meng-hsien for aid.[5] Cheng was able to secure a false Chinese passport using the name T'ang Chi[6] and Ōsugi's photograph.[7] On January 5, Ōsugi departed Shanghai for Marseilles on a French ship, arriving on February 13.[8]

In France, Ōsugi met with a series of disappointments. He headed straight for Paris to make contact with French anarchists, but found he had to go to Lyons to secure an identity card required of all foreigners. The identity card was supposed to include a photograph, both parents' names and birthdates, and the names of four guarantors, two French and two fellow nationals. Any travel was to be entered in the card, which had to be carried at all times, by the local police in each place visited. Ōsugi was very impressed with this system and the restrictions it placed on radical activity, and seemed relieved that a similar effective system did not complicate his movement in Japan.

Late February through late April he spent vainly waiting for the identity card which was never granted, even after extensive questioning. Thus, his presence in France was doubly illegal, since he had entered under a forged passport and since he never procured the required identity card. In Lyons he was given much help by some Chinese anarchists,[9] although he complained that they were humanists, rather than anarchists, who were concerned with avoiding luxuries like smoking and drinking.[10] Ōsugi spent much of his time in France with Hayashi Shizue, a young artist he had previously met in Tokyo.

Ōsugi had hoped to accomplish a number of things besides attending the Berlin Congress. One was to establish and continue communication with Far Eastern and European comrades.[11] Another was to do research. Hayashi wrote that Ōsugi wanted to begin a comparative critique of Romain Rolland, Anatole France (at one time a strong supporter of the Communist Party of France), and Henri Barbusse, a member of the Communist Party. However, he also felt that he should be familiar with their works and he delayed indefinitely meeting any of them.[12] Much more of his time, though, was spent studying the career of Nestor Makhno, a Ukranian peasant who led an anarchist guerrilla army against both the White Russian Armies of Denikin and Wrangel and the Red Army. Makhno had ultimately been defeated and forced to flee Russia and, although Ōsugi did not know his whereabouts, he knew that Berlin was a gathering place of many of the former guerrilla army leaders, including V. M. Eichenbaum (or Voline), one of Makhno's major political advisors. Ōsugi never met these men, but he did collect materials on Makhno, materials he later employed to good effect against the bolsheviks in Japan. He also met some of the Russian émigrés in Paris and heard directly from them about conditions in Russia and the methods of the new government.[13] Meanwhile, wrote Hayashi, he spent much of his time reading until his eyes reddened.[14]

He also inflamed his eyes by long hours spent observing poverty, especially as exemplified by the low-class hotels in which he spent so much of his time, and by the French women he met in their vicinity. He had always insisted, as he did when speaking with representatives of the Comintern in 1920, that each nation's socialist movement must be left to develop independently, implying thereby the essential parity among movements and nations. His stay in France was his first opportunity to know at first hand a developed European nation, to experience the conditions that made France a world power and a major source of anarchist and syndicalist ideas. His experience shocked him, though it is impossible to say whether the shock might have led to any major changes in his ideas or in his reliance on European or American anarchist sources; he died too soon after the event to reflect its influence.

Ōsugi's tight budget forced him into the cheapest hotels available. His first hotel in Paris was in a working-class neighborhood and was filled with poor people and filth.[15] His hotel had advertised electric lights and bathrooms and, although his third floor room had one light, he did not see any bathroom in the room or even on that floor:

> "The bathroom?" I asked the manager who had come up with us, thinking the advertisement a bit of a lie.
>
> "It's by the stairway on the second floor," the manager answered with an indifferent expression.
>
> But when I went and saw that bathroom, I was surprised. It was not the usual sit-you-down Western toilet. Rather, the concrete floor was sloped and there was only a small hole at the low point. You squatted where the slope began. The filthiness cannot be matched in any way by that of Japanese street toilets.
>
> I could not stand using this toilet no matter what; instead I urinated

noisily in a bucket in my room. There was a washstand but no faucet and, accordingly, no running water: water was hauled up little by little from below and then used water was poured into that bucket. Not just me: I could hear the noise [of urination] from rooms everywhere. Defecation was a great problem, but [nearby] I found a pay toilet. If you paid the attendant 50 centimes instead of 20 (about 3 sen), there was a real, clean, Western toilet. [16]

Bathing was another problem, a severe one for a Japanese, for Ōsugi discovered cheap hotels and most homes lacked baths. Consequently, every month or two, most of France had to go to the public baths which charged 2.50 francs (35 sen), a real luxury when a decent meal in the same neighborhood where Ōsugi lived cost only 1 franc. He allowed himself the extravagance of a bath every two or three days. Ōsugi eventually moved into a better hotel, one with a bath, running water, and a proper Western toilet. [17]

Ōsugi's first hotel, in addition to being cheap, was a center of prostitution. Hayashi recalled him saying:

> I was surprised when I was first brought to this hotel by a comrade. If this is what it is like, so be it: I will tolerate it as possibly being interesting. Cheap, prostitute-like women idled away their time and, just when I thought they were singing incessantly, the quarrels began. ... It was inconceivable that I was in Paris: it was as if I had gone to a barbarian country. I had heard that there were places like this, but seeing it is far worse than I had imagined: being like this, Paris has no order, just like hell! [18]

Ōsugi also sent to Kondō Kenji a picture post card featuring a woman and wrote "How's this—look like a woman you would like? For ¥15 a night you will be delighted. Won't you come here?" [19]

Although the number and audacity of the prostitutes surprised him, they also confirmed some of his earlier theories about the effects of a system of private property on women and their relation to men. He related how he became acquainted with a seamstress who was, like many women, a part-time prostitute. Her sewing income was 3,120 francs a year but her expenses were

5,292 francs: prostitution made up the difference. He went on to note two consequences of this. Prostitution called for birth control, and the number of babies being born was indeed falling: 159,790 in 1920, 117,023 in 1921, and 70,674 in 1922. Another result was that marriage figures were also falling: 623,869 in 1920, 456,211 in 1921, and only 383,220 in 1922.[20] It should be noted, however, that Ōsugi does not make any connection between prostitution, the falling birth rate, and the falling marriage rate, on the one hand, and the economic and psychological depression that struck not only France but all of Europe after the slaughter of World War I. In Japan and China the war was a positive, even euphoric catalyst for liberals and radicals alike, but its effect in Europe was the murder, psychologically as well as physically, of a generation.

After finally giving up his Berlin travel plans in late April, Ōsugi went to Paris again in time for May Day. He made arrangements to attend an outdoor meeting sponsored by the Communists in St. Denis, a meeting that was dedicated specifically to protesting the attempt to obtain death sentences in the United States for Nicola Sacco and Bartolomeo Venzetti, two anarchists accused of robbery and murder.[21] Ōsugi was surprised by the relaxed, holiday atmosphere that prevailed among the audience which included many workers' children and wives. When he received permission to address the assembly, he urged the workers to demonstrate more provocatively in the very center of Paris, not in a suburban workers' backwater like St. Denis. At the conclusion of his speech, plain-clothes detectives arrested him, sparking a riot in which over a hundred people were arrested.[22]

Although he tried to avoid being identified as a Japanese, a police interrogator finally said, "You are Ōsugi Sakae, aren't you?" The Japanese government had finally become aware of the possibility that he had gone to Europe and had warned its diplomatic missions to be on the lookout for him. Presumably, the Japanese Embassy in Paris was the source of the police information.[23] He was charged with disruption of the public peace, obstructing a police officer, violation of passport regulations and vagrancy. At his trial, he faced only the charge of violating the passport laws by entering France under a false passport and was sentenced, on May 23, to deportation following three weeks at La Sente Prison where he had already been since soon after his arrest.[24] Consequently, he was released on May 24.

At his trial, Ōsugi was defended by Henri Torres, the "most prominent of the [Communist] Party's lawyers during its first two years of existence."[25] Ōsugi stated that the Communist Party organ, *L'Humanité,* wrote up his arrest but, after discovering that he was an anarchist, mentioned nothing more about him, neither his trial nor his deportation order, implying a great deal of antagonism between the French anarchists and Communists.[26] Such an implication is unwarranted, however, since Ōsugi went to a Communist rally in the company of a French anarchist and was defended by Torres; it is more reflective of Ōsugi's own hostility toward the Japanese bolsheviks.

Ōsugi hoped to escape the order to leave France, but found himself with a police tail. He also hoped to go to Spain, apply for a Japanese passport, and return to France legally, but an official from the Embassy, Sugimura Yōtarō, informed him that Tokyo had prohibited any mission from issuing him any documents.[27] Up until shortly before he was actually deported from Marseille, he considered staying in France illegally, even consulting comrades on the matter, but a letter from Itō finally convinced him he had to return because of "various circumstances" in Tokyo.[28] On June 2, he boarded the *Hakone-maru* and sailed for Kobe the next morning, arriving on July 11.

At least one source close to Ōsugi, Kondō Kenji, has argued that, after his return from Europe, Ōsugi abandoned anarchism. A series of translations done by Ōsugi shortly after arriving in Japan would seem to give some credence to Kondō's conclusion. The translations were of two volumes of the French entomologist, Jean Henri Fabre. Shortly before his departure from Port Said, Ōsugi had written Hayashi asking him to send some of Jean Henri Fabre's books to him in Japan so that he could work on translating them soon after arrival. Fabre was a French entomologist whose accurate studies of insects did much to popularize the subject, and his volumes became popular children's readings in Japan.[29] Ōsugi had made plans to travel to Avignon via the Rhone River to see where Fabre worked, but never made the trip.[30]

Writing shortly after Ōsugi's death, Kondō Kenji said:

> I believe that on the day Ōsugi returned from France he was no longer an anarcho-syndicalist.
>
> The decline of the *temps nouveau* faction of Kropotkin and Reclus who supported the World War; the consequent bankruptcy of anarchism and communism; the rise of an individualistic tendency: these were Ōsugi's stories of his travels on the night he arrived in Kobe. Ōsugi's baggage was a problem, and I witnessed the customs inspector [search it]. It consisted of ratan furniture, girls' clothing, and books. Besides two bundles of newspaper clippings landed by a secret method, the books were mainly on literature, philosophy, sociology, and natural science and only a few on anarchism.
>
> Ōsugi clearly stated that he would close the Rōdō undō sha.
>
> He approached Miyajima Sukeo and Katō Kazuo[31] (and probably Eguchi Kan too) about starting a literary movement. He already had taken the first step.
>
> There is no mistaking the fact that, if he were alive, he would have abandoned long ago the movement as an anarcho-syndicalist, even if his naturally rebellious spirit had not immersed him in biology.[32]

There is nothing in Ōsugi's writings about his trip, however, that indicates a disillusionment with the theory of anarchism; no indication of any personal crisis that might have overflowed into his theories. Rather, his reactions to the French Communist Party imply a continuing hostile attitude toward the Japanese bolsheviks because of what Ōsugi perceived to be slights against himself, an anarchist, by the French Communists and the bolsheviks, while his reaction to France perhaps reflects lingering nationalistic feelings. Indeed, by Kondō's own testimony, there are strong parallels between Ōsugi in the last months of his life and the earlier years: Ōsugi continued to demonstrate through his book purchases his strong interest in natural science, philosophy, and sociology. These were the same subjects he had devoted himself to when first becoming acquainted with anarchism. The proposal to begin a literary movement may have been an ideologically neutral one, but can be associated with his interest in art and with his earlier use of a literary movement, in the form of the first *Kindai shisō,* to overcome the inertia that followed the High Treason Incident. In 1923, he may have been about to turn to that tactic again in order to arouse organized opposition to the bolsheviks. The whole idea, too, cannot be disassociated from his intense interest in Rolland's theories of the people's theater. On the day of his return, Ōsugi may have talked extensively about the pessimism that permeated all Europe as well as the anarchist and syndicalist movements, but there is no indication that he accepted such pessimism himself.

If we consider Ōsugi's publications after his return from Europe, the question of whether or not he was still an anarchist becomes clearer. He returned broke: he had borrowed to get to France, had more money sent by Itō just before he was deported from Marseille and had to repay the Japanese government the cost of his return trip.[33] Writing for money was his immediate task, and in short order he churned out two volumes of Fabre, his own *Nihon dasshutsu ki* (Record of my escapes from Japan), both in serial and book form, and his *Jijōden* (Autobiography) which had previously been serialized in *Kaizō* (Reconstruction) from September 1921 through January 1923. His only serious writing was a single long article entitled "Museifushugi shōgun—Nesutoru Mafuno" (Anarchist general: Nestor Makhno) which puts to rest any suspicion that he had given up anarchism.

As mentioned earlier, Ōsugi's attention had been drawn to the plight of anarchists in Soviet Russia. In fact, much of his attitude toward the Soviets and the Japanese bolsheviks was determined by the treatment meted out to his ideological comrades in Russia. In mid-1922, before going abroad, he began a long article on the Russian anarchist movement which he probably did not finish until late 1922, just before he departed for France.[34] Most of the article is a translation of an article by Alexander Berkman[35] on the untruths propagated about Russian anarchists by the Soviets, together with notes on the parallels between the situation in Russia and Japan which Ōsugi added. One of these lies concerned the career of Nestor Makhno, a Ukrainian anarchist, whom the Soviets accused of initiating pogroms against the Jews in the southern Ukraine. Ōsugi added some information about Makhno in order that Berkman's retort to the charge of anti-Semitism would make some sense to the reader.[36] Ōsugi's description of Makhno and his movement included some misinformation as well as exaggerations, but was generally accurate.[37]

After Ōsugi returned from France, he was able to comment more extensively on Makhno and his movement although he was careful to note that "I have not yet reached a firm conclusion on this question [due to the lack of materials]."[38] Since this is Ōsugi's last major work before his death, it is worthwhile analyzing it to determine his attitude toward anarchism at the end of his life. Before doing so, though, a brief summary of the Makhno movement is necessary.

The Makhno movement in the Ukraine is one of the stranger stories to come out of the aftermath of the Russian Revolution. A Ukrainian government was established after the February Revolution with Kerensky's blessing, although the Bolsheviks did not truly accept the idea of self-determination for the Ukraine. Nevertheless, the Ukrainians sent delegates, recognized by the Soviet Government, to the peace negotiations at Brest-Litovsk with the Central Powers in December 1917. A peace treaty was signed between the Central Powers and the Ukraine on February 9, 1918 but, subsequently, Austrian and German troops occupied it. The Republic and its occupiers were faced with increasing guerrilla warfare waged by wandering bands. In this environment, Nestor Makhno rose to lead a sizeable partisan army that was a major power in the south central Ukraine until 1921.[39]

Makhno, born in 1889, had become a terrorist following the 1905 Revolution and was imprisoned from 1908 to 1917. In prison he was inspired to study anarchism under the direction of Peter Arshinov who, together with V. M. Eichenbaum (Voline), was Makhno's ideological mentor thereafter. After his release by Kerensky's Provisional Government he returned to the Ukraine and exerted himself in redistributing the land to the peasants. At first, Makhno attempted to ally himself with the Soviets but, after they turned against their anarchist allies in other parts of Russia in April and May 1918, he "realized the anarchists could not depend upon the Bolsheviks, whose apparent aim was 'to exploit the Anarchist-Revolutionaries in the struggle against counterrevolution so that those bearers of an unreconciled spirit of anarchism remained at the war front until death.'"[40]

Makhno fought initially against the German and Austrian occupiers of the Ukraine. As the number of his successes grew, so did his band; eventually it became a formally organized army. In September 1918, Makhno had around 50 men, a band that grew to some 22,000 in May 1919, and about 40,000 at the end of that October.[41] During this period of growth, Makhno successfully harassed the Central Powers' troops, and enabled Bolshevik forces to halt and defeat Denikin's White Army through guerrilla action in Denikin's rear area at the moment that Denikin was threatening to destroy the Red Army and capture Moscow. In the middle of 1919, Makhno's alliance with the Bolsheviks broke down, and his army was reduced as it fought both the Bolsheviks and Denikin's successor, Wrangel. The Bolsheviks and the two White generals fought a seesaw war while Makhno fought whichever army was in his locale, alternately aiding and harming both the revolutionary and counterrevolutionary causes through the summer of 1920. In late 1920, Makhno and the Bolsheviks signed a formal instrument of alliance under which they cooperated to eliminate the White forces in November. Before the month was out, Makhno's troops were attacked by the Red Army and the last battles began. Although the Bolsheviks bumbled from one failure to another, Makhno's defeat was only a matter of time. The unequal struggle ended in late August 1921 when Makhno and 83 remaining troops crossed the border into Romania and were disarmed.[42]

Ōsugi gave a garbled version of Makhno's adventures and then offered some conclusions of his own that reveal his attitude toward anarchism and the Russian Revolution. He stated that the movement was "an instinctive movement of the Ukrainian people."[43] It not only opposed the depredations of the counterrevolutionary armies, but strove to protect the Russian Revolution. By this time, Ōsugi was making a firm distinction between the Revolution and the Soviet Government which was stifling the original Revolution through its oppression, he thought. The Makhno movement opposed this oppression and, consequently, protected the Revolution. Its members were "peaceful organizers of entirely autonomous, self-ruling, free soviets,"[44] a slight embroidery on the facts, since the movement had little organization outside of its military and next to no energy to spare from the constant fighting. However, he did reach a conclusion on the military importance of the movement:

> Thus, the meritorious service of Makhno and the Makhno movement to the Russian Revolution was in fact great. Most of the various counter-revolutionary armies and invading foreign armies [that occupied] most of European Russia were driven away by them. You almost cannot conceive of even the establishment of the Bolshevik Government without them.[45]

Ōsugi proudly recounted the military exploits and importance of the Makhno movement from start to final failure, but he placed greatest emphasis on its spiritual aspects. Besides seeing it as an "instinctive movement of the Ukrainian people" to freedom, he saw it as being entirely independent of any leader. Civil war had arisen between landlord and peasant in the Ukraine and armed adventurers, the Bolsheviks, entered the confused scene seeking not to settle the war but to impose their dictatorship over both parties. This dictatorship was in opposition to the people's "instincts and freedom" and was, in fact, counterrevolutionary.[46] In this situation, Makhno and his small band were sought out by the peasants' movement, but he did not create the movement. "Makhno the anarchist did not build the Makhno movement: the revolutionary, rebellious movement (*kakumei-teki ikki undō*), which was based on the instinctive self-defense of the Ukrainian people, simply hunted Makhno up."[47] Fortunately, Makhno's character fit the requirements of the movment and, equally fortunately, so did his anarchism, although Ōsugi might have added, propagandistically, that it would be only natural for an instinctive movement of a people and anarchism to meld perfectly one with the other. This, then, was "the single greatest lesson that the Russian Revolution could furnish us."[48]

Thus isolated from the other Japanese socialists, frustrated by his overseas experiences, and disillusioned and angry at the course of the Russian Revolution, nonetheless Ōsugi returned to Japan from France confirmed in his opinion that anarchism and syndicalism were correct. His praise of Makhno's struggle as the real spirit of the original Russian Revolution was, however, his last gasp.

ELEVEN

The Great Kantō Earthquake and Ōsugi's Murder

On September 1, 1923, a large earthquake struck the heavily pop-
ulated Kantō region, including the cities of Tokyo and Yokohama.
Occurring at 11:58 in the morning, the first gigantic earthquake
was followed by hundreds of smaller tremors over the next couple
of days and by one large quake about twenty-four hours after the
first. Generally referred to as the Great Kantō Earthquake (Kantō
daishinsai, literally "Kantō great disaster"), this event made a
profound impression on residents and affected almost all areas of
human endeavor.[1]

The earthquake was of a magnitude that would have made it
remarkable for years in earthquake-prone Japan had the damage
been restricted to that caused by the earth's movement alone.[2]
The initial shock knocked down a good number of homes and
other buildings and damaged more, especially in Yokohama, which
was nearer than Tokyo to the epicenter in Sagami Bay to the
southwest of Tokyo. Official statistics claim that 10 percent of
all houses in Yokohama were completely destroyed by the initial
tremor, compared to only 1 percent in Tokyo.

The earthquake damage, however, was compounded many times
over by fires. Many people were in the process of preparing lunch,
using wood or charcoal fires. The quake scattered the burning fuel,
which started numerous fires, most often not immediately extinguished because people had fled all structures for the safety of the

open streets. Shortly, these fires burned out of control and proceeded to sweep through large areas of downtown Tokyo and
Yokohama. Ultimately, they devastated the crowded metropolitan
areas. In Tokyo, 73 percent of all houses were damaged and 63
percent were completely destroyed, nearly all by fire. In Yokohama, 95 percent were damaged and 73 percent destroyed and
again fire was the major culprit, fully destroying 63 percent of all
homes. Non-urban areas also suffered considerably with 20 percent
of all homes destroyed, but the statistics show how much more
vulnerable to fire the metropolitan areas were. In Tokyo, 1,604,321
people or 71 percent of the population lost their homes, while in
Yokohama, 378,704 people, 86 percent, were made homeless.

In all, 104,619 people were killed or reported missing, and
another 52,074 were injured. In addition, the ground's movement
and subsequent fires probably left a variety of psychological as
well as physical scars on city residents. Ōsugi's daughter, Mako,
who was about to turn seven, was spending the day with the two
daughters of Yasunari Jirō. When the earthquake struck, the three
girls ran screaming from the house and had to be chased down the
street, caught, and calmed by Yasunari. Mako returned home during the course of that day and visited no more for about six weeks.
Yasunari finally asked her why she had not come over, and Mako
replied "Because your place has earthquakes."[3] Many older people
who were able to generalize their experience must have feared living in Tokyo and Yokohama for the rest of their lives.

For a while after the earthquake, communications were entirely
disrupted, and the government did not realize the exact extent of
the disaster. With so much of Tokyo visibly ablaze, however, it
could guess that immediate emergency measures were in order.
The degree of confusion and disorganization in the city, though,
was complicated by pre-existing disorganization in the Cabinet
itself. Prime Minister Katō Tomosaburō had died a week earlier,
on August 25, and agreement had not emerged by September 1 on
his successor. Hurriedly, Admiral Yamamoto Gonnohyōe was
appointed Prime Minister and a new Cabinet was formed on Sep-

tember 2. It quickly declared martial law and brought thousands
of troops into the metropolitan area to enforce it.

Authorities were faced with a burning, helpless city. The water
system had broken down and was useless for either fighting the
fires or providing drinking water. The telegraph and telephone
systems were knocked out of service, and within the city mes-
sages had to be carried by foot messengers who had to avoid the
fires and cope with great crowds. Initially, communication to the
outside was accomplished partly by airplane and carrier pigeon,
although wireless radios, mainly on ships, soon took over most of
the work. Emergency action was complicated by the destruction
of many official buildings. The following were burned down
completely: the Home Ministry, Ministry of Finance, Ministry of
Education, Ministry of Commerce and Agriculture, Ministry of
Railroads, Ministry of Communications, Metropolitan Police Headquarters, Kanda Ward Office, Kōjimachi Ward Office, Kyobashi
Ward Office, Nihonbashi Ward Office, Shiba Ward Office, Honjo
Ward Office, and Fukagawa Ward Office (a total of seven out of the
fifteen ward offices). Provision of food, shelter, clothing, and water
was an immediate problem, yet solution was hindered by rumors
that spread through the city.

The worst rumor held that Koreans were committing various
crimes, that they were responsible for the many fires that broke
out in a seemingly coordinated fashion at noon, and that they
were poisoning wells that provided what little water was available.
In response to these and other perceived threats of disorder,
various neighborhood organizations formed themselves into
neighborhood self-protection, or vigilante, groups supposedly subject to police control and discipline. Some of these were content
to guard the area and to organize and distribute what few supplies
were available. Others, however, turned murderous and attacked
Koreans and those mistaken for Koreans. Official estimates at the
time claimed only a few hundred were killed in this way, but other
estimates since then have ranged as high as 6,000.[4] Not for several
days were police and military authorities able to regain sufficient

control to put an end to these generalized outrages. Such was the mood in the aftermath of the earthquake.

Martial law provided for punishment of looters and other criminals, of course, but special efforts had to be taken to protect Koreans. On September 5, anti-Korean outbreaks forced the Prime Minister to issue an instruction for the protection of Koreans:

> The present Minister is given to understand that something like apathy is entertained by the citizens toward the Koreans because of the alleged report about riotous acts contemplated by some malcontents among the Koreans, taking advantage of the tumultuous situation occasioned by the dreadful earthquake and fires. Should the Koreans act in such a manner as to confirm the report the public ought to inform the military or police force attending to the preservation of peace and order, and place the matter in their hands. That the multitude themselves should take measures to persecute and threaten the Koreans is not only inconsistent with the principle of Japan-Korean assimilation but such practice, if reported abroad, will certainly produce an unfavourable echo and undesirable effect. It is admitted that the sudden outbreak of the horrible catastrophe and the turbulent situation that followed it has given rise to the undesirable happenings, but the present Minister is anxious that the nation should not lose its usual calmness of mind at this critical moment and take the utmost care to act in a most circumspect way, exercise strong self-control, and endeavor to live up to the principle of peace. The present Minister sincerely hopes the nation will seriously reflect on the matter and maintain an attitude of self-respect.[5]

While the nation "reflected" on its "apathy," the authorities moved to disband the vigilante groups on the one hand, and to place at least some Koreans under detention for their own protection on the other. Gradually, order was restored and physical safety became more predictable, though for many it was too late. The general tone of Prime Minister Yamamoto's instruction, however, implied that the Koreans had only their own compatriots to blame for their troubles. Furthermore, it did not strongly enjoin action by martial law authorities to prevent outrages.

Indeed, while the authorities were supposedly maintaining order, they themselves were subjected to the same fears as the general populace. They may have been inclined to let Koreans get what they "deserved" and therefore been slow to provide protection; this is a question that remains to be studied thoroughly. One can, however, easily imagine individual soldiers and police officers allowing attacks on Koreans or even participating in them if their attitude toward Koreans was similar to the attitude of some soldiers toward leftists.

Police from Kameido Police Headquarters had detained after the earthquake a large and mixed group of troublesome individuals, including four members of vigilante groups and several leaders of a left-wing labor union which had drawn much local attention due to a strike that started before the earthquake occurred. On September 4, a detachment of military police (*kempeitai*) arrived at the Kameido Police Headquarters, took custody of nine prisoners, including the union leaders and the vigilantes, and eventually killed them all. Such behavior was, however, not general, and other unionists and well-known socialists, with one exception, survived the earthquake unscathed.

Ōsugi was that exception. On September 15, he and Itō Noe went to visit his younger sister, Tachibana Ayame, and returned with her son, Munekazu, age six, who had been born in Portland, Oregon. The three of them were arrested the following day by Captain Amakasu Masahiko and his detachment of military police. On September 20, a shake-up in the top echelon of the military police was announced. September 24 brought an explanation for this change: the deaths of some radicals were announced. Although the initial reports had the names of Itō, Ōsugi, and Munekazu deleted, the incident was soon fully publicized.[6] Their bodies were recovered from an abandoned well on September 20, and were eventually turned over to their colleagues.

The cause of death was unclear for years[7] and was variously reported. Amakasu said at his trial for the triple murder that the victims were strangled. Other sources had it that Ōsugi was stabbed in the heart while Itō and Munekazu were strangled.[8] Another story said Ōsugi was shot to death.[9]

On August 26, 1976, the *Asahi* newspaper printed the autopsy report on the three deaths.[10] The report had been in the hands of the wife of Tanaka Ryūichi, the examining doctor who wrote it, since his death in China in 1939. The report said that all three victims died by strangulation and that Ōsugi and Itō were severely beaten. The evidence did not indicate that the beatings necessarily occurred before death; they were clearly not the cause of death. After death, the bodies were stripped, wrapped in straw *tatami* mat coverings, and thrown into an abandoned well. They were recovered and the autopsy performed on September 20-21.

Many have surmised that Ōsugi's death may have been ordered by high authorities of the government or the army.[11] Amakasu was sentenced to ten years in prison, but, in October 1926, he was released and posted with the military police to Manchuria where he was active in the events surrounding the Manchurian Incident of 1931, a course of events that lends circumstantial support to the theory of authoritative orders for Ōsugi's death. Some of Ōsugi's protégés like Wada Kyūtarō concluded that Fukuda Masatarō, the general in charge of martial law in Tokyo initially, was responsible for Ōsugi's murder and plotted unsuccessfully to assassinate him.[12] Some note cryptically that Gotō Shimpei was once again the Home Minister[13] and presumably had a personal interest in getting rid of Ōsugi as well as the means of encouraging Amakasu. No source, however, has offered concrete evidence that any authority higher than Amakasu played a role in the murders.

Indeed, perhaps the most that can be concluded from this series of murders is that high authorities in the government and the military were not scrupulous in maintaining discipline and control of the military and civil police and, through them, the populace. Had the command structure been shaken up and had the culprits involved in the murders of September 4 been severely treated at that time, Ōsugi's death might not have occurred. Instead, one officer and his men acting on their own, under the influence of overwork, lack of sleep and perhaps food, and fear (of socialism and the earthquake both) committed murder.

If this is true, Ōsugi's death is virtually an insignificant accident. Certainly, it was insignificant in terms of leftist thought and action. Anarchism was much eclipsed before September 16, 1923, partly by the failure of violent strikes to achieve the workers' goals during a period of recession and partly by the rise of communism.

Beyond that, Ōsugi's death is but a footnote to the period's history because it makes no statement about the political system or the government. His manner of death brings to mind the execution of Kōtoku Shūsui a dozen years earlier, an execution that had significant impact on the leftist movement and shed light on the legal system. [14] Superficial similarities lead one to conclude that, if Kōtoku was cavalierly executed for being implicated in a plot to kill the Emperor by a government anxious to suppress the left-wing movement altogether, then perhaps Ōsugi's murder was also an execution carried out by the government. Both were anarchists, and both were killed by minions of the government. However, to see a degree of resemblance glosses over the vast differences between the two events.

Kōtoku was implicated in the plot against the Emperor and was guilty to some extent. He had advocated murdering the Emperor to a group which laid plans, constructed bombs, undertook training in throwing the bombs, and reconnoitered various venues for attempting the assassination. Kōtoku's connection with the plot after his initial suggestion is ambiguous. His mistress, Kanno Sugako, was an active conspirator and could have performed the role of messanger between Kōtoku, acting as the leading conspirator, and the rest of the group. She might herself have been the leader, however, and merely pretended to the other conspirators that Kōtoku was the leader. The government's proof of the nature of Kōtoku's role after his initial advocacy was weak, and it is that point in particular that makes Kōtoku's sentence of execution extreme in retrospect. There was, nonetheless, a plot to assassinate the Emperor, and Kōtoku was involved in its initial stages if nothing more. Legal representatives of the government—the police, the procurators, judges, and prison officials—uncovered the plot, investigated it, arrested those involved, tried them, delivered sentences, and executed the sentences. In short Kōtoku's execution was an action sanctioned by law and the legal system. That the execution may have been a gross miscarriage of justice is quite immaterial to the point that it was one arrived at through a complex system of criminal justice.

Ōsugi's case was very different. He was not accused of being involved, even marginally, in any illegal action that the police or military police uncovered. Further, no series of legal organizations took any, much less a long series of, legal steps to arrest, try, and sentence him. Instead, a small group of military policemen under one man's direction committed murder entirely without legal sanction or justification. That fact alone empties the murder of all significance as far as the legal system or the political system goes. Thus, unlike Kōtoku's death, which stated explicitly a number of things about the legal system (it would apprehend, try, and execute assassins, but it would act strictly according to the law) and implicitly other things about the political system (it would condone legal executions of radical conspirators), Ōsugi's murder makes no statement.

Furthermore, in the intellectual arena, the two deaths are starkly different. Following Kōtoku's death, the socialist movement subsided into virtual silence, suspending almost all of its publications, while individual socialists found their essays unwelcome in the liberal press. Even liberal thinkers felt moved to criticize the assassination plot, perhaps partly to put themselves at a distance from the socialists, but also because they were truly shocked by the plot. Nothing of the kind occurred after Ōsugi's death. Most writers in special earthquake issues of liberal journals like *Chūō kōron* (Central review) mentioned Ōsugi's death only in passing, if at all. They devoted their comments to matters they deemed important—descriptions of the destruction, damage to libraries and universities, plans to rebuild Tokyo according to principles of city planning—and Ōsugi's death was not important. His ideas were no longer especially innovative or influential outside his limited following. Moreover, lack of extensive comment on his death implied that no one perceived in it any message about the government or its policy toward dissent. Indeed, even the memorial writings of Ōsugi's friends and colleagues which occupied the better half of the November issue of *Kaizō* (Reconstruction) contained no condemnation of the system for the same reason—individual military policemen, not the system, killed him.

Finally, the mood at the time of Kōtoku's arrest and trial was quite different from that at Ōsugi's murder. Nothing particularly exceptional was happening in 1910–1911—no special crisis was threatening the nation or the government. In 1923, however, fear was prevalent and was exacerbated by rumors. The days following the earthquake were clearly exceptional, and Ōsugi's death was an equally exceptional event.

The Kantō Great Earthquake was a shattering experience and its reverberations continue even to today, if only in preparations in recent years for another earthquake of equally disastrous dimensions. In economic terms, reconstruction efforts stimulated the economy for a while, but damages, which were approximately four times the national government's budget and were entirely uncovered by insurance, nudged the economy toward depression following the initial upswing. The death of Ōsugi and the Kameido murders took on darker meanings when authorities, acting under the Peace Preservation Law of 1925, began earnest and sometimes deadly steps to force Communist Party members to renounce international communism. In retrospect, the crises, emergencies, and assassinations of the late 1920s and 1930s can be seen against the backdrop of the billowing fires sweeping Tokyo in September 1923.

Perhaps it is more accurate, though, to see the earthquake not in terms of what was to come, but in terms of what had been going on. The late Meiji period was one in which uncertainties arose about future goals, leaders, and national symbols because national goals had been largely achieved, the old leaders were dying off, and the symbols of both were passé. The succeeding Taishō period was one of hopeful experimentation with new ideas, new goals, and new leaders, but nothing approaching a consensus on any of these was ever achieved, a consensus that would have given the period an aura of confidence and national self-assurance. Indeed, confusion

and turmoil prevailed throughout the Taishō era, not just following the earthquake.

In politics, the major leaders of the Meiji period left behind
replacements like Katsura Tarō and Saionji Kimmochi, but these
were not of the same stature as their predecessors nor were they
leading the nation toward any agreed-upon goals. Following
Katsura's death in 1913, even this semblance of continuity and
unity was gravely eroded. Considerable power passed to the
political parties and their leaders in the Taishō era, but no leader
emerged to establish a set of principles as national principles.
Indeed, parties were developed in order to achieve power and, with
that as an end in itself, were unable to use that power creatively.
At the same time, no leaders, either within or without the
political parties, emerged who could coordinate, harmonize, and
make work in tandem all the various centers of power, as the
transcendent Meiji leaders had been able to do. The net impression
now, but also at that time, was one of uncertainty, confusion, and
turmoil.

Taishō foreign affairs became more uncertain as time went on.
World War I was in some ways an unmitigated success for Japan:
it had achieved Great Power status without having to become
involved in the meat-grinder of Europe's battlefields, and it had
taken over the German possessions in the Pacific islands and
China. The peace conferences ending the War, however, were a bit
of a slap in the face to Asian aspirations for a declaration of racial
equality. At the same time, the peace brought the beginning of a
new system of international relations—multilateral internationalism
—the implications of which were little understood, though gladly
welcomed. Japan's position in China was expanded with the
newly acquired German concessions and, in the Twenty-One
Demands of 1915, Japan had tried with only partial success to
assert itself as China's protector and advisor. Japan had not, however, had all its desires satisfied and, with the rising Nationalist
Party, Chinese affairs became less predictable as the Taishō era
progressed. The relationship of internationalism to Japan's China
interests was unclear and, as it generally worked out, contrary. The

intervention in Russian Siberia in concert with the other Allies was not clearly defined at the outset and, as Japan's intervention stretched on into 1921 and 1922, the lack of purpose sparked considerable internal debate.

The labor movement remained hampered throughout the Taishō period by Article Seventeen of the Peace Police Law, which made it illegal to undertake collective action against an employer. Nonetheless, the number of labor unions and unionists grew throughout the era. World War I fueled a booming prosperity which drew more and more workers, especially men, into the industrial work force. When the post-war years saw abrupt swings from prosperity to depression and back in a steadily descending downswing, labor disputes and strikes broke out frequently. Leftist, especially anarchist, ideas and leaders contributed to labor militance and to the bitter violence of industrial actions, but the steadily worsening economic picture provoked the same response.

The litany of fields in which uncertainty and turmoil occurred could be extended indefinitely. All areas of life were plagued by them, just as all areas of life were disrupted by the Great Kantō Earthquake. In this context, Ōsugi's murder, though insignificant, is comprehensible.

Conclusion

Ōsugi Sakae's primary concern as an anarchist was with how the individual should live. In fact, although he is labeled an anarchist and was well-versed in anarchist ideas, his relevance to his own era as well as to the present might best be seen in terms of individualism rather than anarchism. The student of Ōsugi's ideas quickly notes that his life and many of his writings ultimately deal with individualism rather than with anarchism; put another way, anarchism provided a philosophical basis to support the rebellious, nonconformist style in which he wished to live. He makes an interesting representative of his generation because, even today, he appears to have been a larger-than-life individual whose eccentricity helps set his era in bold relief. A more willful, independent, unpredictable, intriguing—in short, charismatic—Japanese is hard to imagine. One is either attracted or repelled by him, but never left indifferent.

The theme of individualism appears in all his major writings, whether they center on questions of love and marriage, or on the role of the intellectual in the labor movement, or on the nature of the Russian Revolution. The origins of Ōsugi's need for such a philosophy, however, lie in part in his troubled childhood. In his youth can be found factors that helped make him an anarchist, even if these did not determine that he would become one.

One factor is his family background. Scion of a military elite family, Ōsugi rendered himself unable to follow in his father's footsteps, a circumstance that contributed to his opposition to the authority of all elites. His political writings urged support of the masses and opposition to authority, while his personal behavior demonstrated at every turn contempt for uniformed representatives of the state. In a cruel twist of fate, Ōsugi's life, given to him by one military officer, was taken from him by another.

Ōsugi's relations with his parents typified his domineering manner toward others when he was an adult: he was forever an *enfant terrible.* As a child, he strove for his father's attention but was able to capture it only occasionally and then for negative behavior: he probably nurtured his stammer to attract the concerned interest of his stuttering father. Thus, Ōsugi could not have missed learning that he got his father's attention only by forcing himself on him. Aggressive, attention-getting tactics became an effective, ingrained habit and, when he grew older, a political tactic.

Ōsugi had much closer contact with his mother. Yet, the sense of trust essential for the healthy development of personality was stifled by the competition that raged constantly between them. Her strong character forced her son to develop quickly or be smothered: mother and son competed with each other in a game of wits and strength of will. It was with her that young Ōsugi perfected the tactics he used against his father, in the socialist movement, and against the police.

Ōsugi's friendships underlined the lessons he received in dealing with his parents, for he employed on others the techniques he had contrived to manipulate his parents. His audacious behavior was calculated to gain the attention a leader requires of his followers, while paralyzing those who might challenge him. He enjoyed direct competition, whether it was with opponents from outside his own group or with members of his group in tests of leadership strength. His competitive urge was so highly developed that he was incapable of accepting a position equal or inferior to another child or, in later years, to another socialist.

Ōsugi's disputes with other prominent members of the socialist movement were directly related to this personality trait. He was unable to create warm relationships with his childhood friends, his wives and mistresses, his fellow idealogues. In fact, his friendships and affairs frequently could not withstand the destructiveness of his competitive spirit. Hori Yasuko and Kamichika Ichiko finally broke with him because he could not tolerate their disagreeing with him. By contrast, Itō Noe concurred with his theories and vigorously commended them to the world. With Itō alone Ōsugi achieved a thorough and mutual rapport, but it was firmly grounded in her deference to his theories and to his superior position in the socialist movement.

These personality characteristics render him a fascinating subject to study. Regardless of one's ideological orientation, he is continually interesting because his unpredictable and often outrageous behavior made him a colorful figure. However, a society modeled exclusively on Ōsugi Sakae—for, despite his disclaimers, he certainly saw himself as a personality prototype and an ideological exemplar for others to follow—would be hard to imagine.

Ōsugi's anarchism amounted to a self-centered individualism that is destructive of society as it is commonly assumed to exist. Nonetheless, in his own eyes and for many of his contemporaries in Japan, anarchism offered a prescription for social reform through the liberation of individual human energy. It was a solution not unlike the one urged by leaders in the early Meiji period, when release of the individual from feudal social constraints was viewed as synonomous with and necessary for the promotion of nationalistic goals. Both Ōsugi and the Meiji leaders saw society's major problem as human stagnation caused by multiple layers of habit and social sanction. Ōsugi theorized that, if constraints on individual activity were broken, pent-up energies would be released and these would provide the dynamism for necessary change. Since Ōsugi believed in the existence of a natural social order, he assumed that social reorganization, and not chaos, would result.

There is, of course, a traditional Japanese, as well as a Western source for the idea of a natural social order. It is most clearly present in Confucian thought in the Tokugawa period, and it can be traced from pre-modern roots up through some Meiji and Taishō socialists as well as the rightist movement of the 1930s. Ōsugi's ideas on this point, however, are exclusively Western in origin. It would be incorrect to assume that the existence of a natural order in his thought and in the thought of a military officer reading Confucian texts had the same origin, or that it implied similar political, social, and economic systems. The fact, however, that Ōsugi lived in a society in which a natural social order was assumed no doubt predisposed him to accept easily an ideology based on natural order theory when he encountered it in European anarchist thought.

Ōsugi's anarchism attempted to accomplish the liberation of the individual through two avenues; the individual's own efforts toward expansion of the creative self and the organized action of individuals united in labor unions. Incorporating the extreme individualist and collectivist wings of anarchist theory, his thought seems internally inconsistent; yet his goal remained steady while his means varied between individual and collective action, depending on circumstances. Although he at times appears to have been primarily an individualist, he was an individualist well within the anarchist tradition.

In this sense, then, Ōsugi's anarchism was both extremely individualistic and also socially relevant. It offered a radically new personal and social ethos based on the total rejection of the traditional duty-bound ethics of altruism and self-abnegation. Ōsugi's own behavior demonstrated his belief in the value of bold, forceful, rebellious individualism not only to satisfy personal desires but to forge a new society in which individuals would no longer allow themselves to be docile victims of the state. Thus, Ōsugi's understanding of anarchism was above all else as an idea that legitimized the overthrow of authority—a new form of protest and the legitimization of that protest.

Yet, Ōsugi's reliance on the masses, an integral part of his anarchist theories of revolution, contradicted his personal philosophy. The passive receptivity implied by his version of anarchism constituted a paradoxical reversal of his own personality and his individualism. Instead of providing intellectuals with a new role that would allow them to act boldly, as he so liked to do, he sentenced them to inaction, enjoining them to await the development of an anarchist society from within the people. His essential message was distrust of the intellectuals as leaders of the workers, a distrust that extended to all leaders and all elites. Ōsugi's conclusion that intellectuals were by nature collaborators with the ruling class led naturally to his conviction that thinkers should not take the initiative in reform, but rather should wait for the natural development of new ideas and social systems from among the masses. While this belief by itself cannot be said to have enervated the intellectual class, it surely must have contributed to the uncertainties that continued to plague intellectuals after Ōsugi's death in 1923.

During Ōsugi's lifetime, more conservative members of the elite proved better equipped to mobilize the masses into organizations geared to supporting the goals of the state. They attempted to control and guide the masses by inculcating simplistic nationalistic ideas through these organizations. At the same time, the uncertainties of the intellectuals, to which Ōsugi had contributed, spread to other members of the elite. They were compounded by fears of events—the earthquake of 1923 and the later worldwide economic depression—that appeared beyond the control of the individual, resulting in paralysis at a time when courageous leadership was called for. The rise of mass organization capable of influencing the elite coincided with this paralysis and may have contributed to the events of the 1930s and 1940s. Thus, Ōsugi's significance may weigh as much in the years immediately after his death as before.

Ōsugi continues to be of interest today in terms of interpreting Japan's rapid modernization and present condition. In Western interpretations of Japanese history, it is commonly held that Japan developed quickly and avoided serious problems because of two factors. First, changes during the Tokugawa period (1603–1868) in economic activity, social organization, and political and intellectual concepts and values contributed positively to the modernization process. They established essentially modern modes of action and thought in each field long before pressure as a result of Western penetration forced rapid development. Second, partly because modern and traditional modes co-existed in the Tokugawa period, traditions continued even until the present-day in such a way that they provided a cushion against the effects of modernization, especially the ill-effects. Accordingly, continuities did not contradict modernization but prevented severe dislocation to such a degree that modernization without the continuous traditions is virtually inconceivable.

Ōsugi's example, however, suggests that this interpretation may become less tenable the more completely modernization is accomplished. Whereas his contemporaries received training, education, and values that derived directly and explicitly from Japanese tradition, Ōsugi's values were modern and cannot be attributed to tradition. In other words, one cannot find in Ōsugi the amalgamation of traditional and modern values and attitudes that allowed Meiji figures to move smoothly from "feudal" to "modern" Japan. This fact made him an oddity in Taishō Japan, but his type may be new and increasingly common in present-day Japan.

The implication of seeing Ōsugi as a prototype for the modern Japanese is that many Japanese may no longer be protected by tradition, living instead completely apart from ideas, attitudes, motivations and, probably, social systems that can be accurately related to tradition. This view of his life and thought, then, brings into question the efforts of historians and social scientists to describe "traditional" elements of subjects far removed from the Meiji period. Like Ōsugi Sakae, contemporary Japan might now be best understood only in terms of a complete break with the past.

Notes

Bibliography

Glossary

Index

Notes

1. FAMILY, SCHOOL, AND FRIENDS

1. Ōsugi Sakae, *Jijōden, Ōsugi Sakae zenshū,* Ōsawa Masamichi and others, eds. (Tokyo, 1963–), XII, 10–11. *Ōsugi Sakae zenshū* will be cited as *Zenshū* hereafter.
2. Shakai bunkō, ed., "Shakaishugisha museifushugisha jimbutsu kenkyū shiryō," *Shakai bunko sōsho* (Tokyo, 1964), VII, 283.
3. *Jijōden, Zenshū,* XII, 93.
4. *Shakai bunko sōsho,* VII, 295. The siblings may have lived with Ōsugi off and on: he mentioned his oldest sister as living with him in early 1907. See "Kaineko Natsume," *Zenshū,* XIV, 19. Kawakami Tamio relates that several of the sisters lived abroad, either in America or China, for varying periods and that one brother died of ill health in Hangkow in 1922. See Kawakami Tamio, "Ōsugi Sakae ni tsuite," *Rōdō undō shi kenkyū* 37:39 (July 1963).
5. *Jijōden, Zenshū,* XII, 9.
6. Now called Kamori-chō in Tsushima-shi, Aichi prefecture, Uji is about 10 kilometers due west of the present Nagoya Station of the Japan National Railway.
7. Ōsugi remembered being told he had to absent himself from school for a day during the Sino-Japanese War because of this grandfather's death. *Jijōden, Zenshū,* XII, 9.
8. Ibid., XII, 9–10.
9. Ibid., XII, 10.
10. Ibid., XII, 13–14.
11. Ibid., XII, 31–34.
12. Ibid., XII, 4–5.

13. Ibid., XII, 98–99.
14. Furuya Tsunamasa, "Ōsugi Sakae," *Jimbutsu ōrai* 4. 7:112 (July 1955).
15. Harold Hakwon Sunoo, *Japanese Militarism: Past and Present* (Chicago, 1975), p. 38.
16. Shumpei Okamoto, *The Japanese Oligarchy and the Russo-Japanese War* (New York and London, 1970), p. 48.
17. Ibid.
18. Ibid., pp. 71–74. See also for agreement with Okamoto, Denis Warner and Peggy Warner, *The Tide at Sunrise: A History of the Russo-Japanese War, 1904–5* (New York, 1974), pp. 54–55, 81–125, 154. Roger F. Hackett, *Yamagata Aritomo in the Rise of Modern Japan, 1838–1922* (Cambridge, Mass., 1971), pp. 168–170, 224ff, writes only of high-level politics, never delving into the upper levels of the army, much less the lower echelons. Matsushita Yoshio, *Meiji no guntai* (Tokyo, 1963), pp. 121–127, gives a brief description of the realization in the highest echelon that Russia would be the enemy after 1895 and military expansion in preparation for such a conflict.
19. *Jijōden, Zenshū,* XII, 22–23.
20. Ibid., XII, 7–8.
21. Tada Michitarō, "Ōsugi Sakae," in Kuwabara Takeo et al., eds., *Kindai Nihon no shisōka—nijisseiki o ugokashita hitobito* (Tokyo, 1963), II, 319.
22. *Jijōden, Zenshū,* XII, 81ff.
23. Ibid., XII, 6.
24. Ibid., XII, 19–21.
25. Ibid., XII, 17.
26. Ibid., XII, 56–57.
27. Ibid., XII, 149ff.
28. Ibid., XII, 10.
29. Tada Michitarō, "Ōsugi Sakae," p. 325.
30. *Jijōden, Zenshū,* XII, 111–112.
31. Sakai Toshihiko, "Ōsugi to Arahata," *Kindai shisō* 1. 1:13 (October 1913); and Tada Michitarō, "Ōsugi Sakae," p. 343.
32. Hori Yasuko, "Shoka no Ōsugi kan," in *Mikan Ōsugi Sakae ikō,* Yasutani Kan'ichi, ed. (Tokyo, 1937), p. 494.
33. "Shin chitsujo no sōzō," *Zenshū,* VI, 54.
34. *Jijōden, Zenshū,* XII, 59–60.
35. Ibid., XII, 26–27.
36. Ibid., XII, 60–62.
37. Ibid., XII, 28.
38. Ibid., XII, 50–51, 79.
39. Ibid., XII, 66–67.
40. Ibid., XII, 12, 17–19.

41. Ibid., XII, 63–66.
42. Sakai Toshihiko, "Ōsugi to Arahata," p. 13.
43. F. G. Notehelfer, *Kōtoku Shūsui: Portrait of a Japanese Radical* (Cambridge, England, 1971), pp. 34, 68–70, 74–75; and Gail Lee Bernstein, *Japanese Marxist: A Portrait of Kawakami Hajime, 1879–1946* (Cambridge, Mass., 1976), pp. 30–32, 46–51.
44. *Jijōden, Zenshū,* XII, 76–77, 52; and Tada Michitarō, "Ōsugi Sakae," p. 341.
45. *Jijōden, Zenshū,* XII, 52–53.
46. Ibid., XII, 45–47.
47. Ibid., XII, 79–80.

2. MILITARY ASPIRATIONS

1. The term "Kadet School" will be used for the Japanese *yōnen gakkō* although the common translation is "military preparatory school." T. F. Cook, Jr., has pointed out in private conversation that the term "military preparatory school" is applied in American usage to private schools that have no official relationship with the military establishment. Kadet Schools in Japan, like those in Germany earlier in this century, were maintained and staffed by the army: boys entering them entered the army at the same time and were subject to all army rules and discipline. Hence, the use of the German term avoids confusion with the more amateur and private American military preparatory schools. "Kadet" instead of "cadet" is used to distinguish between the youths in *yōnen gakkō* and the older young men who attend the official military academies in the United States. For a short description of the evolution of the army's educational system, see Matsushita Yoshio and Izu Kimio, *Nihon gunji hattatsu shi* (Tokyo, 1938), pp. 185–190; and Matsushita Yoshio, *Meiji no guntai,* pp. 113–120.
2. *Jijōden, Zenshū,* XII, 80.
3. Ibid., XII, 88–89.
4. Ibid., XII, 90.
5. Graduates of the Nagoya Kadet School have published privately a history of their school. Among the lists of graduates and brief history of the school are reminiscences of its famous graduates, including its most renowned black sheep, Ōsugi Sakae, who is listed in the third entering class. The remembrance of Ōsugi is by Funabashi Shigeru, "Nakidashita Ōsugi Sakae," in *Meiyōkōshi* (Tokyo, 1974), pp. 142–143.
6. *Jijōden, Zenshū,* XII, 100.
7. Ibid., XII, 90–92.
8. Ibid., XII, 103–104.

9. Ibid., XII, 97.
10. Ibid., XII, 77–78.
11. Tada Michitarō, "Ōsugi Sakae," p. 331.
12. Ōsugi had begun smoking during his first year in middle school (age 13), using cigarettes and cigars pilfered from his father; *Jijōden, Zenshū,* XII, 72, 106–109.
13. Ibid., XII, 110–111.
14. Kazuko Tsurumi quotes the following example of punishment in the later period:

> An ex-officer relates his experience of disciplining his new conscripts. "[The purpose of discipline is] to give new conscripts shock treatments. When they first come into the army, they look sloppy and too relaxed. It is hard to explain exactly what is wrong with them. But we somehow feel that way about them. Whenever we find any impropriety in their attitudes, behavior, or speech, we chastise them while keeping them standing at attention. Usually soldiers do not understand what is wrong with them, while they are being punished. The ultimate purpose of shouting at them and hitting them is to make them feel miserable, and thus to hammer it into them that absolute obedience is imperative in the army and that neither criticism nor protest is allowed. When superiors chastise conscripts, the former may ask why the recruits committed this or that blunder. If the conscripts begin to give reasons for their deeds, they are hit for trying to answer. If they keep silent, they are also hit. Either way there is no escape from being beaten. The best they can do is to "Yes, sir" to whatever is said to them.

Kazuko Tsurumi, *Social Change and the Individual: Japan Before and After Defeat in World War II* (Princeton, 1970), p. 116.
15. "Zoku gokuchū ki," *Zenshū,* XIII, 212; and *Jijōden, Zenshū,* XII, 96, 114–115.
16. *Jijōden, Zenshū,* XII, 101–102.
17. Ibid., XII, 115–119.
18. Ibid., XII, 119–121.
19. Ibid., XII, 121–123.
20. Ibid., XII, 124–125.
21. Ibid., XII, 125–132.
22. Ibid., XII, 133–136.

3. SOCIALIST BEGINNINGS

1. "Shikai no naka kara," *Zenshū,* XII, 238.
2. *Jijōden, Zenshū,* XII, 139, 147–148.

3. Ibid., XII, 162.

4. Ibid., XII, 170–171.

5. Ibid., XII, 140–141.

6. Ibid., XII, 171–173.

7. Ibid., XII, 173.

8. Ibid., XII, 154.

9. Ibid., XII, 175.

10. Ibid., XII, 171–174, 178.

11. Ibid., XII, 174.

12. Ibid., XII, 141–143. For brief descriptions of the history of the Ashio Copper Mine and its pollution, see F. G. Notehelfer, "Japan's First Pollution Incident," *Journal of Japanese Studies* 1. 2: 351–383 (spring 1975); and Alan Stone, "The Japanese Muckrakers," *Journal of Japanese Studies* 1. 2: 385–407 (spring 1975). Ōsugi's own indirect contact with the pollution case is detailed in Komatsu Ryūji, "Ashio kōdoku jiken to Ōsugi Sakae," *Jiyū shisō kenkyū* 2: 7–12 (October 1960).

13. *Jijōden, Zenshū*, XII, 176–177.

14. Akiyama Kiyoshi, "Hyōden—Ōsugi Sakae," Part I, *Shisō no kagaku* 49: 78 (July 1975) and *Jijōden, Zenshū*, XII, 182.

15. *Jijōden, Zenshū*, XII, 185.

16. Ibid., XII, 141–144.

17. Ibid., XII, 144.

18. Ibid.

19. The war with Russia was generally a popular one. However, one writer points out that the army's desertion rate after the war rose drastically, a phenomenon perhaps connected to the switch to a longer, two-year conscription period. He continues by saying that "it can not be denied" that the efforts of Ōsugi and others had a great effect too. See Ōsawa Masamichi, "Ōsugi Sakae ron," Part I, *Shisō no kagaku* 21: 73 (September 1960). Of perhaps greater importance than Ōsugi's efforts to higher desertion rates after the Russo-Japanese War, however, was disappointment with the peace treaty, which failed to secure the customary indemnity from Russia, plus disillusionment over the high casualties suffered during the war. Both considerably cooled patriotic ardor much more than could the pacifism of the radicals, which was known in detail by only a small number of people.

20. *Jijōden, Zenshū*, XII, 183. Sakai recalled that Ōsugi introduced himself at this first meeting with attention-grabbing words: "I am the child of a murderer." Quoted in Kawakami Tamio, "Ōsugi Sakae ni tsuite," p. 39.

21. Tada Michitarō, "Ōsugi Sakae," p. 335; and Akiyama Kiyoshi, "Hyōden—Ōsugi Sakae," Part I, p. 82.

22. Mitani Ta'ichirō, "Taishō shakaishugisha no 'seiji kan'—'seiji no hitei'

kara 'seijiteki taikō,'" in "Nihon no shakaishugi," *Nenkan seijigaku,* pp. 66–67, footnote 4 (1968).

23. *Jijōden, Zenshū,* XII, 184.
24. Ibid.
25. Akiyama Kiyoshi, "Hyōden–Ōsugi Sakae," Part I, p. 80, quoting Ōsugi's *Autobiography.*
26. *Jijōden, Zenshū,* XII, 184–185.
27. Ibid., XII, 186.
28. Akiyama Kiyoshi, "Hyōden–Ōsugi Sakae," Part I, p. 83.
29. Miyajima Sukeo, "Ōsugi Sakae ron," *Kaihō* 3. 5:114 (May 1921).
30. *Ōsugi Sakae shokan shū,* Ōsugi Sakae kenkyūkai, ed. (Tokyo, 1974), p. 17–18; hereafter referred to as *Letters.*
31. "Shakaishugi to aikokushin," *Zenshū,* I, 111–132.
32. *Shakai bunko sōsho,* VII, 285.
33. Martin Bernal notes in reference to an article entitled "Bankoku shakaitō taikai ryakushi" (A brief history of the Socialist International) written around this time that, "although the compiler, Ōsugi Sakae, later became an Anarchist, the article was written from an impeccably social democratic standpoint." Martin Bernal, "The Triumph of Anarchism over Marxism, 1906–1907," in *China in Revolution: The First Phase, 1900–1913,* Mary Wright, ed. (New Haven, 1968), pp. 109–110.
34. Takami Jun, "Ōsugi Sakae," in *Nihon no shisōka,* Asahi jūnaru henshūbu, ed. (Tokyo 1963), II, 291. The impact of this increase can be imagined when compared to the daily average income in some occupations in Tokyo at the time: stone mason, 1 yen 28.8 sen; cooper, 72.5 sen; saddler, 1 yen 17.5 sen; tailor (Western clothes), 1 yen 45 sen; tailor (Japanese clothes), 76.8 sen; dyer, 50 sen; paper maker, 37 sen; ship carpenter, 95 sen; weaver (male), 40.5 sen; weaver (female), 26.3 sen; day laborer, 47.5 sen. See Japan, Naikaku, Tōkei-kyoku, *Dai Nihon teikoku tōkei nenkan,* XXVII, 455–458 (1908), Table 256, "Shō yatoi chinsen chihō betsu" (Wages of various occupations, by region).
35. Tada Michitarō, "Ōsugi Sakae," p. 340.
36. *Letters,* p. 18.
37. Kondō Kenji, *Ichi museifushugisha no kaisō* (Tokyo, 1966), p. 11; and Ōsawa Masamichi, *Ōsugi Sakae kenkyū* (Tokyo, 1968), pp. 35–37.
38. "Zoku gokuchū ki," *Zenshū,* XIII, 226–227.

4. PRISON

1. The articles "Shimpei shokun ni atau," an appeal originally in French for conscripts to resist the draft, and "Seinen ni uttau," a tract by Peter Kropotkin, are found in *Zenshū,* I, 138–141 and 3–38, respectively.

2. Opponents of Kōtoku who favored moderate legal tactics formed an opposition group, the Dōshikai (literally, Comrades Group), under the leadership of Katayama Sen, Tazoe Tetsuji, and Nishikawa Kōjirō. See F. G. Notehelfer, *Kōtoku Shūsui*, pp. 118–151, on Kōtoku's conversion to and propagation of direct-action tactics.

3. Ōsawa Masamichi, *Ōsugi Sakae kenkyū*, pp. 45–47, says that higher courts obliged the procurators with heavier sentences, implying that they were either more reactionary or more susceptible to political pressure than the lower courts when dealing with cases brought against left-wing activists.

4. *Shiryō Nihon shakai undō shi*, Tanaka Sōgorō, ed. (Tokyo, 1958), II, 461–472, for sentences and excerpts from the court proceedings.

5. Many sources omit mention of this earlier demonstration, which was not part of the Red Flag Incident itself. Other sources confuse the two demonstrations as to which faction was demonstrating, how many flags were carried, and what the inscriptions on the flags were. See, for one example, Morinaga Eisaburō, "Akahata jiken—taigyaku jiken e no taidō," *Hōgaku zeminā* 209: 85 (April 1974). Eguchi Kan, "Ōsugi Sakae no seikatsu to shisō," in *Gendai Nihon bungaku zenshū* (Tokyo, 1957), LII, 406, claims there was a police spy who incited the entire demonstration, but even Ōsugi fails to support this claim.

6. Katsura was also anxious to topple Saionji from power because he opposed Saionji's ultimate goal, which was to establish the principle of having the majority party in the Lower House, simply because it was the majority party, form the Cabinet. See Robert A. Scalapino, *Democracy and the Party Movement in Prewar Japan: The Failure of the First Attempt* (Berkeley, 1953), pp. 188–189. George M. Beckmann and Okubo Genji, *The Japanese Communist Party: 1922–1945* (Stanford, 1969), pp. 6–7, write that, "when General Katsura, the prime minister who ordered the Socialist Society to disband in 1904, took office again in January 1908, he was determined to destroy the socialist movement and to rid Japan of socialists once and for all," mistaking the inaugural date of the Katsura cabinet by half a year.

7. "Gokuchū ki," *Zenshū*, XIII, 207–209.

8. See below, Chapter 6, for a discussion of the "rules" under which radicals and police both operated in 1911–1923. Both the police and Ōsugi received an early lesson on the rules of tha game when the police questioned him after his arrest in connection with the Red Flag Incident. He felt they were being unnecessarily rough and remonstrated. In reply, they knocked him down and dragged him about, hitting and kicking him. Ōsugi then urinated on one officer and was spread-eagled, naked, on his stomach, and beaten. Furuya Tsunamasa, "Ōsugi Sakae," p. 115.

9. Henry Dewitt Smith, *Japan's First Student Radicals* (Cambridge, Mass., 1972), p. 134.

10. *Letters,* pp. 33, 35. On his Esperanto, see Kondo Kenji, *Ichi museifushugisha no kaisō,* p. 13; and Yamaga Taiji, "Ōsugi Sakae to esuperantogo," *Jiyū shisō kenkyū* 1: 21–22 (July 1960).

11. "Gokuchū ki," *Zenshū,* XIII, 204.

12. *Letters,* pp. 22–23. In another letter, written to Yamakawa Hitoshi on October 13, 1907, he complained that he was bitten by bedbugs in twenty or thirty places each night. *Letters,* p. 40.

13. "Gokuchū ki," *Zenshū,* XIII, 190.

14. Quoted in Akiyama Kiyoshi, "Ōsugi Sakae to bungaku," *Ronsō* 2. 7:133 (December 1960).

15. Ōsawa Masamichi, "Ōsugi Sakae ron," part I, p. 71.

16. Jean Racque Elisee Reclus (1830–1905) was a French geographer and anarchist who participated in the Paris Commune before leaving France for good.

17. Enrico Malatesta (1858–1932) was an Italian anarchist.

18. *Letters,* pp. 38–39.

19. "Dōbutsukai no sōgo fujo," *Zenshū,* IV, 79.

20. See Martin A. Miller, *Kropotkin* (Chicago, 1976), pp. 189–191, and Peter Kropotkin, *The Conquest of Bread* (New York, 1906).

21. Eugene Pyziur, *The Doctrine of Anarchism of Michael A. Bakunin* (Milwaukee, 1955), p. 102.

22. *Letters,* p. 41.

23. See Ōsawa Masamichi, *Ōsugi Sakae kenkyū,* pp. 64–66, for a list of authors and titles Ōsugi mentions having read in his letters from prison.

24. "Gokuchū ki," *Zenshū,* XIII, 203.

25. "Zoku gokuchū ki," *Zenshū,* XIII, 228. In view of Ōsugi's Christian experience, the final phrase might also be translated "a blessing imparted by God." However, since he held such a low opinion of Christians after he abandoned the religion, it seems safe to assume that he was not using *kami* in the sense of the Christian God.

26. *Letters,* p. 46; "Gokuchū ki," *Zenshū,* XIII, 204–206; and "Zoku gokuchū ki," *Zenshū,* XIII, 213.

27. "Gokuchū ki," *Zenshū,* XIII, 206–207; and "Zoku gokuchū ki," *Zenshū,* XIII, 211–214.

28. *Letters,* pp. 59–60.

29. "Zoku gokuchū ki," *Zenshū,* XIII, 228–234, 237–238.

30. *Letters,* p. 19.

31. "Zoku gokuchū ki," *Zenshū,* XIII, 242–247.

5. INTELLECTUAL FOUNDATIONS

1. Komatsu Ryūji, "*Kindai shisō* sōkan zengo," *Jiyū shisō kenkyū* 3: 15 (January 1961); and Ōsawa Masamichi, *Ōsugi Sakae kenkyū*, p. 78.

2. Ōsawa Masamichi, *Ōsugi Sakae kenkyū*, p. 80. In times more favorable to socialism, the rates of renumeration were far better. Around 1919, when interest in socialism was stimulated by the Russian Revolution, *Kaizō* (Reconstruction) and *Kaihō* (Liberation) paid about ¥2–3 per page. In 1923, literary figures like Akutagawa Ryūnosuke received ¥7 per page, while Ōsugi was in even more demand and received around ¥10 a page. Kawakami Tamio, "Ōsugi Sakae ni tsuite," p. 78.

3. *Shakai bunko sōsho*, VII, 204–205.

4. Komatsu Ryūji, "*Kindai shisō* sōkan zengo," p. 14, quoting Sakai's "Nihon shakaishugi undō ni okeru museifushugi no yakuwari," *Rōnō*, December 1958.

5. *Kindai shisō* 1. 1: 21 (October 1912).

6. Kondō Kenji, *Ichi museifushugisha no kaisō*, p. 16; Komatsu Ryūji, "*Kindai shisō* sōkan zengo," p. 15; and *Shakai bunko sōsho*, VII, 207.

7. Paul Fussell, *The Great War and Modern Memory* (New York and London, 1975), p. 8.

8. Irving Louis Horowitz, *Radicalism and the Revolt Against Reason: The Social Theories of Georges Sorel* (New York, 1961), p. 2.

9. Ibid., p. 71. Sorel's theory of violence is contained in Georges Sorel, *Reflections on Violence*, T. E. Hulme, trans., Edward A. Shils, intro. (Glencoe, Illinois, 1950).

10. Horowitz, *Georges Sorel*, p. 122; see also Sorel, *Reflections on Violence*, pp. 186–187.

11. "Sei no kakujū," *Zenshū*, II, 30.

12. Yoshida Seiichi, "Ōsugi Sakae," *Kaishaku to kanshō* 42. 3: 194 (February 1977).

13. Henri Bergson's primary works are *Time and Free Will: An Essay on the Immediate Data of Consciousness*, F. L. Pogson, trans. (New York, 1910); *Matter and Memory*, Nancy Margaret Paul and W. Scott Palmer, trans. (New York, 1911); and *Creative Evolution*, Arthur Mitchel, trans. (New York, 1911). Bergson's ideas are explicated in Algot Ruhe and Nancy Margaret Paul, *Henri Bergson: An Account of his Life and Philosophy* (London, 1914); George Santayana, "The Philosophy of M. Bergson," *Winds of Doctrine* (New York, 1913), pp. 58–109, offers a gentle critique of Bergson.

14. "Rōdō undō to puragumatizumu," *Zenshū*, VI, 233–236.

15. See Max Stirner, *The Ego and his Own: The Case of the Individual*

Against Authority, Steven T. Byington, trans. (New York, 1973), which is Stirner's only significant work.

16. "Yuiitsusha," *Zenshū*, III, 9.
17. "Kindai kojinshugi no shosō," *Zenshū*, III, 85–86.
18. "Yuiitsusha," *Zenshū*, III, 90. Morito Tatsuo, "Ōsugi Sakae chosaku gaihyō," in Yasutani Kan'ichi, ed., *Mikan Ōsugi Sakae ikō* (Tokyo, 1937), p. 393, and Morito Tatsuo, "Ōsugi Sakae-kun no tsuioku," *Kaizō* 6. 4: 52 (April 1924). These two articles are identical; they say Ōsugi turned the contemporary debate on individualism from a strictly psychological orientation to a more social one.
19. See *Kindai shisō* 2. 2: 25 (November 1913); 2. 3: 31 (December 1913); 2. 4: 40 (January, 1914); 2. 5: 26 (February 1914); 2. 8: 32 (May 1914); and 2. 9: 30–31 (June 1914).
20. "Seifuku no jijitsu," *Zenshū*, II, 22 and 23.
21. Ibid., II, 25, 26, 27. Either this last quotation is Ōsugi's translation of the *Manifesto* or else a Japanese version by someone else. Karl Marx and Friedrich Engels, *Basic Writings on Politics and Philosophy*, Lewis S. Feuer, ed. (Garden City, New York, 1959), p. 7, renders the same passage, "Freeman and slave, patrician and plebian, lord and serf, guild master and journeyman."
22. "Seifuku no jijitsu," *Zenshū*, II, 27–28.
23. Ibid., II, 28.
24. *Minshū geijutsu ron*, *Zenshū*, XI, 1–177, and "Atarashiki sekai no tame no atarashiki geijutsu," *Zenshū*, V, 23–45.
25. "Atarashiki sekai no tame no atarashiki geijutsu," *Zenshū*, V, 34–35.
26. Ibid., V, 29–39.
27. Romain Rolland, *The People's Theater*, Barret H. Clark, trans. (New York, 1918), p. 98.
28. "Sei no kakujū," *Zenshū*, II, 30–31.
29. Ibid., II, 35.
30. Ibid., II, 32.
31. Ibid., II, 33.
32. Ibid., II, 33.
33. Ibid., II, 34.
34. "Sei no sōzō," *Zenshū*, II, 54.
35. Ibid., II, 55.
36. Ibid., II, 57.
37. Ibid., II, 58.
38. Ibid.
39. Ibid., II, 59.
40. Ibid., II, 60–61.

6. ŌSUGI AND THE POLICE

1. Portions of this chapter previously appeared in my "Police Constraints on Taishō Radical Movements: The Case of Ōsugi Sakae," Western Conference of the Association for Asian Studies, ed., *Selected Papers in Asian Studies*, 2, 95–109 (1977), and are used here with the permission of the editor, which I gratefully acknowledge.
2. "Sei no sōzō," *Zenshū*, II, 61.
3. "Ōkubo yori," *Zenshū*, XIV, 228.
4. Arahata Kanson, *Shimpan Kanson jiden* (Tokyo, 1965), I, 204–205; and Ōsawa Masamichi, *Ōsugi Sakae kenkyū*, pp. 109–110.
5. Ōsawa Masamichi, *Ōsugi Sakae kenkyū*, p. 117. Ōsawa attributes this story to the column from the editors in *Kindai shisō* 2. 6 (March 1913), but it does not appear in that issue's editor's column as reproduced in "Ōkubo yori," *Zenshū*, XIV, 258–259. Presumably it appears in one of the other infrequent comments the editors made in addition to their regular columns.
6. "Ōkubo yori," *Zenshū*, XIV, 228.
7. See "Rōdōsha no shimbun," *Zenshū*, VI, 58–59; and Ōsawa Masamichi, *Ōsugi Sakae kenkyū*, pp. 132–136.
8. "Heiminsha yori," *Zenshū*, XIV, 280.
9. *Shakai bunko sōsho*, VII, 290.
10. Ibid., VII, 291.
11. Ōsawa Masamichi, *Ōsugi Sakae kenkyū*, pp. 136–137.
12. Ibid., p. 143–148.
13. *Shakai bunko sōsho*, VII, 293.
14. See Ōsawa Masamichi, *Ōsugi Sakae kenkyū*, pp. 232–235, and Hosokawa Karoku, ed., *Nihon shakaishugi bunken kaisetsu* (Tokyo, 1958), p. 109.
15. "Honshi no tachiba," *Zenshū*, XIV, 312–313, and Ōsawa Masamichi, *Ōsugi Sakae kenkyū*, p. 287. Two more *Rōdō undō* were published by Ōsugi's followers after his death.
16. In order to distinguish between the Russian Bolsheviks and Japanese bolsheviks (meaning those who sympathized with and supported communism prior to the founding of the Japanese Communist Party), I will use the upper case Bolshevik for Russians and the lower case bolshevik for the Japanese.
17. Ōsawa Masamichi, *Ōsugi Sakae kenkyū*, pp. 295–306; and "Nihon dasshutsu ki," *Zenshū*, XIII, 23–32.
18. Patricia G. Steinhoff, "Tenkō and Thought Control," paper presented at Annual Meetings of the Association for Asian Studies, Boston, Massachusetts, April 1–3, 1974, p. 1. The full quotation is: "In general [thought control] refers to a power relationship in which one party deliberately

attempts to limit or direct the thoughts and beliefs of some other party. Thought control may be directed only toward overt acts and external expressions of thought, or it may aid to penetrate into the internal state of the individual's mind, reaching even his unexpressed thoughts and beliefs. In addition, thought control may focus either on inculcating good thoughts, on eradicating bad thoughts, or on some combination of the two."

19. Morinaga Eisaburō, *Shidan saiban*, p. 81.
20. *Shakai bunko sōsho*, VII, 285.
21. "Hakkō ken henshūnin kara," *Zenshū*, XIV, 304.
22. *Shakai bunko sōsho*, VII, 287. See Ibid., VII, 288, for information on the Sanjikarizumu kenkyū kai. Reports on other groups are scattered throughout the documents.
23. *Shakai bunko sōsho*, VII, 286, 291; and Ōsawa Masamichi, *Ōsugi Sakae kenkyū*, p. 138.
24. *Shakai bunko sōsho*, VII, 294.
25. Ibid., VII, 285, 296; and "Hakkō ken henshūnin kara," *Zenshū*, XIV, 308.
26. Hemmi Kichizō, "Nihon e kita Bakunin," *Gendai no me* 12, 7: 189–191 (July 1971).
27. Itō Noe, "Aru otoko no daraku," *Itō Noe zenshū*, I, 352–355.
28. Itō Noe, "Kōkin sareru made," *Itō Noe zenshū*, II, 383–394.
29. "Nihon dasshutsu ki," *Zenshū*, XIII, 7–11.
30. Kondō Kenji, *Ichi museifushugisha no kaisō*, pp. 19–20. This incident with Wada is ambiguous in that Ōsugi's choice of the words "contrary to the Way of the Warrior" can be interpreted to mean that he was conforming to his picture of the samurai and to traditional values. On the other hand, he may have simply used the phrase knowing that it would have made a deep impression on Wada; it certainly did on Kondō.
31. Ōsawa Masamichi, *Ōsugi Sakae kenkyū*, pp. 231–232, 242–245; and Morinaga Eisaburō, *Shidan saiban*, p. 30.
32. *Shakai bunko sōsho*, VII, 297; and Ōsawa Masamichi, *Ōsugi Sakae kenkyū*, pp. 231–232. Ōsugi describes this incident in "Gokuchū ki," *Zenshū*, XIII, 161–163. He writes that, on the day following his arrest, the police apologized for arresting him, fed him breakfast, and requested that he never mention the incident. Then the chief of the station arrived and remanded Ōsugi to detention for interfering with policemen carrying out their proper duties. The police record of the incident makes no mention of this, but notes that the incident occurred on February 2, not on March 1. Ōsugi might have made a mistake or the police record may contain a typographical error, since it is a transcribed copy made for the trial of Ōsugi's assassin and not the original record.

33. *Shakai bunko sōsho,* VII, 299. The magazine was entitled *Minshū no geijutsu* (The people's art).
34. Ibid., VII, 300. I can find no mention of the matter in other sources.
35. Ōsawa Masamichi, *Ōsugi Sakae kenkyū,* p. 245; Morinaga Eisaburō, *Shidan saiban,* p. 30; and *Shakai bunko sōsho,* VII, 300–301.
36. Itō Noe, "Kōkin sareru made," *Itō Noe zenshū,* II, 379ff; *Shakai bunko sōsho,* VII, 301, and Ōsawa Masamichi, *Ōsugi Sakae kenkyū,* pp. 242–243.
37. *Shakai bunko sōsho,* VII, 301, and Ōsawa Masamichi, *Ōsugi Sakae kenkyū,* pp. 243–244. The Chief of the Metropolitan Police Detective Bureau accused Ōsugi of defrauding various shopkeepers as well as landlords, and the story was printed in various newspapers. Ōsugi complained to the Chief and filed a complaint with the procurator's office, but the police apparently refused to have the newspapers print a retraction and apology; *Shakai bunko sōsho,* VII, 303, and Ōsawa Masamichi, *Ōsugi Sakae kenkyū,* pp. 244–245. Although no further mention is made of the matter, it appears that the police and Ōsugi reached a tacit or explicit agreement: the police would not press their charges if Ōsugi would not press his. In any case, neither the police, Ōsugi, nor his biographers offer any definite conclusion to this matter.
38. Itō Noe, "Kōkin sareru made," *Itō Noe zenshū,* II, 379ff.
39. Morinaga Eisaburō, *Shidan saiban,* p. 31.
40. *Shakai bunko sōsho,* VII, 294.
41. Ōsawa Masamichi, *Ōsugi Sakae kenkyū,* pp. 294–296.
42. "Gokuchū ki," *Zenshū,* XIII, 164.
43. Ōsawa Masamichi, *Ōsugi Sakae kenkyū,* p. 245.

7. SCANDAL AND ECLIPSE

1. Kamichika Ichiko, "Watakushi no rirekishō," in *Watakushi no rirekisho* (Tokyo, 1965), XXIII, 93.
2. Nancy Andrew, "The Seitōsha: An Early Japanese Women's Organization, 1911–1916, *Papers on Japan* (Harvard University, East Asia Research Center, 1972), 5, 63. See also Ide Fumiko, *"Seitō" no onna-tachi* (Tokyo, 1975), for information on the Seitō-sha.
3. Furuya Tsunamasa, "Kindai bijin den–4–Kamichika Ichiko," *Jimbutsu ōrai* 3. 4: 134–135 (April 1954); and Furuya Tsunamasa, *Ittō josei jūnin no ai* (Tokyo, 1955), pp. 64–71. Kamichika Ichiko writes about her life before meeting Ōsugi in "Rirekisho," pp. 68–113.
4. Morinaga Eisaburō, *Shidan saiban,* p. 46. Ōsawa Masamichi, *Ōsugi Sakae kenkyū,* p. 142, says that there was an advertisement in the first issue of the second *Kindai shisō,* October 1915, soliciting students for Ōsugi's

Furansu bungaku kenkyūkai. Classes were offered in introductory, intermediate, and advanced French for ¥1 per month and were attended by Kamichika, both of the Miyajimas, and Aoyama Kikue, as well as students interested in learning French. Iwasaki Kureo states that the texts in the classes included George Sorel's *Reflections on Violence,* Romain Rolland's *The People's Theater,* and Peter Kropotkin's *Mutual Aid,* indicating Ōsugi's two purposes in teaching language: income and ideological indoctrination. See Iwasaki Kureo, *Hi no onna—Itō Noe den* (Tokyo, 1971), p. 224

5. Ōsawa Masamichi, *Ōsugi Sakae kenkyū,* p. 199; and Morinaga Eisaburō, *Shidan saiban,* p. 46.

6. Kamichika Ichiko, "Rirekisho," p. 114. Other sources indicate the affair began later in 1915. See Furuya Tsunamasa, "Bijin den," p. 135.

7. "Danjo kankei ni tsuite," *Zenshū,* III, 222. See also Ōsawa Masamichi, *Ōsugi Sakae kenkyū,* p. 200.

8. Tada Michitarō, "Ōsugi Sakae," p. 363. A short chronology of Itō Noe's life may be found in Itō Noe, *Itō Noe zenshū,* I, 456–458. A brief biography in English is in Miyamoto Ken, "Itō Noe and the Bluestockings," *The Japan Interpreter* 10, 2: 190–204 (autumn 1975).

9. Tsuji Jun was born in October 1895, and died November 24, 1944. After he dropped out of Kaisei Middle School, he studied English at the Kokumin eigakkai (Citizens' English Study Society) and the Jiyū eigakkai (Free English Study Society), becoming a teacher at Ueno jogakkō. After he was fired, he never again had any fixed job. In 1928, he went to France with his eldest son, returning the following year. See *Nihon bungaku daijiten,* Fujimura Tsukuru, ed. (Tokyo, 1955), p. 701. A short list of his major publications may be found there too. For a short bibliography, see *Nihon jimbutsu bunken mokuroku* (Tokyo, 1974), p. 697. Tsuji is known as a nihilist and a Dadaist. See Matsuo Kuninosuke, *Nihirisuto—Tsuji Jun no shisō to shōgai* (Tokyo, 1967) for information on Tsuji.

10. Ide Fumiko, *"Seitō" no onna-tachi,* pp. 211–212.

11. Itō Noe, *"Seitō* o hikitsugu ni tsuite," *Itō Noe zenshū,* II, 114. For information on *Seitō,* see Ide Fumiko, *"Seitō" no onna-tachi,* pp. 201ff and 260. Ide quotes Hiratsuka Raichō, "Seitō to watakushi" (Bluestockings and I), *Seitō* (January 1915) on p. 204.

12. "'Fujin kaihō no higeki,'" *Zenshū,* III, 204–205, and Ōsawa Masamichi, *Ōsugi Sakae kenkyū,* pp. 196–197.

13. Ōsawa Masamichi, *Ōsugi Sakae kenkyū,* p. 197–198. Ōsugi kissed Itō for the first time while they were strolling in Hibiya Park in February.

14. In addition to writing her own articles and publishing them in *Seitō,* Itō also sparked debates on topics that were of interest to her as a libertarian.

For instance, she led a debate in the pages of *Seitō* on the issues of abortion and contraception. Itō argued, in the February 1915 issue, that a woman should decide to make love or not with the same freedom that a man has in choosing. Yasuda Satsuki, in the same issue, went further and said that, since a woman's body was hers to do with as she pleased, a fetus that was part of that body could be dealt with as she pleased too. In the June issue, Itō contradicted this view and said that a fetus was a child and had its own destiny; a mother could not deal with it as she wished. Hiratsuka Raichō joined the debate in September, pointing out that contraception made the issue of abortion academic and insured that a child would be conceived and born only from love. In the same issue, Yamada Waka argued that both contraception and abortion were criminal because they destroyed "individual happiness" and "national prosperity": they are questions of morality, and one must accept the national morality. Ide Fumiko, *"Seito" no onna-tachi,* pp. 226–230.

15. Ide notes two examples of Tsuji's bloodless reaction to the wider world. After the censure brought down on him by his affair with Itō, Tsuji preferred to yield to forces larger than himself and would abandon things the outside world frowned on in favor of neutral pursuits, like playing the *shakuhachi* (Japanese flute), for which he became famous. In contrast, Ōsugi, even when forced into inaction by the High Treason Incident of 1910, strove to resist and to enlist others in his support by, for instance, publishing the first *Kindai shisō*, even though most colleagues thought it an untimely gesture. Another example was when Itō became concerned about the fate of the inhabitants of Yanaka village, due to be flooded as a means of controlling the pollution from the Ashio Copper Mine. Tsuji made fun of her; he reasoned that so few people in the world are satisfied that if one worried about the unsatisfied people, their problems would be so overwhelming that there would be no time left for private problems. Ide Fumiko, *"Seito" no onna-tachi,* pp. 243–246, 249.

16. Itō Noe, "Jiyū ishi ni yoru kekkon no hametsu," *Itō Noe zenshū,* II, 297–300.

17. "Shikai no naka kara," *Zenshū,* XII, 286. The registration of the marriage might also have had nothing to do with the state of their relationship; they may merely have wanted to please Itō's parents by making their relationship legal.

18. "Danjo kankei ni tsuite," *Zenshū,* III, 222; and Ōsawa Masamichi, *Ōsugi Sakae kenkyū,* pp. 192ff.

19. "Dōbutsu no ren'ai," *Zenshū,* XIV, 8–11.

20. "Yo no sōbō suru jiyū ren'ai," *Zenshū,* XIV, 15. Stephen S. Large misreads his source in a minor way when he says that Ōsugi wrote this article with his wife, Hori. She published the magazine with him, as the

source says, but had nothing to do with the writing of the article "Yo no sōbō suru jiyū ren'ai." See Stephen S. Large, "The Romance of Revolution in Japanese Anarchism and Communism during the Taishō Period," *Modern Asian Studies* 11. 3: 442–443 (July 1977).

21. "Yo no sōbō suru jiyū ren'ai," *Zenshū*, XIV, 14.
22. "'Jogakusei,'" *Zenshū*, III, 200. The earlier "Shūchi to teisō" can be found in *Zenshū*, III, 143–152.
23. "Danjo kankei ni tsuite," *Zenshū*, III, 240–244.
24. When Ōsugi tried to speak to Hori about Itō she began to speak sarcastically about "that fox . . ." ("*ano kitsune-san wa ne . . .*") before he cut her off by placing his hand over her mouth until he went to sleep; *Letters*, p. 138, and "Danjo kankei ni tsuite," *Zenshū*, III, 228.
25. Ōsawa Masamichi, *Ōsugi Sakae kenkyū*, p. 200.
26. "Danjo kankei ni tsuite," *Zenshū*, III, 228. Ōsugi quoted several of her letters to him in this essay.
27. Ibid., III, 230.
28. Ibid., III, 222, 234.
29. *Jijōden, Zenshū*, XII, 207.
30. "Danjo kankei ni tsuite," *Zenshū*, III, 234–239.
31. Furuya Tsunamasa, "Bijin den," p. 135–136.
32. *Jijōden, Zenshū*, XII, 208–209, and "Danjo kankei ni tsuite," *Zenshū*, III, 239–240.
33. Quoted in Ōsawa Masamichi, *Ōsugi Sakae kenkyū*, p. 194.
34. *Jijōden, Zenshū*, XII, 207–208.
35. Ōsawa Masamichi, *Ōsugi Sakae kenkyū*, pp. 144–145.
36. Kamichika Ichiko, "Rirekisho," p. 117. She was not clear about the date of this disruption, but probably referred to the administration of the *Kindai shisō.*
37. Ōsawa concludes that Ōsugi probably rented separate lodgings for Hori and himself the previous month in order to have a place for Itō to move to. Ōsawa Masamichi, *Ōsugi Sakae kenkyū*, p. 200. It is not clear, however, when Itō actually decided to leave Tsuji, so it would be equally possible to conclude that he was simply conforming in reality to his own theory of free love. This conclusion is further supported by the fact that she stayed only a very short time with Ōsugi before departing for Onjuku. See Itō Noe, "'Bekkyo' ni tsuite," *Itō Noe zenshū*, II, 266–277, where she discusses her separation from Tsuji.
38. *Letters*, p. 146.
39. See Ōsawa Masamichi, *Ōsugi Sakae kenkyū*, p. 207.
40. Kamichika Ichiko, "Rirekisho," pp. 114–116. See also Kamichika Ichiko, *Kamichika Ichiko jiden—waga ai, waga tatakai* (Tokyo, 1972), p. 154.

41. Ōsawa Masamichi, *Ōsugi Sakae kenkyū*, p. 201. Iwasaki Kureo, *Hi no onna*, pp. 235–252. quotes passages from some of the letters exchanged by Itō and Ōsugi from April through September, generally reproducing with a few minor differences the text of the letters quoted by Ōsugi in his "Danjo kankei ni tsuite." However, in a letter dated May 7 from Itō to Ōsugi, Iwasaki includes material, pp. 245–246, that Ōsugi does not. According to this, Itō worried about Hori's ability to survive financially and encouraged Ōsugi to take care to support Hori rather than Itō. Itō noted that she had already received money from him, but that she would be able to get along; since she was healthy, she could even work in the factories if necessary.
42. *Letters,* p. 139, 140.
43. Kamichika Ichiko, "Rirekisho," pp. 115–117, 118–119.
44. Furuya Tsunamasa, "Bijin den," p. 136.
45. Kamichika Ichiko, *Kamichika Ichiko jiden,* pp. 153, 155.
46. Quoted in Ōsawa Masamichi, *Ōsugi Sakae kenkyū,* p. 193. The estimate of ¥200 comes from Morinaga Eisaburō, *Shidan saiban,* p. 47.
47. Ōsawa Masamichi, *Ōsugi Sakae kenkyū,* p. 194.
48. *Jijōden, Zenshū,* XII, 214–215.
49. Kamichika Ichiko, *Kamichika Ichiko jiden,* p. 162.
50. Kamichika Ichiko, "Rirekisho," p. 123.
51. Gotō Shimpei (1857–1929), a medical doctor, held a variety of bureaucratic positions. After holding positions in the Home Ministry and the army during the Sino-Japanese War, he was appointed Civil Governor of Taiwan in 1898. Thereafter he headed the South Manchurian Railroad Company, was appointed Minister of Communications in the second and third Katsura Cabinets (July 14, 1908, to August 30, 1911, and December 21, 1912, to February 20, 1913), Home Minister (responsible for religious matters, local administration, health, city planning, publications and copywriting, Diet elections, and the police) in the Terauchi Cabinet (October 2, 1916, to September 29, 1918), Mayor of Tokyo (1920–1922), and Home Minister again in the second Yamamoto Cabinet (September 2, 1923, to January 7, 1924) until he resigned to take responsibility for the Tora no Mon (Tiger Gate) Incident, in which an attempt on the life of the Prince Regent (the present Emperor) was made in the vicinity of the Tora no Mon in Tokyo, December 27, 1923. Some of Ōsugi's biographers leave the reader confused about what Gotō's position was when Ōsugi borrowed money from him: one identifies him incorrectly as the then-mayor of Tokyo. See Tateno Noboyuki, *Kuroi hana* (Tokyo, 1974), I, 26–27. Tateno's work is actually a well-researched piece of historical fiction, usually reliable where not clearly fictive.

Another source merely says Gotō was Home Minister when Ōsugi died: Tadamiya Eitarō, "Ōsugi Sakae: sono gekiteki na sanjūku-nen," *Keizai ōrai* 28. 11: 250 (November 1976).

52. See Ōsawa Masamichi, *Ōsugi Sakae kenkyū*, p. 202; *Jijōden, Zenshū*, XII, 219; and Tada Michitarō, "Ōsugi Sakae," p. 370.

53. *Jijōden, Zenshū*, XII, 218–219.

54. Kondō Kenji, *Ichi museifushugisha no kaisō*, pp. 30–31. Ars published the following books that Ōsugi wrote: *Kuropotokin kenkyū* (Studies on Kropotkin), 1920; *Itazura* (Mischief), 1921; *Mambun manga* (Random notes and caricatures), 1921; *Seigi o motomeru kokoro* (A mind searching for justice), 1921; *Futari no kakumeika* (Two revolutionaries), 1922; *Nihon dasshutsu ki* (Record of my escape from Japan), 1923; *Jizen kagaku no hanashi* (Tales of natural science), translation of the work of Jean Henri Fabre (1823–1915), French entomologist, 1923; *Kagaku no fushigi* (The mysteries of science), translation of another Fabre work, 1923; and *Ōsugi Sakae zenshū* (Collected works of Ōsugi Sakae), 1926.

55. Yamakawa Hitoshi, *Yamakawa Hitoshi jiden—aru bonjin no kiroku*, Yamakawa Kikue and Sakisaka Itsurō, eds. (Tokyo, 1961), pp. 373–374.

56. *Jijōden, Zenshū*, XII, 191, 192–193, 194, 196, 197. Tada Michitarō, "Ōsugi Sakae," pp. 270–271, omits mentioning that Ōsugi suggested that Itō spend a night in Hayama before they even departed from Tokyo, thereby implying they made a spontaneous decision after leaving Chigasaki.

57. Kamichika Ichiko, "Rirekisho," p. 118.

58. Kamichika Ichiko, *Kamichika Ichiko jiden*, pp. 154, 156.

59. *Jijōden, Zenshū*, XII, 202–203.

60. Ibid., XII, 214–215, 220–221.

61. When Ōsugi wrote about the stabbing in "Obake o mita hanashi," he related that recently he had been having bad dreams about it. Frequently, he awoke at three a.m. and saw Kamichika leaving the room, looking at him. He was so scared by these apparitions that Itō had to comfort him as if he were a child. Ibid., XII, 187–189.

62. Ibid., XII, 223–226.

63. Kamichika Ichiko, "Rirekisho," pp. 118–119; and *Kamichika Ichiko jiden*, p. 160.

64. Kamichika Ichiko, *Kamichika Ichiko jiden*, pp. 161–163. Kamichika also wrote a brief and mild remembrance of Ōsugi in "Ōsugi Sakae," *Rōdō hyōron* 3. 1: 27 (January 1948).

65. Morinaga Eisaburō, *Shidan saiban*, pp. 50–51. Akiyama Kiyoshi quotes extensively from the court records of Kamichika's trial in "Sei to jiyū ni tsuite," *Shisō no kagaku* 123: 26–29 (November 1971).

66. Ōsawa Masamichi, *Ōsugi Sakae kenkyū*, p. 202. Hori Yasuko also wrote

about her divorce at greater length in "Ōsugi to wakareru made," *Chūō kōron* (March 1917), reprinted in *Ōsugi Sakae hiroku*, Ōsugi Sakae kenkyū kai, ed. (Tokyo, 1976), pp. 1–24. After her divorce, Hori considered supporting herself by exporting pearls to America. She approached Matsushita Yoshio for a loan, using Sakai as her guarantor, but never concluded a deal. She died shortly after the Kantō Earthquake of 1923. Matsushita Yoshio, "Ōsugi Sakae no kazoku to yōnen gakkō jidai," *Jiyū shisō kenkyū,* 2: 22–23 (October 1960).

67. *Shakai bunko sōsho,* VII, 295.
68. Furuya Tsunamasa, "Ōsugi Sakae," p. 115.
69. Hemmi Kichizō, "'Shi' to 'shi' to 'shi,'" Part I, *Gendai no me* 12. 9: 226–227 (September 1971).
70. Sakai Toshihiko, "Ōsugi-kun no ren'ai jiken," *Shin shakai* 3. 5: 3–4 (January 1917).
71. Takabatake Motoyuki, "Ōsugi jiken to jiyū ren'ai to shakaishugi," *Shin shakai* 3. 5: 5 (January 1917).
72. Yamakawa Hitoshi, "Ren'ai to ninjō to shōsei no kansō," *Shin shakai* 3. 5: 50 (January 1917).
73. "Zakkubaran ni kokuhaku shi yoron ni kotau," *Zenshū,* III, 246.
74. Ibid., III, 252, 256.
75. Ibid., III, 250.
76. Peter Duus and Daniel I. Okamoto, "Fascism and the History of Pre-war Japan: The Failure of a Concept," *Journal of Asian Studies* 39. 1: 68 (November 1979), point out that the modern sector of the economy accounted for 62% of the GNP at the end of World War I.

8. THEORIES ON THE LABOR MOVEMENT AND ART

1. He wrote only six articles in the second half of the year: "Bagabondo tamashii" in May, 1917, found in *Zenshū,* V, 178–199; "Kindai bungaku to shin hanzaigaku" in June, *Zenshū,* V, 200–223; "Minshū geijutsu no gikō" in July, *Zenshū,* V, 46–52; "Jinrui shi jō no dentōshugi" in October, *Zenshū,* IV, 98–120; "Sewa nyōbō" in October, *Zenshū,* XIV, 75–78; and "Hā shintō na koto da" in December, *Zenshū,* XIV, 79–82. The translations were Romain Rolland's *The People's Theater* which appeared in June 1917, and Peter Kropotkin's *Mutual Aid* in October.
2. Itō Noe, "Aru otoko no daraku," *Itō Noe zenshū,* I, 347–349.
3. Ōsawa notes that Ariyoshi was later found to be a police spy and may have formed his Zadankai at the instigation of the police. Ōsawa Masamichi, *Ōsugi Sakae kenkyū,* p. 228.
4. Mizunuma Tatsuo, "Ōsugi Sakae to rōdō undō," Part II, *Jiyū shisō kenkyū* 4: 49–50 (January 1961).

5. Itō Noe, "Aru otoko no daraku," *Itō Noe zenshū*, I, 350–351.
6. On the Shin'yūkai, see Mizunuma Tatsuo, "Ōsugi Sakae to rōdō undō," Part I, *Jiyū shisō kenkyū* 3: 3–7 (December 1960) and Part II, pp. 49–50. On the Seishinkai, see Mizunuma Tatsuo, Ibid., Part II, pp. 52–53. The degree of antagonism that existed between labor and management at this time is reflected in an actively used blacklist maintained by owners of shops until 1940. See Ibid., Part I, p. 5. The Seishinkai later struck the same newspapers in August and September 1920. During the strike, some unionists entered the plant of the *Hōchi shimbun* (The informer) and destroyed ¥88,300 worth of type. This second strike failed too. See Ōsawa Masamichi, *Ōsugi Sakae kenkyū*, p. 263.
7. Akiyama Kiyoshi, *Nihon no hangyaku shisō—museifushugi undō shōshi* (Tokyo, 1960), pp. 82–84.
8. *Shakai bunko sōsho*, VII, 303. The Shin'yūkai along with the Yūaikai and three other organizations were recognized as labor unions by the government for the purpose of dealing with the International Labor Organization. Mizunuma Tatsuo, "Ōsugi Sakae to rōdō undō," Part II, p. 52.
9. Ōsawa Masamichi, *Ōsugi Sakae kenkyū*, p. 264, and Mizunuma Tatsuo, "Ōsugi Sakae to rōdō undō," Part II, p. 51. See also *Shakai bunko sōsho*, VII, 300, for another example.
10. "Shoshinshi teki kanjō," *Zenshū*, VI, 7–18.
11. "Seifuku no jijitsu," *Zenshū*, II, 25. Intellectuals reciprocated Ōsugi's feelings. Ōsugi was on a trolley one day with some friends when he spotted a professor who liked to write about the labor movement. Ōsugi promptly offered to allow the professor to see some materials on the U.S. labor movement he had recently received. The professor silently turned his back and never even glanced at Ōsugi and his friends for the remainder of the ride. Ōsawa Masamichi, *Ōsugi Sakae kenkyū*, p. 176.
12. "Rōdō undō to puragumatizumu," *Zenshū*, VI, 232–243.
13. "Chishiki kaikyū ni atau," *Zenshū*, VI, 27.
14. "Rōdō undō to rōdō bungaku," *Zenshū*, V, 59–61.
15. "Chishiki kaikyū ni atau," *Zenshū*, VI, 26–27; and "Rōdō undō to chishiki kaikyū," *Zenshū*, VI, 33.
16. Yamakawa Kikue, "Chishiki kaikyū to rōdōsha," *Kaihō* 1. 7 (October 1919).
17. "Rōdō undō to chishiki kaikyū," *Zenshū*, VI, 31.
18. "Boku wa seishin ga suki da," *Zenshū*, XIV, 84.
19. "Rōdō undō rironka—Kagawa Toyohiko ron (zoku)," *Zenshū*, VI, 168.
20. "Rōdō undō to chishiki kaikyū," *Zenshū*, VI, 34.
21. "Shakaiteki risōron," *Zenshū*, VI, 43.
22. "Bokura no shugi," *Zenshū*, VI, 65–66.

23. "Shin chitsujo no sōzō," *Zenshū*, VI, 54. Ōsawa says that Ōsugi developed this tactic between July 1918, when *Rōdō shimbun* halted publication, and October 1919, when the first *Rōdō undō* began publication. This period coincided with rapid growth in the labor movement, especially of unions led by conservatives who had the silent approval of the government, which was striving to promote the cooperation of labor and capital. Ōsawa Masamichi, *Ōsugi Sakae kenkyū*, p. 230. This kind of cooperation has often been criticized as being one-sided in favor of capital.

24. "Shin chitsujo no sōzō, *Zenshū*, VI, 51–52.

25. "Shakaiteki risōron," *Zenshū*, VI, 46.

26. Ibid., VI, 46–47.

27. "Kumiai undō to kakumei undō," *Zenshū*, VI, 98.

28. Eguchi Kan (1887–1975) was a novelist and critic active in the socialist movement. He was originally an anarchist, due to the influence of Ōsugi, but later he became a Marxist. He attended Tokyo Imperial University's English Department, but withdrew shortly before graduation in 1916. He entered the socialist movement thereafter, becoming a member of the central executive committee of the Nihon shakaishugi dōmei in December 1920. Later, he was active in the proletarian literature movement.

29. Eguchi Kan, "Ōsugi Sakae no seikatsu to shisō," p. 410.

30. Yoshida Seiichi, "Ōsugi Sakae," p. 184.

31. "Minshū geijutsu no gikō," *Zenshū*, V, 48.

32. "Shakai mondai ka geijutsu mondai ka," *Zenshū*, V, 56.

33. Ibid., V, 56.

34. "Rōdō undō to rōdō bungaku," *Zenshū*, V, 76.

35. Ibid., V, 72, 75.

9. THE RUSSIAN REVOLUTION AND THE ANARCHIST-BOLSHEVIK SPLIT

1. Portions of this chapter originally were presented at the Western Conference, Association for Asian Studies, October 7–8, 1977, Colorado Springs, Colorado, and appeared in *Selected Papers in Asian Studies, New Series* (Tucson, Arizona, 1979), Western Conference, Association for Asian Studies, ed., Paper No. 1, under the title "A Japanese Anarchist's Rejection of Marxism-Leninism: Ōsugi Sakae and the Russian Revolution." I acknowledge gratefully permission from the Western Conference, Association for Asian Studies to republish this material in revised form.

2. See Beckmann and Okubo Genji, *The Japanese Communist Party,* pp. 1-54.
3. Quoted in Asukai Masamichi, "Roshia kakumei to Ōsugi Sakae," *Gendai no riron* 4. 10: 34 (October 1967).
4. Yamakawa Hitoshi, *Yamakawa Hitoshi jiden,* p. 369.
5. Quoted in Asukai Masamichi, "Roshia kakumei to Ōsugi Sakae," p. 34.
6. Mitani Ta'ichirō, "Taishō shakaishugisha no 'seiji' kan." pp. 97-99.
7. See Beckmann and Okubo Genji, *The Japanese Communist Party,* p. 13; and Watanabe Tōru, "Roshia kakumei to Nihon rōdō undō," *Gendai no riron* 4. 10: 21 (October 1967), agreeing with Yamabe Kentarō and Takemura Eisuke, "Jūgatsu kakumei ga Nihon ni ataeta eikyō," *Zen'ei* No. 135 (December 1957).
8. Asukai Masamichi presents an interpretation that differs from that offered here. Asukai argues that Ōsugi clearly supported the Bolshevik Revolution from its start for intellectual and theoretical reasons. Ever since the conjunction of the Russo-Japanese War and the 1905 Russian Revolution, all Japanese socialists could have predicted that a major revolution, probably in Russia, would necessarily follow the Great War. Not only the Japanese socialists, but European socialists also realized this relationship between war and revolution. This was the basis for the Second International adopting the slogan "War against War" in 1907. Ōsugi devoted page 3 of *Heimin shimbun* (Commoners' newspaper) 1. 3 (December 1914) to the Second International's slogan: together with Arahata (Asukai guesses) he wrote that the war which had just begun was the hoped-for opportunity for revolution. Consequently, Ōsugi was greatly disappointed when Kropotkin, like many European socialists, supported this "capitalist" war and he forsook his idol. When, toward the end of the war, the Russian Revolutions occurred as expected, Ōsugi hesitantly supported them. See Asukai Masamichi, "Roshia kakumei to Ōsugi Sakae," pp. 34–42; also Ōsawa Masamichi, *Ōsugi Sakae kenkyū,* p. 273, citing Ōsugi's "Ōshū no tairan to shakaishugisha no taidō," *Zenshū,* I, 156–162.
9. "Kakumei wa itsu kuru ka," *Zenshū,* VI, 105-107.
10. Kondō Kenji, *Ichi nuseifushugisha no kaisō,* p. 79. First reported by Kondō Kenji in "Nihon saisho no Roshia kakumei kinen kai," *Kurohata* No. 24 (December 1, 1957).
11. "Kokusai rōdō kaigi," *Zenshū,* VI, 79.
12. "Nihon ni okeru saikin no rōdō undō to shakaishugi undō," *Zenshū,* VI, 74. This is an unfinished, undated article, probably written in late 1920, according to Komatsu Ryūji writing in the "Kaisetsu," *Zenshū,* VI, 287.
13. Ōsugi gave a brief description of his activities, August 9–19, in a letter that ends by stating he was being held in protective custody by the police.

See *Letters*, p. 193. The scene at the Osaka riot is described in Hemmi Kichizō, "Nihon e kita Bakūnin," pp. 189–191.

14. See Gail Lee Bernstein, "The Russian Revolution, the Early Japanese Socialists, and the Problem of Dogmatism," *Studies in Comparative Communism* 9. 4: 330–335 (winter 1976), for a synopsis of the slowness with which Japanese radicals came to realize the nature of the Russian Revolution and to accommodate their doctrines to it.

15. "Kakumei wa itsu kuru ka," *Zenshū*, VI, 107.

16. This conference remains obscure even in name. Western-language sources commonly omit mentioning any name when referring to it. See, for example, Robert A. Scalapino and Chong-sik Lee, *Communism in Korea* (Berkeley, 1972), 1, 29.

17. Quoted in Asukai Masamichi, "Roshia kakumei to Ōsugi Sakae," p. 36.

18. Takatsu Seidō, "Gyomin-kai zengo no omoide," *Rōdō undō shi kenkyū* No. 12 (November 1958), quoted in Ōsawa Masamichi, *Ōsugi Sakae kenkyū*, pp. 291–292. Takatsu Seidō (1893–1974) was a writer and politician. He was active in the labor and socialist movements after he withdrew from Waseda University, joining the Rōdō nōmin tō (Worker-Farmer Party) and the Nihon musan tō (Proletarian Party of Japan) before World War II. After the war, he was elected to the Diet's Lower House as a member of the Japan Socialist Party, rising to Vice-Speaker of the Lower House. *Nihon kindai bungaku daijiten*, Nihon kindai bungakkan, ed. (Tokyo, 1977–1978), II, 274.

19. "Nihon dasshutsu ki," *Zenshū*, XIII, 17–20. Although Ōsugi describes his trip to Shanghai, many of the details were censored, presumably to prevent other radicals from establishing subversive contacts abroad in a similar manner; see pp. 3–31; and Akiyama Kiyoshi, *Nihon no hangyaku shisō*, p. 92.

20. Kondō Kenji, *Ichi museifushugisha no kaisō*, pp. 23–24, and *Zenshū* XIII, 13. The handbill's text can be found in "Sengen—*Seishinkai* sōgi," *Zenshū*, VI, 178–181.

21. "Nihon dasshutsu ki," *Zenshū*, XIII, 9.

22. Akiyama Kiyoshi, *Nihon no hangyaku shisō*, p. 51; and Moriyama Shigeo, "Ōsugi Sakae—erosu-teki anakizumu," *Bungaku*, 42. 6: 64 (June 1974).

23. Most sources only name Ōsugi, Ch'en, and Yu, but Yi is identified by Scalapino and Lee; *Communism in Korea*, I, 29. Ōsugi labels the Comintern representative "T," but other sources label him Cherin (a transliteration from Japanese); see Eguchi Kan, "Ōsugi Sakae no seikatsu to shisō," p. 407, and Ōsawa Masamichi, *Ōsugi Sakae kenkyū*, p. 292. Scalapino and Lee, *Communism in Korea*, 1, 29, identify him as Grigori Voitinsky (1893–1953), a member of the Comintern's Far Eastern section and frequently in China from 1920 to 1927, when he left the Comintern

following the end of the alliance between China's Kuomintang (Nationalist Party) and the Chinese Communist Party.

24. Scalapino and Lee, *Communism in Korea*, I, 18, n. 30.

25. "Nihon dasshutsu ki," *Zenshū*, XIII, 26.

26. Ibid., XIII, 27-28. Ōsugi had learned Esperanto, Italian, German, and Russian in prison before 1911 and French before that. I do not know when he learned the English in which he held this conversation.

27. Akiyama Kiyoshi, *Nihon no hangyaku shisō*, pp. 87-88. In his "Ōsugi Sakae to ana-boru ronsō," *Chūō kōron* 80. 6: 360 (June 1965), he states that there were only 28 members on the board. See also Tada Michitarō, "Ōsugi Sakae," p. 384.

28. Ōsawa Masamichi, *Ōsugi Sakae kenkyū*, p. 294.

29. Akiyama Kiyoshi, *Nihon no hangyaku shisō*, p. 89.

30. "Nihon dasshutsu ki," *Zenshū*, XIII, 27-29.

31. "Sobieto seifu to museifushugisha," *Zenshū*, VII, 10. Beckmann and Okubo Genji, *The Japanese Communist Party*, p. 31, write that Ōsugi became extremely critical of Marxism-Leninism and the Japanese bolsheviks in the earlier, second *Rōdō undō*, but have mistaken the second for the third journal of that name.

32. "Roshia ni okeru museifushugisha," *Zenshū*, VII, 11-21. Lenin's New Economic Policy (NEP) was approved March 15, 1921, at the Tenth Party Congress. This policy established essentially capitalistic incentives in hopes of increasing faltering agricultural production and insuring the loyalty of the peasantry. The policy was eventually modified and applied to industrial production also. See Ian Grey, *The First Fifty Years: Soviet Russia, 1917-1967* (New York, 1967), pp. 181-195, for a brief survey of the NEP and its period.

33. "Sobieto seifu museifushugisha o jūsatsu su," *Zenshū*, VII, 22-28; "Roshia no museifushugi undō," *Zenshū*, VII, 130-153; "Kuropotokin no sōshiki," *Zenshū*, VII, 5-7; "Kuropotokin o omou—Borushebiki kakumei no shinsō," *Zenshū*, VII, 32-50; and "Kakumei no uragirimono," *Zenshū*, VII, 51-58.

34. "Kuropotokin o omou—Buroshebiki kakumei no shinsō," *Zenshū*, VII, 50.

35. Beckmann and Okubo Genji, *The Japanese Communist Party*, p. 40.

36. See Akiyama Kiyoshi, "Ōsugi Sakae to ana-boru ronsō," pp. 358-366, for a brief description. Komatsu Ryūji, "Taishō-Shōwa shoki ni okeru jiyū rengō shugi rōdō undō to kikan shishi," *Rōdō undō shi kenkyū* 33: 1-14 (September 1962), describes that portion of the labor movement that preferred a decentralized national union organization with local autonomy and lists periodical publications supporting that position.

37. Ōsawa Masamichi, *Ōsugi Sakae kenkyū*, pp. 274-275; and *Nihon no shisōka*, p. 284.

38. Komatsu Ryūji, "Nihon rōdō kumiai sōrengō undō o megutte—ana-boru ronsō no imi suru mono," Part I, *Mita gakkai zasshi* 65. 4: 66–67 (April 1972); and Beckmann and Okubo Genji, *The Japanese Communist Party*, p. 46.
39. "Torotsukii no kyōdō sensen ron," *Zenshū*, VI, 108–114.
40. "Naze shinkōchū no kakumei o yōgo shinai no ka," *Zenshū*, VII, 73.
41. "Borushebiki yonju hachi teura omote," *Zenshū*, VI, 115–126, and "Kumiai teikokushugi," *Zenshū*, VI, 127–140.
42. Most of the charges are a matter of looking at the facts from a slightly different position from Ōsugi's view. For example, with respect to the seating of delegates at the Osaka meeting, what one side considered to be obstructionism was, according to the other side, simply a matter of using the rules of parliamentary procedure to one's advantage. The charges of bribery and profligacy with the Comintern funds were more serious. The bribery charge stemmed from the ¥300 given to Ōsugi at his request by Gotō Shimpei; see Tada Michitarō, "Ōsugi Sakae," p. 325. The money given to Ōsugi by the Comintern was apparently received with the understanding on Ōsugi's part that it would be used for both the new journal and for his own living expenses, since he had no other income at the time. Given Ōsugi's casual attitude toward money and borrowing in general, some of the money may have been invested in good food and wine.
43. See Ōsawa Masamichi, *Ōsugi Sakae kenkyū*, pp. 7–26.
44. "Sei no kakujū," *Zenshū*, II, 31. See also "Sei no sōzō," *Zenshū*, II, 53–62.

10. ŌSUGI IN EUROPE

1. "Nihon dasshutsu ki," *Zenshū*, XIII, 3–4, 7.
2. Arishima Takeo, novelist and a founding member of the Shirakaba (White Birch) literary group, was a socialist sympathizer. He committed suicide on June 9, 1923, just as Ōsugi was returning from France. See Tatsuo Arima, *The Failure of Freedom: A Portrait of Modern Japanese Intellectuals* (Cambridge, Mass., 1969), pp. 99–127 on the Shirakaba group and pp. 128–151 on Arishima.
3. Akiyama Kiyoshi, *Nihon no hangyaku shisō*, p. 109. Other sources add some confusion. Furuya Tsunamasa, "Ōsugi Sakae," p. 117, states that Arishima produced ¥1,500 and adds that it was once rumored that Gotō Shimpei put up the money, forcing Gotō to deny it in a Diet session while serving as Home Minister. Tadamiya Eitarō, "Ōsugi Sakae: sono gekiteki na san-jū-ku-nen," p; 250, says Ōsugi procured another ¥1,000 from a moneylender's son and explains that Gotō had to admit to providing Ōsugi ¥300 seven years earlier to finance *Bummei hihyō*. Yet another source, Yatsugi Kazuo, "Kantō daishinsai to Ōsugi Sakae no shūhen,"

Ekonomisuto 49. 43: 105 (October 12, 1971), truly confuses matters by stating that Gotō gave Ōsugi a letter to deliver to Joffe, the Comintern representative in Peking, on his way to France, but there is no other evidence to support this claim.

4. "Nihon dasshutsu ki," *Zenshū,* XIII, 9–15.
5. Robert A. Scalapino and George T. Yu, *The Chinese Anarchist Movement* (Berkeley, 1961), make no mention of the "F.A.," Ching Mei-chin, or Cheng Meng-hsien. Scalapino and Yu deal mainly with anarchists who went to France or were associated with those who did: presumably Ching and Cheng were not of this group.
6. Had Ōsugi received a little classical education, he might have avoided a very silly mistake. When he was in Shanghai, he used the same surname T'ang and added the given name Shih-min for his pseudonym, at the suggestion of a Korean contact. Since no one in the hotel management could read, there was no problem. In fact, he spoke with the hotel employees in English and was assumed to be half-English. When a member of the Kuomintang came to see him, he inquired if there were a Japanese or a Japanese-looking Chinese in the hotel and was told no. He then took a quick look at the hotel register and identified Ōsugi's pseudonym at a glance. Later, he explained to Ōsugi that he was using the name of the founder of the famous T'ang dynasty (618–907), which only an ignorant foreigner would do. "Nihon dasshutsu ki," *Zenshū,* XIII, 33–35. Li Yuan was the first T'ang emperor, but abdicated in favor of his son, Li Shih-min in 626 after eight years of domination by Shih-min, the real founder of the dynasty. As Sakai Toshihiko had put it, "You cannot say [Ōsugi's] education is wide ... sometimes he writes unexpected rubbish." Sakai Toshihiko, "Ōsugi to Arahata," p. 13.
7. See Kondō Kenji, *Ichi museifushugisha no kaisō,* p. 29; and Akiyama Kiyoshi, *Nihon no hangyaku shisō,* pp. 110–111 on Ōsugi's leaving Japan.
8. "Nihon dasshutsu ki," *Zenshū,* XIII, 74. In an earlier passage, written while he was in France in April and published in July, Ōsugi coyly declined to reveal the details of his trip, only mentioning departure on "a certain day of a certain month" on "a certain ship of a certain nation." Ibid., XIII, 40. He gave the exact details only when writing on August 10 after he had returned to Tokyo. Ōsugi's hope of confusing the police apparently succeeded: while in Shanghai, he recalled that Japanese newspapers speculated that he had gone to Russia, to Europe through Hong Kong, or to a hot spring in Nagano Prefecture. Ibid., XIII, 39.
9. Ibid., XIII, 74, 75–76.
10. Hayashi Shizue, "Furansu ni okeru Ōsugi no seikatsu," in *Mikan Ōsugi Sakae ikō,* Yasutani Kan'ichi, ed. (Tokyo, 1937), p. 311.
11. Akiyama Kiyoshi, *Nihon no hangyaku shisō,* p. 109.

12. Hayashi Shizue, "Furansu ni okeru Ōsugi Sakae no seikatsu," p. 323. See David Caute, *Communism and the French Intellectuals, 1914–1960* (New York, 1964), pp. 73–76 on France and Barbusse.
13. Akiyama Kiyoshi, *Nihon no hangyaku shisō*, p. 112–113.
14. Hayashi Shizue, "Furansu ni okeru Ōsugi Sakae no seikatsu," p. 303.
15. His first hotel cost 100 francs a month (¥12.50) compared with one-half yen per day in Tokyo's working-class slums. "Nihon dasshutsu ki," *Zenshū*, XIII, 44.
16. Ibid., XIII, 47–48.
17. Ibid., XIII, 48, 49–50.
18. Hayashi Shizue, "Furansu ni okeru Ōsugi Sakae no seikatsu," p. 298.
19. Kondō Kenji, *Ichi museifushugisha no kaisō*, p. 36.
20. "Nihon dasshutsu ki," *Zenshū*, XIII, 55–61.
21. Sacco and Venzetti were arrested for the April 15, 1920, payroll robbery in South Braintree, Massachusetts, in which two men were killed. Their first chief counsel, Fred Moore, turned their case into a national and international cause when the trial began on May 31, 1921. The two defendants were finally sentenced to death and executed in 1927. See Corinne Jacker, *The Black Flag of Anarchy: Antistatism in the United States* (New York, 1968), pp. 150–171. The extent to which Moore succeeded in creating a cause can be seen in Ōsugi's comment about "trying to sentence Sacco and Venzetti to death." "Nihon dasshutsu ki," *Zenshū*, XIII, 84.
22. Ibid., XIII, 83–88.
23. Ōsugi claimed that two police officials, one from the Home Ministry and one from Hyogo prefecture (from where he had departed Japan) had been dispatched to Europe to find him. "Nihon dasshutsu ki," *Zenshū*, XIII, 90–93.
24. Ibid., XIII, 64, 109, 111–112. *The New York Times* reported the sentencing of "Sakahe Osugi" following his arrest at the Communist meeting, May 25, 1923, p. 23, col. 1. The *Times* of London said before the trial, "A Japanese journalist arrested for obstructing the police at a Communist meeting in Paris is to be deported from France," May 5, 1923, p. 11, col. 7.
25. Caute, *French Intellectuals*, p. 358.
26. "Nihon dasshutsu ki," *Zenshū*, XIII, 149–150.
27. Ibid., XIII, 120–123. Furuya Tasunamasa, "Ōsugi Sakae," p. 119, provides Sugimura's full name. Sugimura (1884–1939) was the eldest son of Sugimura Fukashi (1848–1906), an official of the Foreign Ministry who became Ambassador to Brazil. After graduating from the Law Faculty of Tokyo Imperial University in political science in 1908, Yōtarō too joined the Foreign Ministry. He was in France from 1923 to 1926 and became Ambassador to Switzerland (1933), Italy (1934), and France (1937).

28. "Nihon dasshutsu ki," *Zenshū*, XIII, 123–126. Presumably, the "circumstances" were strictly private matters, since he never specified what they were.

29. A woman of about fifty told me in 1974 that she knew the name of Ōsugi in two connections: he had been involved in some kind of odd sex scandal and he was the translator of some fabulous volumes on insects that she and her friends grew up reading.

30. Hayashi Shizue, "Furansu ni okeru Ōsugi Sakae no seikatsu," p. 336, 369.

31. Katō Kazuo (1887–1951) was a poet and a critic active in the socialist movement. He became involved in the debate over "people's art," advocating an independent people's art based on Tolstoian humanism and published *Minshū geijutsu ron* (On the people's art) in 1919. His primary anarchist tendency showed in three journals in which he was the main figure: *Kagaku to bungei* (Science and the literary arts), *Rōdō bungaku* (Workers' literature), and *Jiyūnin* (Libertarian), all published in the late 1910s.

32. Kondō Kenji, writing in "Shoka no Ōsugi kan," *Mikan Ōsugi Sakae ikō*, Yasutani Kan'ichi, ed. (Tokyo, 1937), p. 498.

33. "Nihon dasshutsu ki," *Zenshū*, XIII, 126.

34. "Roshia no museifushugi undō," *Zenshū*, VII, 130–153.

35. Alexander Berkman (1870–1936) was born in Russia and became strongly anarchist after moving to America in 1888. He served a prison term for shooting Henry Clay Frick, manager of Carnegie Steel, and later was deported to Russia in 1919. He soon became disillusioned with the Bolshevik methods and left in 1921, finally settling in France until his death by suicide after illness. See Paul Arvich's thumbnail introduction in Alexander Berkman, *What is Communist Anarchism?* (New York, 1972), pp. v–xiv.

36. "Roshia no museifushugi undō," *Zenshū*, VII, 136–140.

37. Ōsugi noted at one point that Makhno was a former schoolteacher. In fact, the uneducated Makhno was frequently identified as a teacher by mistake because he was so labeled on a false passport issued to him by the Soviet government when he was traveling from Moscow to the Ukraine in 1918. See Michael Palij, *The Anarchism of Nestor Makhno, 1918–1921* (Seattle and London, 1976), p. 95.

38. "Museifushugi shōgun," *Zenshū*, VII, 155.

39. See Palij, *The Anarchism of Nestor Makhno*, pp. 3–56, for a summary of the events and the position of the Ukrainian peasants at this time.

40. Ibid., p. 88, quoting Makhno.

41. Ibid., pp. 104–122.

42. The preceding material on Makhno and his movement has been drawn

from Palij, *The Anarchism of Nestor Makhno;* Victor Peters, *Nestor Makhno: The Life of an Anarchist* (Winnipeg, 1970); and Voline, pseud. V. M. Eichenbaum, *The Unknown Revolution (Kronstadt, 1921; Ukraine, 1918–21)*, Holley Cantine, trans. (New York, 1955). Of these Palij is the most comprehensive, deftly fitting Makhno into his time and place. It suffers, though, from ignoring the man's personal failings (alcoholism, abuse of women, inability to control his troops, and a liking for summary executions) which contributed to his charisma and to his repulsiveness. Peters includes such information in a better-balanced biography that, unfortunately, hesitates to deal extensively with the wider political and military environments. Voline tends to polemic diatribes against the Bolsheviks and fails to give a clear picture of the history of the period. Paul Arvich, *The Russian Anarchists* (Princeton, 1967), touches on Makhno only briefly in describing the entire anarchist movement.

43. "Museifushugi shōgun," *Zenshū*, VII, 156.
44. Ibid., VII, 156.
45. Ibid., VII, 167. Palij reached a similar conclusion fifty-three years after Ōsugi wrote this passage: "Paradoxically, although Makhno's struggle against the Bolsheviks may have prolonged the Russian Civil War, by his vital role in the defeat of the forces of Denikin and Wrangel he contributed to the triumph of bolshevism." Palij, *The Anarchism of Nestor Makhno*, p. 252.
46. "Museifushugi shōgun," *Zenshū*, VII, 157.
47. Ibid., VII, 159.
48. Ibid., VII, 152.

11. THE KANTŌ GREAT EARTHQUAKE AND ŌSUGI'S MURDER

1. See Duus and Okimoto, "Fascism and the History of Pre-war Japan."
2. Many of the details of the earthquake presented here are drawn from Japan, Home Office, The Bureau of Social Affairs, comp., *The Great Earthquake of 1923 in Japan* (Tokyo, 1926). Percentage figures that follow have been rounded off.
3. Yasunari Jirō, "Katami no haizara o mae ni," *Kaizō*, 4. 11: 98 (November 1923).
4. See Kyō Tokusō and Kim Jōtō, eds., *Kantō daishinsai to Chōsenjin, Gendaishi shiryō*, Vol. 6 (Tokyo, 1963) for a collection of materials about the experiences of Koreans during the earthquake.
5. Japan, Home Office, *The Great Earthquake*, pp. 558–559.
6. Matsushita Yoshio, *Bōdō chinatsu shi* (Tokyo, 1977), p. 204. A facsimile of the censored newspaper article can be found in *Shimbun shūroku*

Taishō shi (Tokyo, 1978), XI, 384–385, which reproduces the *Kyūshū nippō* (Kyushu daily gazette) article of September 21.

7. See Tadamiya Eitarō, "Ōsugi Sakae: sono gekiteki na san-jū-ku nen," pp. 246–249.
8. Furuya Tsunamasa, "Ōsugi Sakae," p. 120, and the *New York Times*, September 26, 1923, p. 3, col. 2.
9. Kondō Kenji, *Ichi museifushugisha no kaisō*, p. 39.
10. *Asahi shimbun*, August 26, 1976, p. 22, col. 1.
11. Eguchi Kan, "Ōsugi Sakae no seikatsu to shisō," p. 408. One contemporary writer, Mizuno Kōtoku, "Ōsugi satsugai to gunjin shisō," *Chūō kōron* 38. 12: 65–70 (November 1923), regretted Ōsugi's death because such incidents tended to destroy the faith of the citizenry in the army, whose duty it was to lead both the state and society.
12. Furuya Tsunamasa, "Ōsugi Sakae," p. 120.
13. Tadamiya Eitarō, "Ōsugi Sakae: sono gekiteki na san-jū-ku nen," p. 250.
14. See Notehelfer, *Kōtoku Shūsui*, for details on Kōtoku's arrest and trial.

Bibliography

In addition to a recent edition of Ōsugi's writings, substantial biographical research on Ōsugi Sakae in Japanese has been done mainly by two men, Akiyama Kiyoshi and Ōsawa Masamichi. Akiyama is a poet and anarchist who briefly knew Ōsugi when he was a young man. His studies emphasize the spiritual side of Ōsugi, devoting much attention to his theory of life. Akiyama argues that the roots of Ōsugi's anarchism can be traced to his personality as a young boy, even before he came into contact with the ideas of anarchism. According to this approach, Ōsugi's theories of anarchism were the expression of what had always been within him since childhood, not the intellectual constructs of adulthood.

Ōsawa, a much younger man than Akiyama, did not personally know Ōsugi, but he is also an anarchist who works for a major publishing house while doing research on the side. He is most concerned with explaining Ōsugi's attempt to build a new philosophy of knowledge and basis for anarchist action by combining philosophy, literature, and science. This approach makes Ōsugi appear too rational and scientific and minimizes the irrational bases of his thought and life. The studies of both men suffer to a degree because the authors are themselves anarchists espousing their leader's cause, albeit in the subdued manner befitting disinterested scholarship. Nevertheless, there is a tendency for both men to give Ōsugi's every theory and act greater approval than they may deserve.

In English there are only three short studies of Ōsugi Sakae in addition to my own published work. Tatsuo Arima in *The Failure of Freedom* offers a chapter on anarchism dealing primarily with Ōsugi, in which he faults him as a negative influence on the establishment of a working democratic political system owing to his emphasis on violence and destructiveness. Arima's study prevents a fair assessment of Ōsugi, however, because he is solely interested in what aided or eroded the political system of that period.

Bradford L. Simcock devotes his study, "The Anarcho-syndicalist Thought and Activity of Ōsugi Sakae, 1885–1923," to explaining the intimate relationship between Ōsugi's opinions on the labor movement and his philosophy of life—how his activities and labor theory are attempts to force his ideal of individual inner growth to assume an external reality. Being only a brief survey of Ōsugi's entire life and his writings, it is necessarily oversimplified.

Stephen S. Large takes an approach similar to Simcock's in "The Romance of Revolution in Japanese Anarchism and Communism during the Taishō Period," but deals only with one episode in Ōsugi's life—his love affair. He too points out how Ōsugi's life and theory were echoes of each other. Even though Ōsugi found it extremely difficult to make his life conform to his theory of the expansion of life, he nevertheless refused to abandon the theory or the goal of unifying theory and reality.

WORKS CITED

Akiyama Kiyoshi 秋山清. "Ōsugi Sakae to bungaku" 大杉栄と文学 (Ōsugi Sakae and literature), *Ronsō* 論争 (Disputations) 2.7.:132–143 (December 1960).

———. *Nihon no hangyaku shisō—museifushugi undō shōshi* 日本の反逆思想－無政府主義運動小史(Rebellious thought in Japan—A brief history of the anarchist movement). Tokyo, Gendai shichō sha, 1960.

———. "Ōsugi Sakae to ana-boru ronsō" 大杉栄とアナボル論争(Ōsugi Sakae and the anarchist-bolshevik debate), *Chūō kōron* 中央公論(Central review) 80.6:358–363 (June 1965).

———. "Sei to jiyū ni tsuite" 性と自由について (Regarding sex and freedom), *Shisō no kagaku* 思想の科学 (The science of thought) 123:26–34 (November 1971).

———. "Hyōden—Ōsugi Sakae" 評伝 －大杉栄 (A critical biography: Ōsugi Sakae), *Shisō no kagaku* 思想の科学 (The science of thought) 49:75–83 (July 1975).

Andrew, Nancy. "The Seitōsha: An Early Japanese Women's Organization, 1911–1916." *Papers on Japan,* Volume 5. Harvard University, East Asian Research Center, 1972.

Arahata Kanson荒畑寒村. *Shimpan Kanson jiden* 新版寒村自伝 (Autobiography of Kanson: new edition). 2 vols. Tokyo, Chikuma shobō, 1965.

Arima, Tatsuo. *The Failure of Freedom: A Portrait of Modern Japanese Intellectuals.* Cambridge, Harvard University Press, 1969.

Arvich, Paul. *The Russian Anarchists.* Princeton, Princeton University Press, 1967.

*Asahi shimbun*朝日新聞 (Asahi news). August 26, 1976.

Asukai Masamichi 飛鳥井雅道. "Roshia kakumei to Ōsugi Sakae" ロシヤ

革命と大杉栄 (The Russian Revolution and Ōsugi Sakae). *Gendai no riron* 現代の理論 (Theories of modernity) 4.10:34–42 (October 1967).

Beckmann, George M., and Okubo Genji. *The Japanese Communist Party: 1922–1945*. Stanford, Stanford University Press, 1969.

Berkman, Alexander. *What is Communist Anarchism?* New York, Dover, 1972.

Bergson, Henri. *Time and Free Will: An Essay on the Immediate Data of Consciousness*. Translated by F. L. Pogson. New York, Macmillan, 1910.

———. *Creative Evolution*. Translated by Arthur Mitchel. New York, Holt, 1911.

———. *Matter and Memory*. Translated by Nancy Margaret Paul and W. Scott Palmer. New York, Macmillan, 1911.

Bernal, Martin. "The Triumph of Anarchism over Marxism, 1906–1907," in *China in Revolution: The First Phase, 1900–1913*. Edited by Mary Wright. New Haven, Yale University Press, 1968.

Bernstein, Gail Lee. *Japanese Marxist: A Portrait of Kawakami Hajime, 1879–1946*. Cambridge, Harvard University Press, 1976.

———. "The Russian Revolution, the Early Japanese Socialists, and the Problem of Dogmatism," *Studies in Comparative Communism* 9.4:327–348 (winter 1976).

Caute, David. *Communism and the French Intellectuals, 1914–1960*. New York, Macmillan, 1964.

Duus, Peter, and Daniel I. Okimoto. "Fascism and the History of Pre-war Japan: The Failure of a Concept," *Journal of Asian Studies* 39.1:65–76 (November 1979).

Eguchi Kan 江口渙. "Ōsugi Sakae no seikatsu to shisō" 大杉栄の生活と思想 (The life and thought of Ōsugi Sakae), in *Gendai Nihon bungaku zenshū* 現代日本文学全集 (The collected works of modern Japanese literature), Vol. LII. Tokyo, Chikuma shobō, 1957.

Funabashi Shigeru 舟橋茂. "Nakidashita Ōsugi Sakae" 泣き出した大杉栄 (Ōsugi Sakae, who burst out crying), in *Meiyōkōshi* 名幼校史 (A history of the Nagoya Kadet School). Tokyo, Meiyōkai, 1974.

Furuya Tsunamasa 古谷綱正. "Kindai bijin den—4—Kamichika Ichiko" 近代美人伝 – 神近市子 (Biographies of beautiful women—4—Kamichika Ichiko), *Jimbutsu ōrai* 人物往来 (Writings on personages) 3.4:132–139 (April 1954).

————. "Ōsugi Sakae"大杉栄 , *Jimbutsu ōrai* 人物往来 (Writings on personages) 4.7:110–120 (July 1955).

————. *Ittō josei jūnin no ai* 一等女性十人の愛 (The loves of ten superlative women). Tokyo, Tōzai bummei sha, 1955.

Fussell, Paul. *The Great War and Modern Memory.* New York and London, Oxford University Press, 1975.

Grey, Ian. *The First Fifty Years: Soviet Russia, 1917–1967.* New York, Coward-McCann, 1967.

Hackett, Roger F. *Yamagata Aritomo in the Rise of Modern Japan, 1838–1922.* Cambridge, Harvard University Press, 1971.

Hayashi Shizue林佳衛 . "Furansu kangoku oyobi hōtei no Ōsugi Sakae" 仏蘭西監獄及法廷の大杉栄(Ōsugi Sakae in French prisons and courts), *Kaizō* 改造 (Reconstruction) 6.6:94–135 (June 1924).

————. "Furansu ni okeru Ōsugi no seikatsu" フランスに於ける大杉の 生活 (Ōsugi's life in France), in *Mikan Ōsugi Sakae ikō* 未刊大杉栄遺 稿(The unpublished manuscripts of Ōsugi Sakae). Edited by Yasutani Kan'ichi 安谷寛一 . Tokyo, Kinseidō, 1937.

Heimin shimbun 平民新聞 (Commoners' newspaper) 1.3:3 (December 1914).

Hemmi Kichizō 逸見吉三 . "Nihon e kita Bakūnin" 日本へ来たバクー ニン. (Bakunin when he came to Japan), *Gendai no me* 現代の眼 (The eye of our times) 12.7:182–191 (July 1971).

————. "'Shi' to 'shi' to 'shi'"死」と志」と詩」 ("Death" and "will" and "poetry"), *Gendai no me* 現代の眼 (The eye of our times) 12.9:224–233 (September 1971); 12.10:224–233 (October 1971); 12.11:232–241 (November 1971).

Hori Yasuko 堀保子 . "Ōsugi to wakareru made" 大杉と別れるまで (Until separating from Ōsugi), *Chūō kōron* 中央公論 (The central review, March 1917). Reprinted in *Ōsugi Sakae hiroku* 大杉栄秘録 (Memoirs of Ōsugi Sakae). Edited by Ōsugi Sakae kenkyū kai, 大杉栄研究 会 . Tokyo, Kokushoku sensen sha, 1976.

————. "Shoka no Ōsugi kan" 諸家の大杉観 (The views of many people on Ōsugi) in *Mikan Ōsugi Sakae ikō* 未刊大杉栄遺稿 (The unpublished manuscripts of Ōsugi Sakae). Edited by Yasutani Kan'ichi 安谷寛 一. Tokyo, Kinseidō, 1937.

Horowitz, Irving Louis. *Radicalism and the Revolt Against Reason: The Social Theories of Georges Sorel.* New York, Humanities Press, 1961.

Hosokawa Karoku 細川嘉六 , ed. *Nihon shakaishugi bunken kaisetsu* 日本社会 主義文献解説 (A bibliography and commentary on Japanese socialism). Tokyo, Ōtsuki shoten, 1958.

Ide Fumiko 井手文子 . *"Seitō" no onna-tachi* 「青鞜」の女たち (The women of Bluestockings). Tokyo, Kaien shobō, 1975.

Itō Noe 伊藤野枝.*"'Bekkyo' ni tsuite"* 別居」について (On "separation"), in *Itō Noe zenshū* 伊藤野枝全集 (The collected works of Itō Noe), Volume II. Tokyo, Gakugei shorin, 1970. First published September 1916, n.p.

———. *"Seitō o hikitsugu ni tsuite"* 青鞜を引き継ぐについて (On taking over the *Seitō*), in *Itō Noe zenshū*, Volume II. Tokyo, Gakugei shorin, 1970. Originally published in *Seitō* 青鞜 (Bluestockings, March 1917).

———. *"Jiyū ishi ni yoru kekkon no hametsu"* 自由意志による結婚の破滅 (The ruin of a marriage based on free will), in *Itō Noe zenshū*, Volume II. Tokyo, Gakugei shorin, 1970. Originally published in *Fujin kōron* 婦人公論 (Women's review, September 1917).

———. *"Kōkin sareru made"* 拘禁されるまで (Until he is interned), in *Itō Noe zenshū*, Volume II. Tokyo, Gakugei shorin, 1970. First published August 1919, n.p.

———. *"Aru otoko no daraku"* 或る男の堕落 (The depravity of a man), in *Itō Noe zenshū*, Volume I. Tokyo, Gakugei shorin, 1970. First published January 1923, n.p.

———. *Itō Noe zenshū* 伊藤野枝全集 (The collected works of Itō Noe). 2 vols. Tokyo, Gakugei shorin, 1970.

Iwasaki Kureo 岩崎呉夫 . *Hi no onna—Itō Noe den* 火の女 －伊藤野枝伝 (Fiery woman—A biography of Itō Noe). Tokyo, Jiyū kokumin sha, 1971.

Jacker, Corinne. *The Black Flag of Anarchism: Antistatism in the United States.* New York, Scribner's, 1968.

Japan, Home Office, The Bureau of Social Affairs, comp. *The Great Earthquake of 1923 in Japan.* Tokyo, 1926.

Japan, Naikaku, Tōkei-kyoku 内閣統計司 . *Dai Nihon teikoku tōkei nenkan* 大日本帝国統計年鑑 (Imperial Japan statistical yearbook) XXVII (1908); XLV (1926).

Kamichika Ichiko 神近市子. *"Ōsugi Sakae"* 大杉栄 , *Rōdō hyōron* 労働評論 (Labor review) 3.1:27 (January 1948).

———. *"Watakushi no rirekisho"* 私の履歴書 (My life history), in *Watakushi no rirekisho*, Volume XXIII. Tokyo, Nihon keizai shimbun sha, 1965.

———. *Kamichika Ichiko jiden—waga ai, waga tatakai* 神近市子自伝 －わが愛わが闘い (Autobiography of Kamichika Ichiko: My loves, my struggles). Tokyo, Kōdansha, 1972.

Kawakami Tamio 河上民雄. *"Ōsugi Sakae ni tsuite"* 大杉栄について

(About Ōsugi Sakae), *Rōdō undō shi kenkyū* 労働運動史研究(Studies on the history of the labor movement) 37:36–42 (July 1963).

Kindai shisō 近代思想 (Modern thought) 1.1:21 (October 1912); 2.6 (March 1913); 2.2:25 (November 1913); 2.3:31 (December 1913); 2.4:40 (January 1914); 2.5:26 (February 1914); 2.8:32 (May 1914); 2.9:30–31 (June 1914).

Komatsu Ryūji 小松隆二. "Ashio kōdoku jiken to Ōsugi Sakae" 足尾鉱毒 事件と大杉栄 (The Ashio Mine Incident and Ōsugi Sakae), *Jiyū shisō kenkyū* 自由思想研究 (Studies on libertarian thought) 2:7–12 (October 1960).

———. *"Kindai shisō* sōkan zengo"「近代思想」創刊前後(Around the time of the founding of *Kindai shisō*), *Jiyū shisō kenkyū* 自由思想研究 (Studies on libertarian thought) 3:14–16 (January 1961).

———. "Taishō-Shōwa shoki ni okeru jiyū rengō shugi rōdō undō to kikan shishi" 大正昭和初期における自由連合主義・労働運動と機関 紙誌 (The syndicalist labor movement and its newspapers and journals in the Taishō and early Shōwa periods), *Rōdō undō shi kenkyū* 労働運動史 研究 (Studies on the history of the labor movement) 33:1–14 (September 1962); 35:46–48 (March 1963).

———. "Kaisetsu" 解説 (Explanation), in *Ōsugi Sakae zenshū* 大杉栄 全集 (The collected works of Ōsugi Sakae). Edited by Ōsawa Masamichi 大沢正道 and others. Volume VI. Tokyo, Gendai shichō, 1963.

———. "Nihon rōdō kumiai sōrengō undō o megutte— ana-boru ronsō no imi suru mono" 日本労働組合総・連合運動をめぐって—アナ・ボル論争 の意・味するもの (1922 movement for General Federation of Japanese Labor Unions: Historical Significance of Conflict of "Anarchism vs. Bolshevism"). *Mita gakkai zasshi* 三田学会雑誌 (Journal of the Mita Academy) 65.4:66–74 (April 1972); 65.5:66–73 (May 1972).

Kondō Kenji 近藤憲二. "Shoka no Ōsugi kan" 諸家の大杉観 (The views of many people on Ōsugi), in *Mikan Ōsugi Sakae ikō* 未刊大杉栄遺 稿(The unpublished manuscripts of Ōsugi Sakae). Edited by Yasutani Kan'ichi 安谷寛一. Tokyo, Kinseidō, 1937.

———. Nihon saisho no Roshia kakumei kinen kai" 日本最初のロシヤ革命 記念会 (Japan's first meeting to commemorate the Russian Revolution), *Kurohata* 黒旗 (Black flag) No. 24 (December 1, 1957).

———. *Ichi museifushugisha no kaisō* 一無政府主義者の回想. (Memoirs of an Anarchist). Tokyo, Heibonsha, 1966.

Kropotkin, Peter. *The Conquest of Bread*. New York, Vanguard, 1906.

Kyō Tokusō 姜徳祖 and Kim Jōtō 琴東洞, eds. *Kantō daishinsai to Chōsenjin* 関東大震災と朝鮮人 (The Great Kantō Earthquake and the Koreans), *Gendaishi shiryō* 現代史資料(Materials on modern history), Volume 6. Tokyo, Misuzu shobō, 1963.

Large, Stephen S. "The Romance of Revolution in Japanese Anarchism and Communism during the Taishō Period," *Modern Asian Studies* 11.3:441–467 (July 1977).

Marx, Karl, and Friedrich Engels. *Basic Writings on Politics and Philosophy.* Edited by Louis S. Feuer. Garden City, Anchor, 1959.

Matsuo Kuninosuke 松尾邧之助. *Nihirisuto—Tsuji Jun no shisō to shōgai* ニヒリスト －辻潤の思想と生涯 (Nihilist—The thought and life of Tsuji Jun). Tokyo, Orion, 1967.

Matsushita Yoshio 松下芳男. "Ōsugi Sakae no kazoku to yōnen gakkō jidai" 大杉栄の家族と幼年学校時代 (Ōsugi Sakae's family and Kadet School days), *Jiyū shisō kenkyū* 自由思想研究 (Studies on libertarian thought) 2:19–25 (October 1960).

———. *Meiji no guntai* 明治の軍隊 (The Meiji military). Tokyo, Shibundō, 1963.

———. *Bōdō chin'atsu shi* 暴動鎮圧史 (A History of the suppression of rebellion). Tokyo, Kashiwa shobō, 1977.

Matsushita Yoshio and Izu Kimio 松下芳男・伊豆公夫. *Nihon gunji hattatsu shi* 日本軍事発達史 (A history of the development of Japanese military affairs). Tokyo, Mikasa shobō, 1938.

Miller, Martin A. *Kropotkin.* Chicago, University of Chicago Press, 1976.

Mitani Ta'ichirō 三谷太一郎. "Taishō shakaishugisha no 'seiji kan'—'seiji no hitei' kara 'seijiteki taikō'" 大正社会主義者の「政治観」－「政治の否定」から「政治的対抗」へ (Changing attitudes toward "politics" among the socialists of Taishō Japan: From "Rejection of politics" to "Political confrontation"), in "Nihon no shakaishugi" 日本の社会主義 (Socialism in Japan). *Nenkan seijigaku* 年鑑政治学 (The Annals of political science, 1968).

Miyajima Sukeo 宮島資夫. "Ōsugi Sakae ron" 大杉栄論 (On Ōsugi Sakae), *Kaihō* 解放 (Liberation), 3.5:112–116 (May 1921).

Miyamoto Ken. "Itō Noe and the Bluestockings," *The Japan Interpreter* 10.2:190–204 (autumn 1975).

Mizuno Kōtoku 水野広徳. "Ōsugi satsugai to gunjin shisō" 大杉殺害と軍人思想 (The Murder of Ōsugi Sakae and the military mind), *Chūō kōron* 中央公論 (Central review) 38.12:65–70 (November 1923).

Mizunuma Tatsuo 水沼辰夫. "Ōsugi Sakae to rōdō undō" 大杉栄と労働運動 (Ōsugi Sakae and the labor movement), *Jiyū shisō kenkyū* 自由思想研究 (Studies on libertarian thought) 3:3–7 (December 1960); 4:49–54 (January 1961).

Morinaga Eisaburō 森長永三郎. "Akahata jiken—taigyaku jiken e no taidō" 赤旗事件－大逆事件への胎動 (Red Flag Incident—Moving toward the High Treason Incident), *Hōgaku zeminā* 法学ゼミナー (Law seminar) 209:84–87 (April 1974).

————. *Shidan saiban* 史談裁判 (Historic trials). Tokyo, Nihon hyōron sha, 1966.

Morito Tatsuo 森戸辰夫 . "Ōsugi Sakae-kun no tsuioku" 大杉栄君の追憶 (Recollections of Ōsugi Sakae), *Kaizō* 改造 (Reconstruction) 6.4:41–75 (April 1924).

————. "Ōsugi Sakae chosaku gaihyō" 大杉栄著作概評 (General comments on the works of Ōsugi Sakae). Edited by Yasutani Kan'ichi 安谷寛一 , in *Mikan Ōsugi Sakae ikō* 未刊大杉栄遺稿 (The unpublished manuscripts of Ōsugi Sakae). Tokyo, Kinseidō, 1937.

Moriyama Shigeo 森山重雄 . "Ōsugi Sakae—erosu-teki anakizumu" 大杉栄 —エロス的アナキズム (Ōsugi Sakae—Erotic anarchism), *Bungaku* 文学 (Literature) 42.6:63–77 (June 1974).

New York Times. May 25, 1923, p. 23, col. 1; September 26, 1923, p. 3, col. 2.

Nihon bungaku daijiten 日本文学大辞典 (Dictionary of Japanese literature). Edited by Fujimura Tsukuru 藤村作 . Tokyo, Shinchō sha, 1955.

Nihon jimbutsu bunken mokuroku 日本人物文献目録 (A bibliographic catalogue of Japanese figures). Edited by Hōsei daigaku bungakubu shigaku kenkyūshitsu 法政大学文学部史学研究室 . Tokyo, Heibonsha, 1974.

Nihon kindai bungaku daijiten 日本近代文学大事典 (Dictionary of modern Japanese literature). Edited by Nihon kindai bungakkan 日本近代文学館 . 6 vols. Tokyo, Kōdansha, 1977–1978.

Nihon no shisōka 日本の思想家 (Japanese intellectuals). Tokyo, Asahi shimbun, 1963.

Notehelfer, F. G. *Kōtoku Shūsui: Portrait of a Japanese Radical.* Cambridge, Cambridge University Press, 1971.

————. "Japan's First Pollution Incident," *Journal of Japanese Studies* 1.2: 351–383 (spring 1975).

Okamoto, Shumpei. *The Japanese Oligarchy and the Russo-Japanese War.* New York and London, Columbia University Press, 1970.

Ōsawa Masamichi 大沢雅道. *Ōsugi Sakae kenkyū* 大杉栄研究 (A study of Ōsugi Sakae). Tokyo, Dōseisha, 1968.

————. "Ōsugi Sakae ron" 大杉栄論 (On Ōsugi Sakae), *Shisō no kagaku* 思想の科学 (The science of thought), September 1960, pp. 66–78; October 1960, pp. 88–96; November 1960, pp. 89–96.

Ōsugi Sakae 大杉栄 The following works are included in *Ōsugi Sakae zenshū* (The collected works of Ōsugi Sakae). Edited by Ōsawa Masamichi 大沢雅道 et al. 14. vols. Tokyo, Gendai shichō, 1963. Each is cited by volume number and place of original publication.

"Shakaishugi to aikokushin: 社会主義と愛国心` (Socialism and patriotism), Volume I. *Chokugen* 直言 (Plain speaking) 2.29 through 3.2 (August 20 through September 10, 1905).

"Dōbutsu no ren'ai" 動物の恋愛 (Love among the animals), Volume XIV. *Katei zasshi* 家庭雑誌 (Home Journal) 5.1 (November 1906).

"Shimpei shokun ni atau" 新兵諸君に与ラ (To all the new conscripts), Volume I. *Hikari* 光 (Light) 1.28 (November 1906).

"Yo no sōbō suru jiyū ren'ai" 予の想望する自由恋愛 (The free love I yearn for), Volume XIV. *Katei zasshi* 5.2 (December 1906).

"Kaineko Natsume" 飼猫ナツメ (Natsume, the family cat), Volume XIV. *Katei zasshi* 5.3 (January 1907).

"Seinen ni uttau" 青年に訴ラ (An appeal to youth), Volume I. *Nikkan heimin shimbun* 日刊平民新聞 (Daily commoners' newspaper), Nos. 42, 45–47, 50–56 (March 8–23, 1907).

"Yuiitsusha" 唯一者 (The egotist), Volume III. *Kindai shisō* 近代思想 (Modern thought) 1.3 (December 1912).

"Ōkubo yori" 大久保より (From Ōkubo), Volume XIV. *Kindai shisō* 1.3 (December 1912).

"Shūchi to teisō" 羞恥と貞操 (Shame and chastity), Volume III. *Kindai shisō* 1.6 (March 1913).

"'Jogakusei'" 女学生 (The schoolgirl), Volume III. *Kindai shisō* 1.9 (June 1913).

"Seifuku no jijitsu" 征服の事実 (The reality of conquest), Volume II. *Kindai shisō* 1.9 (June 1913).

"Sei no kakujū" 生の拡充 (The expansion of life), Volume II. *Kindai shisō* 1.10 (July 1913).

"Sei no sōzō" 生の創造 (The creation of life), Volume II. *Kindai shisō* 2.4 (January 1914).

"Ōkubo yori" 大久保より (From Ōkubo), Volume XIV. *Kindai shisō* 2.6 (March 1914).

"Fujin kaihō no higeki" 婦人解放の悲劇 (The tragedy of women's liberation), Volume III. *Kindai shisō* 2.8 (May 1914).

"Ōshū no tairan to shakaishugisha no taido" 欧州の大乱と社会主義者の態度 (The European upheaval and the attitude of the socialists), Volume I. *Daisan teikoku* 第三帝国 (The third empire) No. 7 (August 1914).

"Heiminsha yori" 平民社より (From the Heiminsha), Volume XIV. *Heimin shimbun* 平民新聞 (Commoners' newspaper) No. 4 (January 1915).

"Rōdōsha no shimbun" 労働者の新聞 (The newspaper of the workers), Volume VI. *Heimin shimbun* No. 6 (March 1915).

"Rōdō undō to puragumatizumu" 労働運動とプラグマティズム (The

labor movement and pragmatism), Volume VI. *Kindai shisō* 3.1 (October 1915).

"Dōbutsukai no sōgo fujo" 動物界の相互扶助 (Mutual aid in the animal world), Volume IV. *Shin shōsetsu* 新小説 (The new novel, November 1915).

"Kindai kojinshugi no shosō" 近代個人主義の諸相 (Various aspects of modern individualism), Volume III. *Waseda bungaku* 早稲田文学 (Waseda literature) No. 120 (November 1915).

"Danjo kankei ni tsuite" 男女関係について (On relations between the sexes), Volume III. *Onna no sekai* 女の世界 (The woman's world, June 1916).

"Atarashiki sekai no tame no atarashiki geijutsu" 新しき世界のための新しき芸術 (A new art for a new world), Volume V. *Waseda bungaku* 早稲田文学 No. 131 (October 1916).

"Zakkubaran ni kokuhaku shi yoron ni kotau" ザックバランに告白し世論に答う (Confessing candidly and answering public opinion), Volume III. *Shin nihon* 新日本 (The new Japan) 7.1 (January 1917).

"Bagabondo tamashii" ヴァガボンド魂 (Soul of a vagabond), Volume V. *Shin shōsetsu* (May 1917).

"Kindai bungaku to shin hanzaigaku" 近代文学と新犯罪学 (Modern literature and the new criminology), Volume V. *Shin shōsetsu* (June 1917).

"Minshū geijutsu no gikō" 民衆芸術の技巧 (The art of the people's art), Volume V. *Minshū no geijutsu* 民衆の芸術 (The art of the people, July 1917).

"Jinrui shi jō no dentōshugi" 人類史上の伝統主義 (Traditionalism in the history of man), Volume IV. *Shin shōsetsu* (October 1917).

"Sewa nyōbō" 世話女房 (Helpful wife), Volume XIV. *Onna no sekai* (October 1917).

"Hā shintō na koto da" はあ真当なことだ (Indeed, it is the truth), Volume XIV. *Waseda bungaku* No. 145 (December 1917).

Minshū geijutsu ron 民衆芸術論 (The people's theater), Volume XI. Originally published under the same title. Tokyo, Oranda shobō, 1917.

"Hakkō ken henshūnin kara" 発行兼編集人から (From the publisher and editor), Volume XIV. *Bummei hihyō* 文明批評 (Critique of civilization) No. 1 (January 1918).

"Boku wa seishin ga suki da" 僕は精神が好きだ (I like spirit!), Volume XIV. *Bummei hihyō* No. 2 (February 1918).

"Hakkō ken henshūnin kara" 発行兼編集人から (From the publisher and editor), Volume XIV. *Bummei hihyō* No. 2 (February 1918).

"Shoshinshi teki kanjō" 小紳士的感情 (Petit bourgeois sentiments), Volume VI. *Bummei hihyō* No. 2 (February 1918).

"Gokuchū ki" 獄中記 (Record of imprisonment), Volume XIII. *Shin shōsetsu* (January–February 1919).

"Zoku gokuchū ki" 続獄中記 (Record of imprisonment: continued), Volume XIII. *Shin shōsetsu* (April 1919).

"Bokura no shugi" 僕等の主義 (Our ideology), Volume VI. *Rōdōsha* 労働者 (The worker, August 1919).

"Shikai no naka kara" 死灰の中から (From amidst the ashes), Volume XII. *Shin shōsetsu* (September 1919).

"Kokusai rōdō kaigi" 国際労働会議 (International Labor Conference), Volume VI. The first *Rōdō undō* 労働運動 (The labor movement) No. 1 (October 1919).

"Honshi no tachiba" 本誌の立場 (The standpoint of this journal), Volume XIV. The first *Rōdō undō* No. 1 (October 1919).

"Chishiki kaikyū ni atau" 知識階級に与う (To the intellectual class), Volume VI. The first *Rōdō undō* No. 3 (January 1920).

"Rōdō undō rironka—Kagawa Toyohiko ron (zoku)" 労働運動理論家一賀川豊彦論続 (Labor movement theorist Kagawa Toyohiko [continued]), Volume VI. The first *Rōdō undō* No. 3 (January 1920).

"Rōdō undō to chishiki kaikyū" 労働運動と知識階級 (The labor movement and the intellectual class), Volume VI. The first *Rōdō undō* No. 3. (January 1920).

"Shin chitsujo no sōzō" 新秩序の創造 (The creation of the new order), Volume VI. The first *Rōdō undō* No. 6 (June 1920).

"Shakaiteki risōron" 社会的理想論 (Social idealism), Volume VI. The first *Rōdō undō* No. 6 (June 1920).

"Kumiai undō to kakumei undō" 組合運動と革命運動 (The union movement and the revolutionary movement), Volume VI. The first *Rōdo undō* No. 8 (August 1920).

"Sengen—Seishinkai sōgi" 宣言 —正進会争議 (Proclamation on the Seishinkai dispute), Volume VI. Originally published as a handbill and distributed on October 15, 1920, then published in *Seishin* 正進 (Righteous progress) No. 7 (November 1920).

"Kakumei wa itsu kuru ka" 革命はいつ来るか (When will the revolution come?), Volume VI. The second *Rōdō undō* No. 3 (February 1921).

"Shakai mondai ka geijutsu mondai ka" 社会問題か芸術問題か (A social question or an artistic question?), Volume V. *Bummei hihyō* No. 9 (September 1921).

Jijoden 自叙伝 (Autobiography), Volume XII. *Kaizō* 改造 (Reconstruction, September 1921 through January 1923).

"Rōdō undō to rōdō bungaku" 労働運動と労働文学 (The labor movement and workers' literature), Volume V. *Shinchō* 新潮 (The new tide, October 1921).

Ōsugi Sakae. "Sobieto seifu to museifushugisha" ソヴィエト政府と無政府
主義者 (The Soviet Government and anarchists), Volume VII. The third
Rōdō undō No. 1 (December 1921).

"Roshia ni okeru museifushugisha" ロシアにおける無政府主義者
(Anarchists in Russia), Volume VII. The third *Rōdō undō* Nos. 2 and 3
(February and March 1922).

"Sobieto seifu museifushugisha o jūsatsu su" ソヴィエト政府無政府主義
者を銃殺す (The Soviet government is shooting anarchists), Volume VII. The third *Rōdō undō* No. 4 (April 1922).

"Kuropotokin o omou—Borushebiki kakumei no shinsō" クロポトキンを想.
う—ボルシェヴィキ革命の真相　　(Considering Kropotkin: The truth
of the Bolshevik Revolution), Volume VII. *Kaizō* (July 1922).

"Kakumei no uragirimono" 革命の裏切者 (Betrayers of the revolution), Volume VII. The third *Rōdō undō* No. 6 (August 1922).

"Naze shinkōchū no kakumei o yōgo shinai no ka" なぜ進行中の革命
を擁護しないのか(Why am I not championing the revolution
that is in progress?), Volume VII. The third *Rōdō undō* No. 7 (September
1922).

"Obake o mita hanashi" お化を見た話　(A story about seeing a
spook), Volume II. *Kaizō* (September 1922).

"Torotsukii no kyōdō sensen ron" トロッキーの協同戦線論 (Trot-
sky's united front line), Volume VI. The third *Rōdō undō* No. 7 (September 1922).

"Borushebiki yonjūhachi te ura omote" ボルシェヴィキ四十八手裏表　(A
chart of all the Bolshevik tricks), Volume VI. The third *Rōdō undō* No. 9
(November 1922).

"Kumiai teikokushugi" 組合帝国主義　　(Union imperialism), Volume VI. The third *Rōdō undō* No. 9 (November 1922) and *Kaizō* (November 1922).

"Kuropotokin no sōshiki" クロポトキンの葬式　　(Kropotkin's funeral
ceremony), Volume VII. Ōsugi Sakae and Itō Noe, *Futari no kakumeika* 二人の
革命家(Two revolutionaries), Tokyo, Ars, 1922.

"Roshia no museifushugi undō," ロシアの無政府主義運動 (The
Russian anarchist movement), Volume VII. Unknown where first published. First known to be published in Ōsugi Sakae, *Museifushugisha no
mita Roshia kakumei* 無政府主義者の見たロシア革命　　(The Russian
Revolution as viewed by an anarchist), Tokyo, Sōbunkaku, 1922.

"Nihon dasshutsu ki" 日本脱出記 (Record of my escape from
Japan), Volume XIII. Two parts, "Nihon dasshutsu ki" and Nyūgoku kara
tsuihō made" 入獄から追放まで　　　(From imprisonment to
deportation), were originally published in *Kaizō* (July and September

1923). The remainder first appeared in Ōsugi Sakae, *Nihon dasshutsu ki* 日本脱出記(Record of my escape from Japan), Tokyo, Ars, 1923.

"Museifushugi shōgun" 無政府主義将軍(Anarchist shōgun), Volume VII. *Kaizō* 改造 (September 1923).

"Nihon ni okeru saikin no rōdō undō to shakaishugi undō" 日本における最近の労働運動と社会主義運動 (The recent labor and socialist movements in Japan), Volume VI. Ōsugi Sakae, *Jiyū no senku* 自由の先駆 (Pioneers of freedom), Tokyo, Gendai shichō, 1963–.

Ōsugi Sakae hiroku 大杉栄秘録 (Memoirs of Ōsugi Sakae). Edited by Ōsugi Sakae kenkyū kai 大杉栄研究会 . Tokyo, Kokushoku sensen sha, 1976.

Ōsugi Sakae shokan shū 大杉栄書簡集 (A collection of Ōsugi Sakae's letters). Edited by Ōsugi Sakae kenkyū kai. Tokyo, Kaien shobō, 1974.

Palij, Michael. *The Anarchism of Nestor Makhno, 1918–1921.* Seattle and London, University of Washington Press, 1976.

Peters, Victor. *Nestor Makhno: The Life of an Anarchist.* Winnipeg, Echo Books, 1970.

Pyzuir, Eugene. *The Doctrine of Anarchism of Michael A. Bakunin.* Milwaukee, Marquette University Press, 1955.

Rolland, Romain. *The People's Theater.* Translated by Barret H. Clark. New York, Henry Holt, 1918.

Ruhe, Algot, and Nancy Margaret Paul. *Henri Bergson: An Account of His Life and Philosophy.* London, Macmillan, 1914.

Sakai Toshihiko 堺利彦 . "Ōsugi to Arahata" 大杉と荒畑 (Ōsugi and Arahata), *Kindai shisō* 近代思想 (Modern thought) 1.1:13 (October 1913).

———. "Ōsugi-kun no ren'ai jiken" 大杉君の恋愛事件 (Ōsugi's love scandal), *Shin shakai* 新社会 (The new society) 3.5:2–4 (January 1917).

———. "Nihon shakaishugi undō ni okeru museifushugi no yakuwari" 日本社会主義運動における無政府主義の役割り (The role of anarchism in the Japanese socialist movement), *Rōnō* 労農 (Worker and farmer), December 1958.

Santayana, George. "The Philosophy of M. Bergson," in *Winds of Doctrine.* New York, Scribner's, 1913.

Scalapino, Robert A. *Democracy and the Party Movement in Prewar Japan: The Failure of the First Attempt.* Berkeley, University of California Press, 1953.

Scalapino, Robert A., and Chong-sik Lee. *Communism in Korea.* 2 vols. Berkeley, University of California Press, 1972.

Scalapino, Robert A., and George T. Yu. *The Chinese Anarchist Movement*. Berkeley, Center for Chinese Studies, Institute of International Studies, University of California, 1961.

Shakai bunko sōsho 社会文庫叢書 (Shakai Bunko Library) Shakai bunko 社会文庫. 8 vols. Tokyo, Kashiwa shobō, 1964.

Shimbun shūroku Taishō shi 新聞集録大正史 (A history of Taishō compiled from newspapers). 13 vols. Tokyo, Taishō shuppan, 1978.

Shiryō Nihon shakai undō shi 資料日本社会運動史 (The history of the Japanese socialist movement in documents). Edited by Tanaka Sōgorō 田中惣五郎. 2 vols. Tokyo, Tōzai, 1958.

Simcock, Bradford L. "The Anarcho-syndicalist Thought and Activity of Ōsugi Sakae, 1885–1923." *Papers on Japan*, Voume 6. Harvard University, East Asian Research Center, 1970.

Smith, Henry Dewitt. *Japan's First Student Radicals*. Cambridge, Harvard University Press, 1972.

Sorel, Georges. *Reflections on Violence*. Translated by T. E. Hulme. Introduction by Edward A. Shils. Glencoe, Free Press, 1950.

Stanley, Thomas A. "Police Constraints on Taishō Radical Movements: The Case of Ōsugi Sakae." *Selected Papers in Asian Studies*, Volume 2. Western Conference, Association for Asian Studies, Albuquerque, 1977.

———. "A Japanese Anarchist's Rejection of Marxism-Leninism: Ōsugi Sakae and the Russian Revolution." *Selected Papers in Asian Studies,* Volume 3. Western Conference, Association for Asian Studies, Albuquerque, 1979.

Steinhoff, Patricia G. "Tenkō and Thought Control." Paper presented at Annual Meeting of the Association for Asian Studies, Boston, Massachusetts, April 1–3, 1974.

Stirner, Max. *The Ego and his Own: The Case of the Individual Against Authority*. Translated by Steven T. Byington. New York, Libertarian Book Club, 1963.

Stone, Alan. "The Japanese Muckrakers," *Journal of Japanese Studies* 1.2: 385–407 (spring 1975).

Sunoo, Harold Hakwon. *Japanese Militarism: Past and Present*. Chicago, Nelson, Hall, 1975.

Tada Michitarō 多田道太郎. "Ōsugi Sakae" 大杉栄, in *Kindai Nihon no shisōka—nijisseiki o ugokashita hitobito* 近代日本の思想家 ― 20世紀を動かした人々 (Thinkers of modern Japan: People who have moved the twentieth century). Edited by Kuwabara Takeo 桑原武夫 et al. 2 vols. Tokyo, Kodansha, 1963.

Tadamiya Eitarō 田田官英太郎. "Ōsugi Sakae: sono gekiteki na sanjū-ku-nen" 大杉栄、その劇的な三十九年 (Ōsugi Sakae: his dramatic thirty-nine years), *Keizai ōrai* 経済往来 (Writings on economics) 28.11:246–257 (November 1976).

Takabatake Motoyuki 高畠素之 . "Ōsugi jiken to jiyū ren'ai to shakaishugi" 大杉事件と自由恋愛と社会主義 (The Ōsugi scandal and free love and socialism), *Shin shakai* 新社会 (The new society) 3.5:5–6 (January 1917).

Takami Jun 高見順 . "Ōsugi Sakae" 大杉栄 , in *Nihon no shisōka* 日本の思想家 (Thinkers of Japan). Edited by Asahi jānaru henshūbu 朝日ジャーナル編集部 (Editorial staff of the *Asahi Journal*). 3 vols. Tokyo, Asahi shimbun sha, 1963.

Takatsu Seidō 高津正道. "Gyōmin-kai zengo no omoide" 暁明会前後の思い出 (Memoirs of the enlightened persons' [Communist] society), *Rōdō undō shi kenkyū* 労働運動史研究 (Studies on the history of the labor movement) No. 12 (November 1958).

Tateno Noboyuki 立野信之. *Kuroi hana* 黒い花 (Black flower). 2 vols. Tokyo, Perikan sha, 1974.

Times of London, The. May 5, 1923, p. 11, col. 7.

Tsurumi Kazuko. *Social Change and the Individual: Japan Before and After Defeat in World War II.* Princeton, Princeton University Press, 1970.

Voline, pseud. V. M. Eichenbaum. *The Unknown Revolution (Kronstadt, 1912; Ukraine, 1918–1921).* Translated by Holley Cantine. New York, Libertarian Book Club, 1955.

Warner, Denis, and Peggy Warner. *The Tide at Sunrise: A History of the Russo-Japanese War, 1904–5.* New York, Charterhouse, 1974.

Watanabe Tōru 渡部徹 "Roshia kakumei to Nihon rōdō undō" ロシア革命と日本労働運動 (The Russian Revolution and the Japanese labor movement), *Gendai no riron* 現代の理論 (Theories of modernity) 4.10:21–33 (October 1967).

Yamabe Kentarō 山辺健太郎 and Takemura Eisuke 竹村英輔 . "Jūgatsu kakumei ga Nihon ni ataeta eikyō" 十月革命が日本に与えた影響 (The influence of the October Revoultion on Japan), *Zen'ei* 前衛 (Vanguard) No. 135 (December 1957).

Yamaga Taiji 山鹿泰治. "Ōsugi Sakae to esuperantogo" 大杉栄とエスペラント語 (Ōsugi Sakae and Esperanto), *Jiyū shisō kenkyū* 自由思想研究 (Studies on libertarian thought) 1:21–22 (July 1960).

Yamakawa Hitoshi 山川均 . "Ren'ai to ninjō to shōsei no kansō" 恋愛と刃傷と小生の感想. (Love and bloodshed and my thoughts), *Shin shakai* 新社会 (The new society) 3.5:50–51 (January 1917).

———. *Yamakawa Hitoshi jiden—aru bonjin no kiroku* 山川均自伝_ ある

凡人の記録 (Autobiography of Yamakawa Hitoshi—chronicle of an ordinary man). Edited by Yamakawa Kikue 山川菊栄 and Sakisaka Itsurō 向坂逸郎. Tokyo, Iwanami shoten, 1961.

Yamakawa Kikue 山川菊栄 . "Chishiki kaikyū to rōdōsha" 知識階級と 労働者 (The intellectual class and the workers), *Kaihō* 解放 (Liberation) 1.7 (October 1919).

Yasunari Jirō 安成二郎 . "Katami no haizara o mae ni" (With a keepsake ashtray in front of me) かたみの灰皿を前に , *Kaizō* 改造 (Reconstruction) 4.11:97–101 (November 1923).

Yatsugi Kazuo 矢次一夫 . "Kantō daishinsai to Ōsugi Sakae no shūhen" 関東大震災と大杉栄の周辺 (The Great Kantō Earthquake and Ōsugi Sakae's district), *Ekonomisuto* エコノミスト (The economist) 49.43: 102–109 (October 12, 1971).

Yoshida Seiichi 吉田精一. "Ōsugi Sakae" 大杉栄 , *Kaishaku to kanshō* 解釈 と鑑賞 (Explanation and appreciation) 42.3:188–199 (February 1977).

Glossary

Note: This list excludes the authors of works cited in the Bibliography.

Abe Isoo 安部磯雄
Akahata jiken 赤旗事件
Akutagawa Ryūnosuke
芥川竜之助
Amakasu Masahiko 甘粕正彦
ana-boru ronsō アナ・ボル論争
Andō Chūgi 安藤忠義
Andō Kiyoshi 安藤清
ano kitsune-san wa ne
あの狐さんはね
Aofuku 青服
Aoyama (Yamakawa) Kikue
青山（山川）菊栄
Arahata Kanson 荒畑寒村
Arishima Takeo 有島武郎
Ariyoshi Sankichi 有吉三吉
Arusu アルス

Baibunsha 売文社

Batabata Kyanson
バタバタキャンソン
boku 僕
Bummei hihyō 文明批評
bushidō 武士道

Chian keisatsu hō
治安警察法
Chigasaki 茅ヶ崎
chōmin 町民
Chūō kōron 中央公論
Chūō yōnen gakkō
中央幼年学校

dōki 動機
Dōshikai 同士会

Ebina Danjō
海老名弾正

fukoku kyōhei 富国強兵
Fukuda Masatarō 福田雅太郎
fukushū 復讐
Furansu bungaku kenkyūkai
仏蘭西文学研究会
gashin shōtan 臥薪嘗胆
Gembun-sha 玄文社
geshuku 下宿
geta 下駄
gohyaku-en 五百円
Gotō Shimpei 後藤新平

haikara ハイカラ
Hakone-maru 箱根丸
Hayama 葉山
Hayashi Shizue 林倭衛
Heimin-sha 平民社
Heimin kōenkai 平民講演会
heimin rōdōsha 平民労働者
Heimin shimbun 平民新聞
hibachi 火鉢
Hikari 光
Hirano Kuniomi 平野国臣
Hiratsuka Raichō 平塚らいてふ
Hisaita Unosuke 久板卯之助
hitsudan 筆談
Hōchi shimbun 報知新聞
hōfuku 報復
Hokufūkai 北風会
Hori Yasuko 堀保子

ii kimochi いい気持

inshō 印象
Ishikawa Sanshirō
石川三四郎

Jiji shimpō 時事新報
jikkō 実行
Jimbō-chō 神保町
jissai undō 実際運動
Jiyū eigakkai 自由英学会
jiyū kyōsan no seidō
自由共産の制度
Jiyūnin 自由人
jōgen 上弦
juku 塾
Junten chūgakkō 順天中学校

Kagaku to bungei 科学と文芸
Kagawa Toyohiko 賀川豊彦
kagekiha-ka 過激派化
kagen 下弦
Kaihō 解放
Kaizō 改造
kakumei-teki ikki undō
革命的一揆運動
kami 神
Kameido 亀戸
Kamori-chō 神守町
Kanda 神田
kangun 官軍
Kanno Sugako 管野須賀子
Kantō daishinsai
関東大震災

Katayama Sen 片山潛
Katei zasshi 家庭雜誌
Katō Kazuo 加藤一夫
Katō Tomosaburō 加藤友三郎
Katsura Tarō 桂太郎
Kawakami Hajime 河上肇
Kawakami Kiyoshi 河上清
kempeitai 憲兵隊
kendō 劍道
kenkyū kai 研究会
kenryoku ishi 権力意志
Kindai shisō 近代思想
Kinoshita Naoe 木下尚江
Kinshi kunshō 金鵄勲章
Kin'yōkai 金曜会
Kitahara 北原
Kogetsukai (Kogetsugumi) 湖月会（湖月組）
kokka shakaishugisha 国家社会主義者
Kokumin eigakkai 国民英学会
Kokuryūkai 黑龍会
Kondō Eizō 近藤栄蔵
Kondō Kenji 近藤憲二
Kōtoku Shūsui 幸徳秋水
Kume Masao 久米正雄
Kuomintang 国民党
Kusui Rikimatsu 楠井力松
Kusui Yutaka 楠井豊
Kuwabara Rentarō 桑原錬太郎

kyōchōkai 協調会
Kyokutō shakaishugisha kaigi 極東社会主義者会議
kyōsan seidō 共産制度

Meiji 明治
minshū geijutsu 民衆芸術
Miyajima Reiko 宮島麗子
Miyajima Sukeo 宮島資夫
Momose Susumu 百瀬晋
Morioka 森岡
mura hachibu 村八分

nakama no hitobito 仲間の人々
Nakanishi Inosuke 中西伊之助
Nihon musan tō 日本無産党
Nihon rōdō rengōkai 日本労働連合会
Nihon shakai tō 日本社会党
Nihon shakaishugi dōmei 日本社会主義同盟
ningen seikatsu 人間生活
Nishikawa Kōjirō 西川光二郎
Nishimura Torajirō 西村虎次郎

Ōhai 大ハイ
Oka Asajirō 丘浅次郎
Onjuku 御宿
Osaka mainichi shimbun 大阪毎日新聞

Ōsugi Aki 大杉秋

Ōsugi Ayame 大杉アヤメ

Ōsugi Azuma 大杉東

Ōsugi Inoko 大杉猪

Ōsugi Kenkyūrō (Kenshichirō)
大杉権九郎 (権七郎)

Ōsugi Mako 大杉魔子

Ōyūkai 欧友会

Rei-chan 礼ちゃん

Rikugun daigaku 陸軍大学

Rōdō bungaku 労働文学

Rōdō mondai enzetsukai
労働問題演説会

Rōdō mondai kenkyūkai
労働問題研究会

Rōdō mondai zadankai
労働問題座談会

Rōdō nōmin tō 労働農民党

Rōdō shimbun 労働新聞

Rōdō undō 労働運動

rōdō undō no jissai
労働運動の実際

Rōdōsha 労働者

Rōdōsha sōdanjo
労働者相談所

Roshia kakumei kinenkai
ロシア革命記念会

Saigō Takamori 西郷隆盛

Saionji Kimmochi
西園寺公望

Sakai Bokehiko 堺ボケ彦

Sakai Toshihiko 堺利彦

sambyaku-en 三百円

Sanjikarizumu kenkyūkai
サンディカリズム研究会

sei 生

seimeiryoku 生命力

Seinan (Satsuma) Rebellion 西
南 (薩摩) 戦争

seinendan 青年団

seishin-ka 精神家

Seishinkai 正進会

Seitō 青鞜

Seitō-sha 青鞜社

Seitō-sha kōenkai
青鞜社講演会

Shakai kakumei tō
社会革命党

Shakai minshu tō 社会民主党

shakai seikatsu 社会生活

Shakai shimbun 社会新聞

Shakaishugi kenkyūkai
社会主義研究会

shakaishugi-ka 社会主義化

shakuhachi 尺八

Shimbunshi hō 新聞紙法

Shin shakai 新社会

Shinjinkai 新人会

Shinka ron kōwa 進化論講話

Shin'yūkai 進友会

Shirakaba 白樺

shishi 志士

shōji 障子

Shōwa 昭和

shōya 庄屋

Sōdōmei (Nihon Rōdō Sōdō-mei) 総同盟 (日本労働総・同盟)

Sugamo 巣鴨

Sugimura Fukashi 杉村濬

Sugimura Yōtarō 杉村陽太郎

Sunda koto wa mō shikata ga nai. 済んだ事はもう仕方がない

Suzuki Bunji 鈴木文治

Tachibana Ayame 橘アヤメ

Tachibana Munekazu 橘宗一

Tachibana Sōsaburō 橘惣三郎

Taigyaku jiken 大逆事件

Taishō 大正

Tanaka Kunishige 田中国重

Tanaka Ryūichi 田中隆一

T'ang Chi 唐継

tatami 畳

Tazoe Tetsuji 田添鉄二

tenkō 転向

tōfu 豆腐

Tōkyō asahi shimbun 東京朝日新聞

Tōkyō chūgakkō 東京中学校

Tōkyō gaikokugo gakkō 東京外国語学校

Tōkyō gakuin 東京学院

Tōkyō mainichi shimbun 東京毎日新聞

Tōkyō nichinichi shimbun 東京日々新聞

Tora no Mon 虎の門

Tosaka 登坂

Tsuda eigo juku 津田英語塾

Tsuji Jun 辻潤

Tsuji Makoto 辻一

Tsuji Ryūji 辻流二

Tsushima-shi 津島市

Uchimura Kanzō 内村鑑三

Uji 宇治

Ueno jogakkō 上野女学校

Uno Kōji 宇野浩二

Wada Kyūtarō 和田久太郎

Watanabe Masatarō 渡辺政太郎

Yamada Hōei 山田保永

Yamada Ryōnosuke 山田良之助

Yamada Waka 山田わか

Yamaga Taiji 山鹿泰治

Yamaguchi Gizō (Koken) 山口義三 (狐劍)

Yamakan Hitoshi 山カン均

Yamakawa (Aoyama) Kikue
山川（青山）菊栄

Yamamoto Gonnohyōe
山本権兵衛

Yamato-damashii teki kurisuto-
kyō 大和魂的キリスト教

Yanaka 谷中

Yane-jō jiken 屋根上事件

Yasuda Satsuki 安田皐月

Yasunari Jirō 安成二郎

Yomiuri shimbun 読売新聞

yōnen gakkō 幼年学校

Yorozu chōhō 万朝報

Yoshida Hajime 吉田一

Yoshida Shōin 吉田松陰

Yoshikawa Akimasa 芳川顕正

Yoshikawa Kaneko 芳川鎌子

Yoshino Sakuzō 吉野作造

Yūaikai 友愛会

Yūki Reiichirō 結城礼一郎

Zen'ei 前衛

zokugun 賊軍

Index

Abe, Isoo, 35, 37

Akahata jiken. *See* Red Flag Incident

Amakasu Masahiko, 159–160

Anarchism, 57–64; and the Great Kantō Earthquake, 160–163; and Japanese society, xi; and Marxism-Leninism, x–xi; and modernization, x; and Ōsugi Sakae, 46, 59–61, 72, 167, 169–170; and self-identity, x; in the socialist world, 57; theory of, xi. *See also* Marxism-Leninism; Socialism

Anarchists: cooperation with Japanese bolsheviks, 79, 132, 135–136; in Russia, 150–154. *See also* Anarcho-bolshevik dispute

Anarcho-bolshevik dispute, 121, 127–129, 136–141, 148, 149, 198 n.31, 199 n.42; bolshevik attacks on Ōsugi Sakae, 140; Ōsugi Sakae on bolsheviks, 139–140; Ōsugi Sakae's opposition to bolshevism, 127–128, 129, 137–138, 139–141; roots in Ōsugi Sakae's love affairs, 139

Anarcho-syndicalism. *See* Anarchism; Syndicalism

Andō Chūji, 41–42

Andō Kiyoshi, 86, 87

Aoyama Kikue. *See* Yamakawa Kikue

Arahata Kanson, 94, 133, 136; and censorship, 75, 76; and the first *Kindai shisō*, 56, 64; and the masses, 114; and the second *Kindai shisō*, 100; pro-bolshevism of, 127; Ōsugi Sakae's criticism of, 121; and Red Flag Incident, 45

Arishima Takeo, 143, 199 n.2

Ariyoshi Sankichi, 193 n.3; and the masses, 114

Army officer corps, elite group, 18

Army University, 20; and Ōsugi Sakae, 42

Arrests of Ōsugi Sakae, 30, 36, 41–42, 147–148

Ars Publishing Company, 103

Arshinov, Peter, 151

Art: debate on, 1920–1921, 122; and the labor movement, 123–125; and Ōsugi Sakae, 66; Ōsugi Sakae's theory of, 122–125

Ashio Copper Mine. *See* Yanaka Village Copper Poisoning Incident

Authority, Ōsugi Sakae and, 141

Autobiography of Ōsugi Sakae, xii, 1, 150

Autopsy of Ōsugi Sakae, 159–160

Baibunsha, 55–56

Bakunin, Michael Aleksandrovich, 48, 49

Barbusse, Henri, 144

Bergson, Henri, 59; thought of, 61–62

Berkman, Alexander, 138, 150, 202 n.35

Bluestockings. *See* Seitō; Seitōsha

Bolsheviks (Japanese), and cooperation with anarchists, 79; and Ōsugi Sakae, 127–128, 132, 135–140

Bummei hihyō (Cultural review), 78, 111

Bushidō, 21

Harvard East Asian Monographs

1. Liang Fang-chung, *The Single-Whip Method of Taxation in China*
2. Harold C. Hinton, *The Grain Tribute System of China, 1845–1911*
3. Ellsworth C. Carlson, *The Kaiping Mines, 1877–1912*
4. Chao Kuo-chün, *Agrarian Policies of Mainland China: A Documentary Study, 1949–1956*
5. Edgar Snow, *Random Notes on Red China, 1936–1945*
6. Edwin George Beal, Jr., *The Origin of Likin, 1835–1864*
7. Chao Kuo-chün, *Economic Planning and Organization in Mainland China: A Documentary Study, 1949–1957*
8. John K. Fairbank, *Ch'ing Documents: An Introductory Syllabus*
9. Helen Yin and Yi-chang Yin, *Economic Statistics of Mainland China, 1949–1957*
10. Wolfgang Franke, *The Reform and Abolition of the Traditional Chinese Examination System*
11. Albert Feuerwerker and S. Cheng, *Chinese Communist Studies of Modern Chinese History*
12. C. John Stanley, *Late Ch'ing Finance: Hu Kuang-yung as an Innovator*
13. S. M. Meng, *The Tsungli Yamen: Its Organization and Functions*
14. Ssu-yü Teng, *Historiography of the Taiping Rebellion*
15. Chun-Jo Liu, *Controversies in Modern Chinese Intellectual History: An Analytic Bibliography of Periodical Articles, Mainly of the May Fourth and Post-May Fourth Era*
16. Edward J. M. Rhoads, *The Chinese Red Army, 1927–1963: An Annotated Bibliography*
17. Andrew J. Nathan, *A History of the China International Famine Relief Commission*
18. Frank H. H. King (ed.) and Prescott Clarke, *A Research Guide to China-Coast Newspapers, 1822–1911*
19. Ellis Joffe, *Party and Army: Professionalism and Political Control in the Chinese Officer Corps, 1949–1964*
20. Toshio G. Tsukahira, *Feudal Control in Tokugawa Japan: The Sankin Kōtai System*